The Pleadings Game

The Pleadings Game

An Artificial Intelligence Model of Procedural Justice

by

Thomas F. Gordon
GMD-German National Research Center for
Information Technology

KLUWER ACADEMIC PUBLISHERS
DORDRECHT / BOSTON / LONDON

Library of Congress Cataloging-in-Publication Data

Gordon, Thomas F.
    The pleadings game   an artificial intelligence model of
procedural justice / by Thomas F. Gordon.
        p.   cm.
    Includes bibliographical references and index.

    1. Law--Methodology. 2. Logic. 3. Reasoning. 4. Artificial
intelligence.   I. Title.
    K213.G68   1995
    340'.11--dc20   95-30098

ISBN 978-90-481-4591-1

Published by Kluwer Academic Publishers,
P.O. Box 17, 3300 AA Dordrecht, The Netherlands.

Kluwer Academic Publishers incorporates
the publishing programmes of
D. Reidel, Martinus Nijhoff, Dr W. Junk and MTP Press.

Sold and distributed in the U.S.A. and Canada
by Kluwer Academic Publishers,
101 Philip Drive, Norwell, MA 02061, U.S.A.

In all other countries, sold and distributed
by Kluwer Academic Publishers Group,
P.O. Box 322, 3300 AH Dordrecht, The Netherlands.

Printed on acid-free paper

*To my mother, for the self-confidence needed to begin
and to my wife, Ines, and children, Dustin and Caroline,
for the patience needed to finish*

Contents

viii

Preface

The British philosopher Stephan Toulmin, in his *The Uses of Argument*, made the provocative claim that "logic is generalized jurisprudence". For Toulmin, logic is the study of norms for practical argumentation and decision making. In his view, mathematical logicians were preoccupied with formalizing the concepts of logical necessity, consequence and contradiction, at the expense of other equally important issues, such as how to allocate the burden of proof and make rational decisions given limited resources. He also considered it a mistake to look primarily to psychology, linguistics or the cognitive sciences for answers to these fundamentally normative questions.

Toulmin's concerns about logic, writing in the 1950's, are equally applicable to the field of Artificial Intelligence today. The mainstream of Artificial Intelligence has focused on the analytical and empirical aspects of intelligence, without giving adequate attention to the normative, regulative functions of knowledge representation, problem solving and decision-making. Normative issues should now be of even greater interest, with the shift in perspective of AI from individual to collective intelligence, in areas such as multi-agent systems, cooperative design, distributed artificial intelligence, and computer-supported cooperative work. Networked "virtual societies" of humans and software agents would also require "virtual legal systems" to fairly balance interests, resolve conflicts, and promote security.

This book draws upon jurisprudence and moral philosophy to develop a formal model of argumentation, called the Pleadings Game. From a technical perspective, the Pleadings Game can be viewed as an extension of recent argumentation-based approaches to nonmonotonic logic: 1) The game is dialogical instead of monological; 2) The validity and priority of defeasible rules is subject to debate; and 3) Resource limitations are acknowledged by rules for fairly dividing the burdens of representation and proof among the players.

Rather than starting with abstract preconceptions about argumentation, the approach taken here is to first evaluate some important jurisprudential theories of argumentation and reasoning in the context of a particular legal domain, the U.S. commercial law on secured transactions. This leads to a better appreciation of the variety and types of priority relationships between rules than one would have expected from a survey of the literature on argumentation or nonmonotonic logic alone. More importantly, it also leads to the identification of the proper division of power between legislative and judicial branches of government as being the main issue in legal philosophy driving the search for adequate models of reasoning and argumentation. (No special legal knowledge is needed to understand this book. All of the law and legal theory needed to understand the issues and examples is contained here.)

The division of power issue is usually phrased in terms of the limits of judicial discretion. Where is the border between a judge's power to decide cases by applying the law and his power to create law? How can it be decided whether or not a judge has exceeded the limits of his discretion? What methods can be applied to construct decisions which are correct or justified, given these limits? The Pleadings Game may be of interest to legal theorists to the extend it helps to shed light on issues such as these.

Most prior work in AI and Law has been founded on the prominent legal philosophy of H.L.A. Hart. In the basic version of Hart's theory, judicial discretion begins where the literal meaning of authoritative legal texts, such as legislation and case books, ends. To use a standard example, if a law prohibits vehicles from a public park, then a judge would not have discretion to allow a tank, even if it is to be used as a war memorial. AI and Law models typically try to represent the meaning of legislation and cases using some formal language, often a variant of first-order predicate logic. In this approach, the task of modeling discretion is reduced to finding an inference relation such that precisely the decisions which the judge may reach are derivable from the representation of the law and the facts of the present case.

It is argued here that relational models of this kind cannot capture the essence of judicial discretion, as they fail to take seriously the problem of representing the knowledge of such inherently political and dynamic domains as the law, where opinions and values differ so widely and consensus is unlikely to ever be definitely established. These models also fail to acknowledge the intractability of inference relations for languages expressive enough to represent legal knowledge. How can such a relational model serve as a practical check on discretion when no efficient inference procedure for the model can exist?

The Pleadings Game takes another approach, founded in the discourse theory of legal argumentation developed by Robert Alexy, a contemporary German legal philosopher. In Alexy's theory, it is not the meaning of the law alone which delimits judicial discretion, but rather the discourse norms of rational argumentation. These norms regulate the *process* by which arguments are presented and compared. The relational or descriptive model is replaced by a procedural model: a judicial decision is assumed to be correct if there is no reason to believe that the procedure by which it was reached was not fair.

The particular legal proceeding modeled by the Pleading Game is civil pleading, where the parties exchange arguments and counterarguments to identify the issues to be decided by the court. In the model, the arguments a judge may make when deciding a case are constrained by the arguments made by the parties during pleading. The rules of the game are designed to promote efficiency and assure that no player can prevent termination. The concepts of issue and relevance are used to focus pleading and avoid superfluous arguments. A tractable inference relation is used to commit players to some of the consequences of their claims. The concept of an issue is formalized using the dialectical structure of arguments which have been made pro and contra the main claim of the case. The task of identifying issues is shown to be an abduction problem.

A prototype mediation system for the Pleadings Game has been implemented. A mediator is a neutral third-party. Its job is to manage the record of the proceeding and help assure that rules of procedure are not violated, by advising the parties about their rights and obligations. This book contains a high-level description of the Pleadings Game mediation system sufficient to reimplement it, in the programming language of your choice.

The Pleadings Game has been tested using examples from Article Nine of the Uniform Commercial Code of the United States, which covers secured transactions. A typical transaction of this type is a loan by a bank to purchase a car, where repayment of the loan is secured by the bank retaining a security interest in the car. Article Nine is full of various kinds of exceptions and priority relations between conflicting rules. In an appendix, the rule language of the Pleadings Game is shown to be suitable for modeling statutes of this kind, by representing significant portions of Article Nine.

Let us end this preface by returning to Toulmin and his view of logic. To avoid confusion with the now dominant conception of logic within AI, it might be preferable to call Toulmin's broader view of logic "dialectics". The study, within Artificial Intelligence, of the theory, design and implementation of systems which mediate discussions and arguments between agents, artificial and human, might then be called "Computational Dialectics". This field would be closely related to what Carl Adam Petri, the German computer scientist, proposed calling "formal pragmatics". The Pleadings Game is a contribution to Computational Dialectics.

Acknowledgements

For providing me with the opportunity to pursue the dissertation which resulted in this book, and for his encouragement, support and careful editing, I would first of all like to thank heartily my principal thesis advisor, Wolfgang Bibel. Thanks also are due to other members of my thesis committee, L. Thorne McCarty and Adalbert Podlech.

This book began in 1981 at the School of Law of the University of California, Davis. For supporting my interest in legal philosophy, I would like to thank several of my former law professors, John Ayer, Florian Bartosic, Gary Goodpaster, John Poulos and, last but not least, Thomas Ulen. Special thanks go to John Ayer, for having actively sponsored my artificial intelligence and law independent-study project, despite his own deep skepticism, and for teaching me more about writing than I have ever learned, before or since.

Bernard Schlink introduced me to Herbert Fiedler shortly after my arrival in Germany in 1982. Professor Fiedler gave me my start at the German National Research Center for Computer Science (GMD), for which I am deeply grateful. I would also like to thank him for the independence he allowed me during the several years I worked in his Information Law and Legal Informatics group at GMD.

Several colleagues and friends have commented on various versions of this book: Barbara Becker, Trevor Bench-Capon, Gerhard Brewka, Joachim Hertzberg, Christoph Lischka, Ron Loui, Lothar Philipps and Henry Prakken. I am indepted to them all. Special, warm thanks go to my friends Gerhard and Joachim for having taken the trouble to carefully read the whole manuscript. Of course, I remain solely responsible for all errors and omissions.

For giving me the time to write the thesis and then revise it for the book, I thank the director of the Artificial Intelligence Division of GMD, Thomas Christaller.

Finally, I would like to thank the anonymous reviewers for their evaluations and constructive criticism.

Chapter 1   Introduction

In modern democratic states, political power is divided among the executive, legislative and judicial branches of government. When resolving concrete legal disputes, there is also a division of power between the parties and the courts. What are the limits of judicial discretion? How should it be decided whether these limits have been respected? Are there methods for constructing decisions which are sure to fall within these limits?

This book presents a formal, computational model of adversarial legal argumentation, called the Pleadings Game, which is intended to shed some light on these questions. Whereas most previous AI models of legal reasoning have been based on the Anglo-American school of analytical jurisprudence, especially the work of H. L. A. Hart [52], the Pleadings Game is founded primarily in Robert Alexy's discourse theory of legal argumentation [3; 4]. Hart draws the line of judicial discretion at the border between clear and hard cases. In the simplest form of his theory, a case is clear just when the facts of the case are subsumed by the context-independent, conventional meaning of the applicable law. To use his standard example, if a rule prohibits vehicles in the park, a judge would not have discretion to decide that cars are permitted. In Alexy's theory, it is not the meaning of the law which delimits judicial discretion, but rather the discourse norms of rational argumentation, which regulate the process by which arguments are presented and compared.

To compare the Pleadings Game with other AI models of legal reasoning, it is important to first emphasize a few aspects of models in general. A model can be classified along several dimensions: 1) its purpose, 2) the object modeled, and 3) its analytical, empirical and normative claims.

The purpose of a model can be theoretical or practical. A theoretical model is intended to help clarify the properties of some theory. Rather than proving theorems of the theory, one manipulates the model and observes how it performs. A practical model is intended to be useful in some application, such as planning, design or diagnosis.

Regarding the second aspect, models can be built of any object or system, no matter how abstract or concrete, from the structure of a system of morals to the aerodynamic characteristics of an automobile. It is important to remember that models only share some properties of the objects they are intended to model. The Styrofoam shape in the wind canal is not an automobile.

The analytical claims of a model are its commitments about the structure and relationship of the components of the object modeled. The Styrofoam mock-up of a car makes no commitments about the structure of an automobile's motor or drive train. Whether the claims made for a model are empirical or normative depends on the standard adopted to evaluate the model. In the case of empirical models, the actual behavior of the object modeled sets the standard. In the case of normative models, these roles are

1

reversed. The behavior of the object is judged by comparing it with the ideal represented by the model. Notice that normative models require justification independent of the actual behavior of the object modeled.

Empirical models are of several types. If the goal is to *simulate* the behavior of the object, then it is not sufficient that the model display the same functionality as the object; it must do so in a comparable way. (In AI models of mental behavior, this is called the "cognitive adequacy" of the model.) Airplanes do not simulate flying birds. In other words, a simulation model is an empirical model which also makes strong analytical claims about the internal structure of the object modeled. If the goal is only performance, then the principle of *Occam's razor* may be used to prefer simpler models. In the history of computers and law, the early *jurimetrics* models where entirely behavioral; they had neither analytical nor normative ambitions. The race of the defendant in a criminal trial may be sufficient to effectively predict the verdict.

Talking about the purpose, object and claims of the model is somewhat misleading, as these are not inherent properties of the model, but are better understood as a relationship between an agent and the model. Thus, when I speak of the purpose of a model, I really mean the purpose intended by the model's author.

Let's see how a few AI and Law models fit into this classification scheme. Anne Gardner's model, which identified the issues of law school examination questions, clearly had a theoretical purpose [40, p. 1]: "to create a model of the legal reasoning process which makes sense from both jurisprudential and AI perspectives." We can safely assume the system was not intended to assist law students with their exams. The program was evaluated by comparing its performance with the correct solutions published in a study aid for students, rather than with the answers of students, so it is a normative model. She does make strong analytical claims [40, p. 2]: "The design of the program is intended to reflect lawyers' own understanding of the nature and use of legal materials — in other words, to accord with a legally plausible conceptualization of the domain. The result is a conceptual analysis of legal reasoning, not a psychology." In the conclusion [40, p. 189], Gardner writes: "This book has presented a computational framework for legal reasoning." It is surely legitimate to try to generalize the results of an experiment or model, but one must keep in mind the extent to which the generalization is supported by the model.

Kevin Ashley's HYPO program used a representation of a set of cases to construct arguments in the domain of trade secret law. Ashley evaluated the performance of HYPO [12, p. 8] "by comparing the outputs to the arguments that lawyers and judges made in the actual legal cases on which the example fact situations were based." So the model is empirical. Ashley explicitly confirms that the model is not intended to simulate the problem-solving behavior of lawyers [12, p. 1] : "The goal is not necessarily to design a program that reasons in the same way as a human but whose outputs are, within certain constraints, as intelligent as those of a human reasoner." Both practical and theoretical "ramifications" are claimed for the model.

Henry Prakken's recent dissertation on *Logical Tools for Modelling Legal Argument* [97] is the last model I'd like to mention here. He develops a framework for defeasible reasoning in which conflicts between rules may be resolved by ordering them using a combination of factors, such as specificity, authority and time. Given a set of default rules, a set of nondefeasible first-order sentences, and a priority relationship on defaults, the framework defines a nonmonotonic inference relation. This work is mostly analytical: it makes claims about the structure of defeasible rules and their relationships without making strong empirical or normative commitments. This is not to say that the work does not have empirical and normative aspects. The model of the structure of defeasible rules is arrived at by examining actual legal rules and principles. And the defeasible entailment relation proposed is justified by normative arguments, using standard examples which are claimed to display intuitively correct results. Nonetheless, its normative claims are weak, as Prakken stops short of arguing that legal rules and arguments should be structured in this way for some class of tasks. Rather, the goal of the book is to show how defeasible reasoning *can* be accomplished using his logic, and to explicate its mathematical properties. This is valuable, as it provides others who may wish to argue that the system should be used for some task with information which may be necessary for justifying their normative claims.

All three of these models can be viewed as instances of an abstract structure, which I will call the *relational model of legal reasoning*, as shown in Figure 1.1.

This figure requires some explanation. One must be careful not to jump too quickly to hypotheses about the reasons for my choice of symbols here. On the left side of the arrow there are two boxes, one for some representation of the law, the other for some representation of the facts of a particular case. No commitment is being made here about how these are to be represented. The law may be represented, e.g., by a set of cases modeled using dimensions, as in HYPO, or as a set of defeasible rules and a priority ordering, using Prakken's approach, or in any other possible way, including neural networks. This also applies to the representation chosen for the facts of the case.

On the right side of the arrow is a box labelled "argument". Here too, it is unimportant just how arguments are represented in the model. I've chosen the term "argument", rather than "decision", to allow for the possibility of modeling issue-spotting or the construction of alternative plausible arguments, in addition to just deciding the case. (The latter can be viewed as a special case, where the argument includes a justification for the decision.)

The plus sign and arrow symbol are intended to mean that representations of the law and facts together stand in some *relation* to the set of arguments. That is, no input/output direction is intended to be suggested by this arrow. One might imagine using models of this type in any number of ways, such as representing an argument and the facts and asking the system to produce appropriate representations of the law.

No commitment is made here about the mathematical properties of this relation. I am intentionally avoiding calling this an inference relation, let alone a consequence relation, as the properties of this relation are completely irrelevant for my current purposes. The relationship can be one of classical entailment, probability, plausibility, Fuzzy Logic, defeasible inference, mere association, or any other relation.

Finally, it is just as irrelevant how this relation is implemented in the computational model, whether, for example, sequentially on a normal single-processor computer, or using connectionistic methods on a massively-parallel architecture. It is also unimportant whether the implementation is correct, complete or approximate.

Given these preliminaries, I would like to point out two problems all relational models

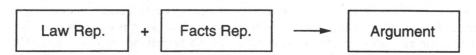

Figure 1.1. Relational Model of Legal Reasoning

of legal reasoning must face, and then state a conjecture regarding their suitability for modeling judicial discretion.

The two problems are what I call the *burden of representation* and the *burden of proof*. In AI, the first of these problems is also known as the *knowledge acquisition* problem. Representing all of the relevant law and facts (or arguments) can be a very major undertaking, requiring at worst the representation of all of common sense, in addition to the positive law itself, depending on the purpose and task of the model. Some knowledge representation schemes may be less burdensome than others, but even machine learning or case-based reasoning approaches, e.g., require the set of relevant dimensions or concepts to be designed, and all of the training cases to be encoded.

But the burden of representation is not primarily a problem due to the quantity of knowledge to be represented. More significantly, reasonable persons will disagree about whether or not the representation is adequate for the intended purposes of the model. For this reason, it may be more appropriate to speak of the *right of representation*, because those who have the privilege of programming the knowledge base can fashion it according to their own world view and interests.

Allowing multiple, competing representations, although necessary for some kinds of applications, only increases the difficulty of this task.

In computer science, the burden of proof is more precisely divided up into the problems of decidability and computational complexity. The question is, given a model which is an instance of this framework, how difficult is it to generate tuples which are members of the relation, or to test whether a given tuple is a member?

Here too, however, the problem is not solely a question of how difficult these tasks may be, but a question of *who* shall bear this burden of computation. In computer science, the answer is usually, implicitly, the computer. But when the problems are undecidable or intractable, this answer may not be *fair*. When the answer is approximate, or possibly wrong, the interests of the person affected by the decision should be taken into consideration, in order to decide which risks to take. When more than one agent is affected by the decision, they may have competing interests, which lead to different evaluations of risk.

Whether or not these problems are significant depends on the purpose and task of the model. For example, it can be assumed that both the quantity of knowledge to be represented and the burden of proof presented significant problems in Gardner's and Ashley's models. However, I suspect that in both cases the more significant burden was the effort required to represent the domain. On the other hand, neither of these problems were significant for Prakken, as it was not his goal to apply his framework to some particular legal task. However, anyone using his framework would have to face these problems.

In none of these models did the fact that reasonable persons may have different opinions and interests play a role. Gardner's system modeled the problem-solving behavior of a single student; Ashley's system modeled the behavior of a single lawyer constructing an argument from cases. Also, they were the only users of their models, which were constructed primarily for theoretical purposes.

In some of the proposed applications of AI and Law technology, such as legal analysis systems, planning systems, and conceptual retrieval of case law [79], these problems are more serious, as the interests and opinions of the system developers may conflict with those of users. For this reason, Trevor Bench-Capon has proposed that knowledge bases be incrementally constructed through a dialogue game with the user [17; 18].

Finally, when the task is to construct a correct or just legal decision, or to review such a decision, the interests and views of the various agents involved must be a part of the model. Here is the conjecture:

No relational model of legal reasoning can adequately model judicial discretion.

Obviously, this is another one of those conjectures which cannot be proven with certainty, because of the nice little qualifier *"adequately"*, and because a constructive proof may require some way to iterate over all possible relational models, to test whether or not they are adequate.

Nonetheless, there are good arguments supporting this conjecture, some of which have been pointed out by various other researchers within AI and Law, such as Berman and Hafner [19] and Bench-Capon and Sergot [14]. These arguments will be presented in detail in the body of this dissertation, but the main reason is this: relational models all fail to fairly allocate the burdens (and rights) of representation and proof.

Following Alexy, I approach these problems by modeling the procedural norms which regulate the allocation of the burdens of representation and proof, instead of modeling the legal domain. Models of this type are formal *games*, for one or more players, where the rules of the game regulate access and modification of the representations of law and facts, and distribute the rights and obligations to draw inferences from these representations. The number and roles of the players, the analytical structure of the knowledge base constructed during the game, and the types of inference relations used will vary considerably from game to game, depending on the type of proceeding to be modeled.

Others in AI and Law have had similar insights. Fiedler, e.g., expressed the view that legal reasoning is a process of theory construction [37], but did not propose modeling the norms which regulate this process. Similarly, McCarty, when recently reflecting on his Prototypes and Deformations theory of case-based legal argumentation, came very close to my position when he wrote [83]:

> Since lawyers are more likely to agree on what counts as a plausible argument than to agree on the appropriate outcome, we decided it would be more fruitful to develop a theory of legal argument than to develop a theory of correct legal decisions.
>
> ...
>
> What determines the choice of the prototype? What are the criteria for constructing transformations? It was clear that the set of transformations had to be tightly constrained, or else anything could be "transformed" into anything. But what are the source of these constraints?

The source of these constraints are the norms of procedural justice.

Alexy proposes a very abstract set of norms he contends should regulate all legal discourse. This is one point where I disagree. The norms should depend on the nature and purpose of the particular type of legal proceeding, and the rights and responsibilities of the participants should depend on their role, such as plaintiff, defendant, or judge. Notice that these procedural norms not only limit the discretion of the judge, but also regulate the behavior of the other participants in the proceeding.

For this reason, my model is not of legal argumentation in the abstract, but of a particular kind of legal proceeding: civil pleading. (To demonstrate how judicial discretion is restricted, there is also a simple model of trial.) It would be difficult to draw a diagram which abstractly characterizes all games, comparable to the previous figure for relational models of legal reasoning. However, Figure 1.2 displays the general structure of the particular games developed here.

The purpose of pleading is to identify the *issues* to be decided by the court. My model of pleading is more akin to common law practice than to the "modern" law of civil procedure in the United States. At common law, the goal of pleading was to reduce the issues to be tried to a minimum. In the modern law of civil procedure, the parties do not explicitly make legal arguments during pleading, but merely assert or deny "essential" facts which are believed to entitle them to legal relief, such as monetary compensation for damages, or are believed to constitute a defense.

To get an initial understanding of the purpose of pleading, consider the following hypothetical exchange of allegations, loosely based on Article Nine of the Uniform Commercial Code of the United States, which covers secured transactions.[1] No familiarity with commercial law should be required to appreciate this example.

The plaintiff, Smith, and the defendant, Jones, have both loaned money to Miller for the purchase of an oil tanker, which is the collateral for both loans. Miller has defaulted on both loans, and the practical question is which of the two lenders will first be paid from the proceeds of the sale of the ship. These facts are uncontested. One subsidiary issue is whether Smith *perfected* his security interest in the ship or not. (Roughly, the interest is

---

[1]The Uniform Commerical Code is not federal law, but rather state law which has been enacted in almost the same form by most of the 50 states of the United States. Commercial law regulates commerce and trade. There is a glossary of legal terms in the appendix.

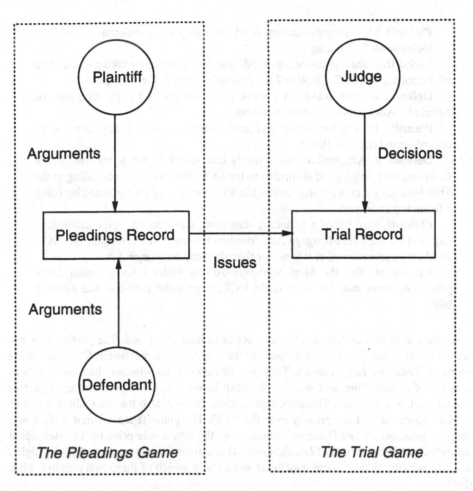

Figure 1.2. General Structure of the Pleadings and Trial Games

perfected when sufficient steps have been taken to make it effective.) This is where we enter the pleadings.

Plaintiff. My security interested in Miller's ship was perfected.

Defendant. I do not agree.

Plaintiff. A security interest in goods may be perfected by taking possession of the collateral (UCC § 9-305). I have possession of Miller's ship.

Defendant. What makes you think ships are goods for the purposes of Article 9? Also, prove you have possession.

Plaintiff. Except for money and instruments, movable things are goods, according to UCC § 9-105-h.

Defendant. Although a ship is surely movable, I do not agree that this is sufficient for being a good according to the UCC. Furthermore, according to the Ship Mortgage Act, a security interest in a ship may only be perfected by filing a financing statement.

Plaintiff. I have filed a financing statement. But I do not agree that this is required by the Ship Mortgage Act. Moreover, even if you are right, the UCC would take precedence, as it is newer than the Ship Mortgage Act.

Defendant. But the Ship Mortgage Act is Federal Law, which takes precedence over state law such as the UCC, even if the state law was enacted later.

At the end of this exchange several issues have been identified. The parties disagree about whether or not Smith has possession of the ship, and whether he has filed a financing statement. These are factual issues. They also disagree about whether ships are goods in the sense of Article Nine, and whether the Ship Mortgage Act requires filing to perfect a security interest in a ship. These are legal issues. There is also the issue about whether the Ship Mortgage Act has priority over the UCC. The plaintiff argued that it does not, using the principle of *Lex Posterior*, which gives the newer rule priority. The defendant responded with the principle of *Lex Superior*, which gives the rule supported by the higher authority priority. Finally, there may be an issue about which of these two principles has priority.

Notice that in this exchange, the parties are arguing about the validity and priority of conflicting legal rules. To handle this, the Pleadings Game *uses* a nonmonotonic logic, Geffner and Pearl's logic of *conditional entailment* [41]. Thus, this book lends further support to the claim about the importance of logic, and in particular nonmonotonic logic, for legal reasoning and argumentation.

Although the Pleadings Game is primarily a normative model of legal reasoning, it also has its analytical and empirical aspects. Some have argued against the use of nonmonotonic logics for legal reasoning. Alchourroun and Bulygin, for example, write [2, p. 25] :

... we agree with MacCormick that in principle no kind of logic is needed in order to cope with the problems of legal justificatory reasoning other than the ordinary (classic) deductive logic. It is not necessary and scarcely convenient to go beyond the limits of deductive logic, as has been suggested by many authors in the field of Artificial Intelligence. ... However — as has been convincingly demonstrated by D. Makinson — [defeasible reasoning] can be coped with by ordinary deductive logic by means of explication of the implicit or suppressed premises. ...

It is one thing to claim that legal decisions *can* be justified using ordinary deductive logic, it is another thing altogether to claim that decisions *are in fact* justified this way, and still another thing to argue that they *should be*. Sartor has presented considerable empirical evidence that the law is in fact organized using defeasible rules [107]. I have argued elsewhere that this is as it should be [45]. (These arguments are repeated in later in this book.) However, as Alchourron and Bulygin are less concerned with how the statutes are organized than with how judicial decisions are justified, these previous results in favor of nonmonotonic logic for legal reasoning are only indirectly relevant. This deficit is addressed in this book; empirical and normative arguments are made supporting the claim that nonmonotonic reasoning is and should be used for constructing and reviewing the justifications of judicial decisions.

The rest of the book is organized as follows. Chapter 2 is an overview of Article Nine of the Uniform Commercial Code, about secured transactions. The legal examples will all be from this area of law. The chapter serves two functions: 1) It is intended to provide just enough information about the law of secured transactions to make the examples understandable to non-lawyers, and to lawyers who may not be familiar with this particular subject; 2) It also provides further empirical evidence for the variety and extent of defeasible rules in the law. Chapter 3 is a critical survey of several theories from legal philosophy concerning the limits of judicial discretion. It focuses on the theories of Hart, Rödig, and of course Alexy. Although Hart's theory is well-known in AI and Law, it is presented again here for the sake of comparison with Alexy's discourse theory. Rödig was a German legal logician who, in the earlies 70's, made the most thoughtful and forceful arguments to date defending the goal of axiomatizing the law using formal logic. He was also a strong *opponent* of nonmonotonic logics, long before this was a subject of interest in AI. I criticize Rödig's positions on axiomatization and nonmonotonic logic, but agree with his assessment of the value of formalization. The goal of this chapter on philosophy is to justify and defend my model of adversarial legal argumentation. It provides the basis for a "semantics" or "foundation" of the model. Chapter 4 discusses several previous formal models of argumentation, including Lorenzen's Dialogue Logic, Pollock's OSCAR model, and the nonmonotonic logics of Simari and Loui and of Geffner and Pearl. These systems were the main source of techniques and methods for my own formal model of argumentation. To understand the Pleadings Game, one must at least be familiar with Geffner and Pearl's logic of conditional entailment, at the level of detail presented here. Chapter 5 is the formal specification of the Pleadings Game. It also includes several examples from Article Nine. Chapter 6 describes the implementation of my computational model. The system does not play the game, but is rather a mediator which enforces the rules of the game. The level of description should be sufficient to allow any AI programmer to reimplement the system. Chapter 7 is the conclusion. It critically evaluates the model and suggests directions for future work. There are two appendices. The first is a simplified version of Article Nine of the Uniform Commercial Code, called A9W, which also includes example representations of code sections using the formal language developed in Chapter 5. The other appendix is the glossary of legal terms.

To reiterate, this book presents a formal, computational model of adversarial legal argumentation, the Pleadings Game, whose purpose it is to support, illustrate and clarify some fundamental theoretical claims about the nature of legal reasoning and argumentation. These claims are of three types:

Analytical Claims.
Relational models of legal reasoning alone cannot account for the limits of judicial discretion. Rather, to understand judicial discretion, legal procedures must be modeled as language games, where the rules of each game are designed to further the purpose of the proceeding. The rights and obligations of each party to a proceeding depend on his or her role.

One such proceeding, civil pleading, can be modeled as a nonmonotonic, dialogue logic, where the parties exchange arguments of various kinds to identify the issues of the case. Arguments can be constructed by formulating and applying defeasible legal rules. Conflicting arguments can be resolved by ordering the rules used in them according to a variety of principles, such as specificity, authority and age. There is no need for a formal distinction between legal principles and other rules. By reifying rules, principles can be modeled as rules about other rules, at any level. The validity and priority of rules can also be subject to discussion during pleading.

Empirical Claims.
Article Nine of the Uniform Commercial Code consists of defeasible legal rules of various kinds, with both explicit and implicit exceptions. Many of the legal rules of Article Nine are higher-order: they explicitly refer to other legal rules.

Normative Claims.
The deductive theory of justification is wrong: A deductive argument is neither sufficient nor necessary to justify a judicial decision. Rather, the issues raised by arguments actually made by the parties during pleading should be taken into consideration when evaluating the sufficiency of the argument constructed by the judge to justify the decision.

Legislation should be formulated using defeasible rules for a nonmonotonic logic, as this furthers the normative and conflict resolution purposes of the law.

Finally, judicial discretion should be limited by fair procedural rules for deciding issues raised by the parties during pleading, rather than by an objective theory of the meaning of legal texts.

Chapter 2   The Legal Domain: Article Nine

The main source of examples for the theory of argumentation developed in this book will be Article Nine of the Uniform Commercial Code (UCC) of the United States, covering "Secured Transactions". Although quite complex in its entirety, Article Nine is *relatively* self-contained, so that I hope to be able to explain the code in sufficient depth for our purposes here within a few pages. The goal is to provide just enough information about Article Nine to allow non-lawyers to understand and appreciate the legal arguments we will be using as examples.[1]

Of course, an abbreviated description of Article Nine will be wholly inadequate for analyzing actual secured transactions problems. Most of the examples will be about hypothetical cases drawn from a standard text book on the Uniform Commercial Code [118] and should require no more knowledge of the law than provided here. The examples are intended to be "realistic", but not real. That is, they will demonstrate certain aspects of real legal reasoning, while at the same time abstracting away from distracting details. In this way they will be similar to the law school examination questions used in Anne Gardner's work on Artificial Intelligence and legal reasoning [40].

Another reason for choosing Article Nine is that the Uniform Commercial Code *is* a code; it is statutory law. Although the cases are still quite important, as Speidel, Summers and White point out in their casebook [118, p. 34], the code is the primary source of applicable law:

> The lawyer who practices commercial and/or consumer law badly may begin his research on a legal problem in the "relevant" case law. He thus indulges in the common law assumption that "the law is all in the cases." This assumption is fallacious. ... In this field, statutes are the primary, principal, and often preemptive source of law.

Why choose a legal domain for my artificial intelligence model which is principally statutory? There are several reasons. Firstly, although cases are traditionally stressed in common law countries, especially during law school, statutes are of central importance in civil law countries such as Germany. As evidenced by the UCC, statutes are also of increasing importance in common law jurisdictions. Hopefully, a theory of legal argumentation using statutes will be of equal interest in both types of jurisdictions.

Secondly, as there are many difficult representational problems for statutes and cases

---

[1]Appendix A contains a simplified version of Article Nine sufficient for the examples, called A9W, along with a partial formalization using the rule language developed in Chapter 5 .

[78; 103; 11] it would be too ambitious to try to deal with them all. One of the open problems in representing statutes, how to represent rules with exceptions while preserving the original structure of the legal code, is a subject I would like to address in this work.[2]

Finally, the formalization developed in this book is primarily intended to be a model of civil law pleading. In this context, the choice between statutory and case law is of only minor significance. During pleading, the parties assert general rules, which may be backed by references to cases or statutes. These references may be modeled in a uniform way, even if it would not be possible to uniformly represent the cases and statutes to which they refer.

The choice of Article Nine as our domain does not in any way preclude us from extending the investigation to aspects of case-based reasoning as opportunities present themselves. The Uniform Commercial Code, like all texts, is not self-applying. Despite all efforts of the drafters to be clear and precise, none other than Karl Llewellyn was the chief reporter, the code is full of the usual problems of statutory interpretation.[3] Cases have been plentiful.

Having decided to focus on statutory law, Article Nine is a good choice. The Uniform Commercial Code is somewhat unusual in that it was not drafted by a legislative committee, but by a group of distinguished legal scholars including, as mentioned above, Karl Llewellyn. (Allison Dunham and Grant Gilmore were the principal draftsmen of Article Nine.) The project began in 1944 and was sponsored jointly by the National Conference of Commissioners on Uniform State Laws and the American Law Institute.[4] The first complete draft took six years to complete. Between 1953 and 1955, the New York State Law Revision Commission spent, according to White and Summers [129, p. 4], "several hundred thousand dollars" studying the code and making recommendations for revision, many of which eventually found their way into the official text.

Thus, the UCC is, or at least should be, an exceptionally well drafted code. At least this has been a guiding assumption in my attempt to model the code in an AI program. I have assumed that there is method in the madness of the code's organization and try to find representations preserving this structure, rather than presumptuously attempting to "rationally reconstruct" the code. As will be discussed later, a structure preserving representation, what Bench-Capon has called "isomorphic" modeling [15; 16], is important in any event, so as to be able to trace statements in the model to their authority in the code. This is considerably more difficult if there is not a one-to-one mapping from statements to code sections.

Another reason to use the UCC in a work on AI and legal reasoning, intended for the still rather small audience of lawyers and AI scientists distributed throughout the world,

---

[2]Although Gardner has claimed that "It would be unrealistic to work with statutes to the exclusion of case law." [40, p. 6], it cannot be my aim to model all the aspects of legal reasoning that a realistic account would require.

[3]Llewellyn wrote several books on jurisprudence in the realist tradition, including [67].

[4]The American Law Institute also sponsored the Restatement of the Law of Contracts, which Anne Gardner used as her main source of "black letter" law for offer and acceptance problems.

is that it has been enacted, in some form, by almost all of the states of the United States. As substantive law varies greatly from state to state, and of course country to country, it is difficult, perhaps impossible, to find a set of laws understood by all lawyers. This is a disadvantage of the law, compared to fields such as mathematics or the natural sciences, where knowledge is universally applicable. So, although European lawyers cannot be expected to be familiar with the UCC, it is nonetheless relatively well known.

Also, despite the fact that Article Nine radically simplified the prior law on secured transactions, according to Quinn it "remains one of the most difficult and complex articles to apply ..." [98, p. 9-2]. This complexity may make Article Nine a good candidate for a legal expert system or, less ambitiously, some kind of decision support system, such as a hypertext information retrieval system.

Finally, Article Nine is "planner's law" [118, p. 57] :

> ... security is a planner's concept and security law predominately planner's
> law — law to structure the future, not merely to abide by.

It is hoped that an Article Nine knowledge base will prove useful later in an AI-supported system for drafting security agreements, using methods such as those described in [48].

2.1 Introduction to Article Nine

Let's start with a story adapted, with minor changes, from Speidel, Summers and White's textbook [118, pp. 58-67] .

> George Potts, a middle-aged construction worker, had been out of work for two months. He needed $800 to make installment payments on some appliances and a television set he and his wife had bought. He owned a used car worth $1,200, but apart from clothing, furniture, and other personal effects, little else. He had assurance from his union that he would have work by June 1, 1978. It was then May 15.
>
> On May 16, Potts talked to Ben Adams of a local finance company, Adams Finance Co. After an interview and a general investigation of Potts's credit standing with local department stores, Adams agreed to and did lend Potts $800. Potts signed a promissory note for that amount providing for repayment of the $800, with interest at 12 per cent, on July 15, 1978.

In addition, let us suppose that the same day, May 16, Potts and Adams signed a document including the following text [118, p. 64] :

George Potts ("Debtor"), whose residence is ... hereby grants to Adams
Finance Co. ("Lender"), whose address is ... a security interest in the following
described motor vehicle, together with all accessories, attachments and
equipment now or hereafter attached thereto or used in connection therewith
("Collateral"):

One Ford four-door sedan, License No. 7J3336, Serial No. L8694371. This
security interest is to secure payment of a note ... executed and delivered by
Debtor to Lender, in the sum of Eight Hundred Dollars ($800.00), payable as to
principal and interest as provided therein.

Upon default by Debtor in the discharge of his liability to Lender, Lender
will have all the rights and remedies of a secured creditor under the Uniform
Commercial Code and any other applicable laws, including the right of Lender
to take possession of the Collateral.

In this story, Potts is the *debtor*, Adams is the *creditor* and the *secured party*, the Ford
sedan is the *collateral* and the document signed on May 16 is a *security agreement*. If
all goes well, Potts will have paid Adams the money owed under the promissory note by
July 15th. If Potts *defaults*, however, for example by not paying back the money due on
time, then the security agreement gives Adams certain *remedies* under Article Nine. For
example, he may go and take the car, if "this can be done without breach of the peace",
§ 9-503, and, after notifying Potts, may sell it at a public auction, § 9-504.

According to Speidel, Summers and White [118, p. 83], there are five basic types
of problems in the field of secured transactions: 1) deciding whether Article Nine is
applicable; 2) creating a valid security agreement between the creditor and debtor; 3)
perfecting the security interest created by the agreement; 4) resolving *priority conflicts*
between multiple interests in the collateral; and 5) deciding which remedies are available
upon default. Rather than trying to explain all of these aspects of the law, a task for which
Speidel, Summers and White require 368 pages (!), the primary focus will be on points
1 and 4 here. The other aspects will be discussed only as required to make sense of the
examples we'll be using. Priority conflicts will be handled first, while the facts so far of
Pott vs. Adams are fresh.

In the two sections which follow, we will be discussing rules for resolving conflicts of
two different kinds, at the "object" level and the "meta" level. The object-level rules, to be
discussed next, are Article Nine priority rules for ordering conflicting interests in collateral.
The meta-level, or second order, rules help to resolve conflicts between object-level rules,
such as between sections of Article Nine, or between Article Nine and other sources of
law, such as federal law.

2.2 Article Nine Priority Rules

Let us continue with the Potts and Adams story, but with a few alternative future
developments.

Case One.

Suppose that George Potts sells the Ford to Joachim Strauß on May 30. If George defaults, whose interest in the Ford is superior, Joachim's or Adams Finance Co.'s?

Case Two.

Suppose that Potts, in addition to his debt to Adams, owed Norbert Vogel $1000, due June 1. On Potts' failure to pay, Vogel filed a complaint in Superior Court, which Potts failed to answer. Vogel obtained a default judgment, and then procured a writ of execution from the Clerk of the Court. Pursuant to this writ, a sheriff of the county took possession of the Ford and sold it at an auction to Vogel, for $450. Whose interest in the Ford has priority, Vogel's or that of Adams Finance Co.?

Case Three.

Suppose that Helmut Blum also had loaned money to Potts, on June 15th, secured by the same Ford, and that Blum had properly filed a *financing statement* on June 16th. If Adams Finance Company did not file a financing statement, does Blum's security interest have priority?

These three alternative versions of the story illustrate some of the kinds of priority conflicts that can arise. In the first case, there is a conflict between a *property claimant*, Strauß, and Adams, who does not claim to own the Ford, but only to have a security interest. In the second case, Vogel is a *judgment lien creditor*. In the third case, the contest is between Blum's *perfected* security interest and Adams' *unperfected* security interest. (Blum's interest was perfected by filing the financing statement.)

Three factors are especially significant for solving Article Nine priority problems:

Role of each Party.

What is the role of each party in the transaction creating its interest? Is he, for example a purchaser of the collateral, a lender of property secured by the collateral, a trustee in bankruptcy, a judgment lien creditor, or perhaps a seller of the collateral, where the purchase price is secured by the property sold?

Type of Collateral.

What kind of property is the collateral? Is it stocks or bonds, equipment, goods, accounts, inventory, proceeds from a sale, or even farm products? A complicating factor here is that the type of the collateral depends on its role in the transaction creating the interest. The car serving as collateral for a business loan from a bank to a car dealership is *inventory*, but the same car in the sale to a customer of the dealership is a *consumer good*.

Attachment and Perfection.

The priority of a security interest often turns on the timing of certain events, in particular the time of its *attachment*, and of *perfection*. Briefly, the interest does not necessarily attach at the time of the security agreement, but only after the debtor has *rights* in the collateral and the secured party has given *value*. A security interest may be perfected by filing a *financing statement*, which puts the rest of the world on notice that the security interest exists in the collateral, or by taking possession of the collateral. In some cases, only possession is effective to perfect the interest, and in certain other cases perfection is automatic without having either filed or taken possession.

2.3 Higher-Order Conflicts Between Rules

The first problem to be addressed when analyzing a secured transactions problem is to determine whether Article Nine is applicable. This is a problem of Article Nine's *scope*. I consider this problem of scope to be just one instance of the more general problem of resolving conflicts between legal rules. A variety of conflicts of this kind, and some means of resolving them, will be addressed in this section, starting with the scoping problem.

Article Nine limits the scope of its own applicability. The basic scoping provision is § 9-102. It states, in part:

(1) Except as otherwise provided in Section 9-104 on excluded transactions, this Article applies (a) to any transaction (regardless of form) which is intended to create a security interest in personal property ... including goods, documents, instruments, general intangibles, chattel paper or accounts; and also (b) to any sale of accounts or chattel paper. ...

§ 9-104 lists twelve exceptions, including:

(c) to a right represented by a judgment ...
(j) ... to the creation or transfer of an interest in real estate, including a lease or rents thereunder ...

But the ability of any law to delimit its own applicability is modest. The law is like a ball of yarn: if you start pulling on one end it is only a matter of time before you have the whole ball in your hand. So too with Article Nine. To thoroughly consider all possibilities when analyzing a secured transactions case, it is not enough to just consider Article Nine, or even the whole of the UCC. Conflicting rules which may override the provisions of Article Nine can come from above, from Federal law, below, by agreement of the parties, or the side, from other state law.

As the UCC is state law, any applicable Federal laws may come from above to supercede Article Nine. (The traditional name for this principle is *lex superior derogat inferior*, or simply *Lex Superior*, which means rules from a superior authority take precedence over those from an inferior authority.) For example, the Ship Mortgage Act, a Federal statute, governs the creation of security interests in ships. There may also be conflicts between the UCC and Federal bankruptcy law.

The UCC allows the parties to a transaction great freedom to override the UCC, from the bottom, so to speak [118, p. 22] :

> As one authority put it, "... businessmen are free to make their own law. They do so expressly through contract, implicitly through a course of dealing, collectively through custom and resultant business understanding." By their own agreement, then, the parties to a commercial deal can vary most the provisions of the code.

This right of the parties to make their own deal is made explicit at a number of places within the UCC. Section 1-102(3) states, in part:

> The effect of provisions of this Act may be varied by agreement, except as otherwise provided in this Act and except that the obligations of good faith, diligence, reasonableness and care prescribed by this Act may not be disclaimed by agreement ...

And § 9-501(3) of Article Nine states:

> To the extent that they give rights to the debtor and impose duties on the secured party, the rules stated ... below may not be waived or varied ... but the parties may by agreement determine the standards by which the fulfillment of these rights and duties is to be measured if such standards are not manifestly unreasonable: ...

Potential conflicts coming from the side include provisions in other articles of the UCC, such as the buyers right to rejection and certain other non-consensual security interests created under Article Two on sales, and other state law, outside of the UCC. For example, there may be a state law with special requirements for perfecting a security interest in a motor vehicle, or there may be special consumer protection laws governing transactions between businesses and consumers.

Another source of state law to be aware of are the equity doctrines, such as estoppel and waiver. UCC § 1-103 explicitly states that equity principles shall "supplement" the code:

Unless displaced by the particular provisions of this Act, the principles of
law and equity, including ... estoppel, fraud, misrepresentation, duress, coercion,
mistake, bankruptcy, or other validating or invalidating cause shall supplement
its provisions.

In the case of multistate commercial transactions, there may be a *conflict of laws*
problem in the narrow, legal sense; it may not be clear which state's law applies. § 9-103 of
Article Nine itself resolves some of these issues, but may only be applicable if both states
have adopted the UCC, and have not modified or interpreted this section disparately, in
some significant way.

There are still two other kinds of conflicts between rules I would like to mention,
between different sections and versions of Article Nine itself.

The problem of conflicts between sections of the same Article is the problem of rules
with exceptions. Sartor has cataloged a variety of forms exceptions can take [107], and
I have speculated about reasons for structuring the law in this way, rather than simply
including all sufficient and perhaps necessary conditions for some legal predicate in
one place [45]. The theory, on the importance of nonmonotonicity for legal reasoning, is
reiterated in this book, in section 3.2.1. For the moment, let us just briefly describe the
types of exceptions to be handled by the computational model and give a few examples
from Article Nine.

Exceptions may be explicit or implicit. In the case of explicit exceptions, there are three
possibilities: either the general rule mentions the exception, the exception mentions the
general rule, or they refer to each other. Otherwise the exceptions are implicit.

For an example of a general rule mentioning an exception, consider § 9-102, which
was reprinted in part above: "(1) Except as otherwise provided in Section 9-104 on
excluded transactions ...". Another example is § 9-301, which states, in part, that "Except
as otherwise provided in subsection (2), an unperfected security interest is subordinate to
the rights of (a) persons entitled to priority under Section 9-312; ...". Article Nine is full
of this type of exception.

There are several kinds of implicit exceptions. UCC § 1-103, for example, which was
reprinted above, can be considered a *blanket exception*. Recall that it states that equity
principles, such as fraud, can be used to override sections of the UCC. It begins "Unless
displaced by the particular provisions of this Act ...", but the poor lawyer is left to look for
the particular provisions on his own.

Another form of implicit exception occurs when one rule is more *specific* than some
conflicting rule. The principle known as *Lex Specialis* states that when a general rule
conflicts with a more specific rule, the specific rule has priority. For example, in Article
Nine there are general rules which apply to all security interest, with more specific rules
for particular types of collateral, such as consumer goods.

Finally, in this last example, § 9-113 states an implicit exception to § 9-302, on the
necessity of filing to perfect the security interest. § 9-302 also fails to mention § 9-113.
That is, neither the exception nor the general rule mention the other:

A security interest arising solely under the Article on Sales (Article 2) is subject to the provisions of this article except that to the extent that and so long as the debtor does not have or does not lawfully obtain possession of the goods ... (b) no filing is required to perfect the security interest; and ...

The problem of conflicts due to different versions of the UCC has two aspects, one jurisdictional and one temporal. Although the UCC has been enacted in 49 states, the version of the code enacted is not precisely the same in each state. The states which did enact the UCC often made minor modifications before doing so. This is just another aspect of the conflict of laws problem discussed above.

The temporal aspect here concerns the major revisions made to the UCC in 1972, especially to Article Nine. Not all states have enacted these amendments. Of course, these revisions override the 1962 version of the UCC to the extent they conflict. There is a Latin name for this principle too: *Lex Posterior*.

Quite a variety of sources of conflicting law have been identified, and case law has yet to even be mentioned. The usual uncertainty caused by competing interpretations of the code by different courts is also a fact of life for the law secured transactions. Where the doctrine of *stare decisis* is adhered to, as in the United States, then the opinions of the higher courts, to the extent that they are not *dicta*, are binding on the lower courts, and therefore take precedence. This is another application of *Lex Superior*. Between courts at the same level, such as different appellate courts in the State of California, or the supreme courts of different states, such as Nevada and California, the opinions of another jurisdiction may provide guidance, but are not binding.

Several generally accepted legal principles for ordering conflicting rules have been mentioned: *Lex Specialis*, *Lex Superior* and *Lex Posterior*. These principles can be considered second-order rules *about* the rules of some legal field, which are first-order. These two levels are not sufficient for legal reasoning, as there may well be conflicts between the second-order rules which need to be resolved. For example, in a conflict between an earlier Federal law and a later State law, which should have priority? This can be viewed as a conflict between *Lex Superior* and *Lex Posterior*. Generally, authority takes precedence over time. However, here too there may be exceptions. The rules for ordering conflicting defeasible rules may themselves be defeasible. Although three levels seem sufficient for most purposes, a completely general system for legal reasoning would place no arbitrary limits on the number of levels which can be handled.

To sum up:

1. Legal rules are *defeasible*; they may conflict with other valid legal rules in some cases.

2. Second-order rules or principals, such as *Lex Specialis*, *Lex Posterior* and *Lex Superior*, regulate the resolution of conflicts between first-order rules.

3. These second-order rules are themselves defeasible; they may also conflict with one another. These conflicts are resolved by appealing to still higher-level principles.

Chapter 3   Philosophy of Legal Reasoning

Practical legal reasoning and argumentation, as is all behavior, are subject to resource limitations. Decisions and judgments are usually made under time pressure, for example. Of particular interest here, however, are limitations on information and knowledge about the law, about the facts of a case, and more generally on our ability to experience, understand and reason rationally about the world. The theory and computational model of legal reasoning to be developed in this book attempts to take some of these pragmatic limitations on rationality into consideration. This chapter and the next discuss certain theories and models of legal philosophy and Artificial Intelligence, respectively, to see what they can contribute to our understanding of legal reasoning in the face of such limitations. After a critical examination of this previous work, my own theory of legal argumentation will then try to take into account the lessons learned.

As a rational activity, book writing too is subject to practical limitations. It is not possible here to discuss the relevant legal philosophy literature in much depth. My plan is to focus on a few issues, and then review what several selected theorists have had to say about just these issues. Thus, there can be no claim of comprehensiveness for the comparative study of legal philosophy in this chapter. Its purpose is to provide just enough jurisprudence to support the formal theory and computational model which forms the core of the book.

The issues selected are the following:

- Which *kinds of pragmatic limitations* does the theory of legal argument identify or recognize?

- What does the theory consider a *correct* or *justified* legal decision or judgment to be, given the limitations on rationality it accepts?

- Which *methods* does the theory propose, if any, for *identifying* or *constructing* legal decisions meeting these criteria for correctness or justification?

The jurisprudential foundation of the most prominent English-language works on AI and legal reasoning [77; 40; 119] has been limited to Anglo-American schools of legal philosophy, especially Hart's form of *analytical jurisprudence*. For the sake of comparison, I will include a discussion of Hart's philosophy in this chapter, but my focus will be certain contemporary German jurisprudential thought, in particular Rödig's work on *Legal Logic* and Alexy's *Discourse Theory of Legal Argumentation*. Some other theories, mainly of historical interest, such as *Conceptualism* (Begriffsjurisprudenz) will be discussed briefly, in passing.

This selection may seem somewhat arbitrary. Kaufmann lists 15 "newer directions"

(Neuere Strömungen) in Legal Philosophy, each stemming from some philosophical root, such as phenomenology, Marxism, existential philosophy, hermeneutics, system theory, or "critical rationality" [58]. But it cannot be the aim here to provide encyclopedic coverage of the subject. The theories chosen, as we will see, are directly relevant to the issues of interest, concerning limitations of practical reason.

3.1   Hart's Analytical Jurisprudence

Analytical jurisprudence is sometimes identified with *legal positivism* and contrasted with *legal realism*. Following Mazurek [58, pp. 164-173], however, realism and analytical jurisprudence can both be viewed as forms of positivism. For Hart, the central feature of positivism is the claim that laws are separate from morals [52, p. 181]: "We shall take Legal Positivism to mean the simple contention that it is in no sense a necessary truth that laws reproduce or satisfy certain demands of morality ..." The difference between realism and analytical jurisprudence concern the nature of the events and objects which they are willing to label "law".

The American realists, Oliver Wendell Holmes and Karl Llewellyn were the leading figures, take a sociological perspective. The law is what the courts and other authorities decide in fact. In [40, p. 21] we see that Holmes wrote: "The prophecies of what the courts will do in fact, and nothing more pretentious, are what I mean by the law." On the same page is this quotation from Llewellyn: "What ... officials do about disputes is, to my mind, the law itself." I suspect we should be careful about overinterpreting such isolated statements. Nonetheless, a superficial analysis of realism would lead us to conclude that its preferred theories of the law are those which best *predict* legal decisions. The appropriate methods for studying the law would appear to be those of the empirical social sciences, such as surveys, experiments and statistical models.

Although the prediction of judicial decisions is a legitimate interest, and the methods of social science are surely appropriate for this purpose, the utility of realism is quite limited. It neither provides methods for deciding legal cases, nor for critically evaluating legal decisions. Lawyers do not argue their case before a court by publicly predicting the judge's decision. Nor do judges predict their own behavior when deciding cases or justifying their decisions. Thus, for this task, realism is of little assistance to an attorney, and even less to a judge. Moreover, realism does not acknowledge that decisions can be wrong. It does not develop criteria for testing the "correctness" of judgments. To sum up, realism limits its attention to *descriptive* and *predictive* theories of law, to the exclusion of its normative and synthetic aspects.

Analytical jurisprudence addresses some of these limitations of realism by viewing the law as a system of rules. Its leading proponent is H.L.A. Hart [52]. Following Dworkin [30, p. 38], the principal claims of Hart's form of positivism include:

1.   The law is of a set of rules, which can be identified by applying a fundamental secondary *rule of recognition*. This secondary rule concerns the *authority* or "pedigree" of the primary rules, not their content.

2.   At any point in time, the set of valid rules is "exhaustive of the law". Usually, cases
     are decided by "applying the law". These are clear cases. But, in *hard cases*, those not
     clearly covered by one of the rules, a judge must decide the case by "manufacturing a
     new rule" or "supplementing an old one". This power is called "judicial discretion".

     The first point asserts that the ultimate source of law is not reason, ethics or morality,
but the sovereign power of the state. This it has in common with realism. It is the authority
of judges which entitles their decisions to be characterized as law. This view of law is
rooted in Hobbes philosophy [54]. Thus, positivism, in both forms discussed here, cleanly
separates legal and moral questions. Legally justified judicial decisions can be morally
doubtful. Positivism does not assert that there is no connection between law and morality.
The legislative and judicial powers of a state should enact laws which do not conflict with
moral principles, and moral arguments can be made to criticize law. But this is not the
place to deepen this discussion about the relationship between morals and positive law.
     The important point here is that analytical jurisprudence claims to have addressed to a
certain extent one of the limitations of realism mentioned above: it provides legal criteria
for evaluating the "correctness" of judicial decisions. A judgment is justified either by a
demonstration that its decision was reached by an application of valid legal rules, or by
showing that the case was "hard", falling outside the range of application of the existing
rules. To this extent, analytical jurisprudence is a normative theory of legal reasoning.
     However, like realism, analytical jurisprudence is also an empirical theory of law.
Whether or not a rule is *valid* is viewed as a second-order factual question, to be answered
by interpreting sources of law, such as statutes and published cases. Pure reason alone is
not sufficient. The validity of a rule must be grounded in evidence of some appropriate
action, such as the decision of a previous case or the enactment of a statute, by a legal
authority. That is, as Dworkin notes, legal rules are validated not by their truth, but by their
"pedigree".
     Interestingly, this establishes a link between analytical jurisprudence and Wittgen-
stein's theory of *language games* (Sprachspiele). In his "Philosophical Investigations"
[131], the so-called "late Wittgenstein" was one of the first to recognize that language is
behavior; that it is not used just to describe the world, but also to command, to direct, to
tell stories, to entertain, to persuade, and so on. I will discuss Wittgenstein's philosophy
in a bit more detail later, as well as the "speech act" theories which descend from it, in the
section on Alexy's discourse theory of legal argumentation. For now, it is enough to note
that Hart, building on Wittgenstein's philosophy, recognized that legal utterances can be
of different kinds, definitional, empirical (descriptive) and normative, and that different
methods are required for establishing the appropriateness of each kind of utterance, depending on the context of its use. This insight is reflected in his secondary rule of recognition, which as just mentioned, appeals to authority, rather than truth or purely formal criteria, to validate legal rules.[1]

---

[1]Hart acknowledges his debt to Wittgenstein [53, p. 274] : "the main stimulus" of the modern phase of analytical
jurisprudence "has been provided by two philosophers very much concerned with language: Wittgenstein and

American realism was an (over-) reaction to *conceptualism* (Begriffsjurisprudenz), which Pound called "mechanical jurisprudence". Anne Gardner notices that "consistent practitioners of mechanical jurisprudence are hard to find" [40, p. 19]. This may be true of Anglo-American jurisprudence, but it is not difficult to find German conceptualists. It was the dominant legal philosophy in Germany during the second half of the 19th century. According to Michael Marx [58, pp. 92-95] its leading figures were Puchta, Windscheid and von Jhering.[2] It is usually understood today as a deductive theory of legal reasoning.

But, of course, conceptualism was prevalent before the development of formal logic, so it was not really "mechanical" in a modern sense. From an AI perspective, conceptualism appears to have more in common with terminological reasoning, in the KL-ONE sense [21] than with propositional reasoning. Consider this description of the "conceptual pyramid" from Larenz[58, p. 92] :

> From level to level the pyramid becomes less wide, but gains in height.
> ... The ideal of the logical system is completely realized when there is an
> abstract concept at the top of the pyramid under which all other concepts can be
> subsumed.

According to Puchta, the law "becomes visible as the product of scientific deduction" using the conceptual pyramid. The complete set of legal "sentences" were considered to be implicit within the closed structure of the conceptual pyramid, just as the theorems of an axiomatic theory are implicit in the axioms. Hart writes [53, p. 269]:

> The fundamental error [of conceptualism] consists in the belief that legal
> concepts are *fixed* or *closed* in the sense that it is possible to define conditions;
> so that for any real or imaginary case it is possible to say with certainty whether
> it falls under the concept or does not ... it is logically closed (begrenzt). This
> would mean that the application of a concept to a given case is a simple logical
> operation conceived as a kind of unfolding of what is already there, and, in the
> simpler Anglo-American formulation, it leads to the belief that the meaning of
> all legal rules is fixed and predetermined before any concrete questions of their
> application arises.

Puchta named conceptualism "lawyer's law", as the professional "scientific" skills of lawyers were required to make explicit the law inherent in this structure.

Notice that conceptualism is itself an especially strong form of legal positivism.

Professor John L. Austin".

[2]Jhering later became a critic of conceptualism and founded *interest jurisprudence*. According to Hart, Holmes criticism of conceptualism was in part a reaction to Jhering's earlier work, the *Geist des Römischen Rechts* and was similar in many respects to Jhering's own later criticism of conceptualism, in *Im Juristischen Begriffshimmel*. But Hart [53, p. 267] states there is no indication that Holmes "ever recognized that Jhering had uttered protests ... similar to his own ..."

The conceptual pyramid *is* the law. But, according to Michael Marx [58, pp. 89-111], conceptualism was only the culmination of an entire century of positivism in German jurisprudence. The first half of the century was dominated by the positivism of Friedrich Carl von Savigny. By negative implication, one might suppose that positivism has been on the decline in Germany since then, long before Hart's *The Concept of Law* [52] was published in 1961. But then Fritjof Haft writes "legal positivism is, despite all criticism, still the dominant view." [58, p. 112].

The main concern of the American Realists was that judges not be unduly constrained by such abstract conceptual ideals [55, p. 5]: "... the felt necessities of the time, the prevalent moral and political theories, intuitions of public policy, avowed or unconscious, even the prejudices which judges share with their fellow men, have had a good deal more to do than the syllogism in determining the rules by which men *should* be governed." (Emphasis added.)

Thus, it is clear that realism was not a cynical recognition that judges will decide cases as they will, and that all one can do to protect oneself from their whim is to attempt to predict their behavior so as to enable the avoidance of unfavorable decisions. Rather, realism was motivated by the moral conviction that justice can demand the "necessities of the time" be given greater priority than the maintenance of an elegant "conceptual pyramid".

Although conceptualism is usually ridiculed today, it is interesting to speculate about the interests conceptualist ideals serve. Their emphasis reminds me of the goals of modern software engineering: transparency, maintainability, modularity, fault tolerance, and so on. That is, the focus of conceptualism was the structural attributes of a system of laws, independent of the purposes or demands of any particular legal domain.

Hart's analytical jurisprudence lies somewhere between conceptualism and realism, with respect to the amount of power it delegates to the judiciary. German positivism, including conceptualism, tries to limit "discretion" to the point that "all arbitrariness is eliminated, so that the judge's sole task is a purely logical interpretation of the law." [58, p. 90] An indication that this view of judging is still prevalent, is the fact that German judges begin their careers shortly after finishing law school. Good judging is apparently considered a skill that can be learned in professional school, rather than something requiring substantial experience. As mentioned previously, whereas realism does not provide any criteria for constraining judicial power, Hart's theory limits judicial discretion to *hard cases*.

What is a "hard case"? This is a hard question. The problem has two aspects, both concerning Hart's secondary "rule of recognition". It's job is to identify the valid legal rules. But what is a rule? Susskind's distinction between "law-statements" and "law-formulations" is helpful here [119, pp. 36-37]. A law-formulation is an *authoritative* expression of law, such as the actual statutes and case reports. Susskind states that these "in a sense, belong to the external physical world". Consider UCC § 9-105 (1) (c):

(c) "Collateral" means the property subject to a security interest, and includes accounts and chattel paper which have been sold;

Is this a law-formulation? Although I've made an effort to quote § 9-105(1)(c) exactly, perhaps I've made an error. So, as this book is not an authoritative expression of the UCC, it is not a law-formulation. Rather it is a law-statement. However, a quotation of a paragraph from a statute such as this is not typical. A law-statement is usually a reformulation intended to clarify the meaning of the law for a particular audience.

The first, and easier, aspect of Hart's rule of recognition distinguishes between authoritative and nonauthoritative expressions of the law, i.e., between law-formulations and law-statements. It is a factual problem. In the example, one need only go to the law library and obtain a copy of the most recent version of the Uniform Commercial Code. Cases present greater problems. Although an authoritative case report is as easy to locate as a code book, cases, unlike statutes, need not contain explicit statements of rules. As Hart says [53, p. 131], "... there is no single method for determining the rule for which a given authoritative precedent is an authority. ... there is no authoritative or uniquely correct formulation of a rule to be extracted from cases." The rule of a case must first be found by interpretation.

It is this problem of interpretation which poses the most difficulty for Hart's secondary rule of recognition. Clearly, as rules must first be "extracted" from cases by interpretation, it is not the literal text of the case which is the legal rule in Hart's theory, but rather its *meaning*. Arguably, the difference between statutes and cases is not so great as it might at first appear. Although statutes purport to state rules explicitly, they too must first be interpreted [9]. Law-formulations, be they cases or statutes, are the "sources" of legal rules, which are gained through interpreting the sources. As there is no way to express the rules which are the meaning of these formulations other than by using language, the rules themselves remain intangible, beyond direct experience.[3] This raises a host of semantical questions, such as Jørgensen's dilemma about the "truth value" of normative statements, but we will have to ignore most of these issues here. Let us focus on two sources of the nondeterminancy of interpretation recognized by Hart: the problem of *open-textured* terms, which is an instance of the more general problem of the *defeasibility* of legal rules, and the problem of conflicting norms.

Hart's notion of open-texture can again be traced back to Wittgenstein, by way of Waismann [53, p. 274], who called it the "Porösität der Begriffe". The claim expressed by the notion of open-texture is that "there can be no final and exhaustive definitions of concepts, not even in science". Waismann's example was: "Suppose I come across a being that looks like a man, speaks like a man, behaves like a man, and is only one foot tall, shall I say he is a man?" Hart writes:

---

[3]Actually, the rules can also be "communicated" by following them, i.e., by behaving according to them. Supposedly, in practice most legal rules are learned indirectly, by conforming to prevailing practices, some of which can be traced back to legal acts.

However complex our definitions may be, we cannot render them so precise so they are delimited in all possible directions and so that for any given case we can say definitely that the concept either does or does not apply to it. ... As we can never eliminate such possibilities of unforeseen situations emerging, we can never be sure of covering all possibilities. We can only redefine and refine our concepts to meet the new situations as they arise.

The open texture of particular terms is a special case of the more general problem of the defeasibility of legal rules. Hart recognized [52, p. 135] that rules have, or at least can have, "exceptions not exhaustively specifiable in advance". In "The Ascription of Responsibility and Rights" [51], before "The Concept of Law", Hart noted that even rules which seem to be unqualified, absolute statements are actually subject to the risk of implied exceptions. Every rule, he said, has an unwritten "unless" at the end.

However, defeasibility is not so much a limitation on language, although it is also this, as a limitation on knowledge. In his view, defeasibility and open-texture are not defects of natural language that we should try to correct [52, p. 125] : "... we should not cherish, even as an ideal, the conception of a rule so detailed that the question whether it applied to a particular case was always settled in advance, and never involved, at the point of application, a fresh choice between open alternatives." Why not? Because, "we are men, not gods." We neither have complete knowledge of the world, nor are we ever completely certain about our goals and purposes. The ability of natural language to be imprecise allows legislatures to postpone decision on many potential issues, allowing the law to develop in the courts, where there is considerably more information about the potential advantages and disadvantages of alternative refinements of some abstract rule.

Regarding conflicting rules, Hart writes [52, p. 98]:

> In a modern legal system where there are a variety of 'sources' of law, the rule of recognition is correspondingly more complex: the criteria for identifying the law are multiple and commonly include a written constitution, enactment by a legislature, and judicial precedents. In most cases, provision is made for possible conflict by ranking these criteria in an order of relative subordination and primacy. It is in this way that in our system 'common law' is subordinate to 'statute'.

Here we see that Hart recognized that primary rules may conflict, whatever procedure is used to interpret the individual sources to arrive at these rules, and that some secondary rule for ranking or prioritizing them would be necessary. However, it seems odd to me to consider this ordering rule to be a part of the rule of recognition. Surely Hart does not mean that the subordinate rules are not valid rules, or less valid than higher priority rules. Also, the ordering relationship mentioned here is based solely on the authority of the source. Although this is certainly one factor to be considered, it is hardly exhaustive of the principles used to order conflicting rules in practice. This does not seem to be a subject which Hart has given much attention.

Hart's harshest critics are not rationalists, as one might expect, questioning his adoption of Wittgenstein's insights about the nondeterminancy of the meaning of language. On the contrary, they are primarily realists, who oddly claimed that language is still even less certain than Hart admitted. In "The Concept of Law" [52, pp. 132-144], Hart presents and responds to various forms of "rule skepticism". But I find the realist's position on this issue to be incoherent for another reason. Hart claims that despite the indeterminacy of language, sentences do have a "core of certainty". That is, there are "clear cases" where there can be no serious question that the sentence (or term) is applicable. That is, in logical terms, there are worlds which clearly satisfy some statement. In particular, there are prototypical cases. For example, a passenger car is a prototypical "vehicle". The realists deny that this is possible while at the same time asserting that predictive theories of judicial behavior, which they identify with "the law", are possible. But how are these predictions stated if not in language, and how can they be predictive of anything if language is as uncertain as they claim? How would one evaluate whether the predicted behavior occurred? Would such theories be falsifiable? In short, the realists accept uncritically a correspondence theory of meaning, with its much stronger assumptions about the power and certainty of language, while at the same time rejecting Hart's claim that statements of law can even have a "core of certainty".

Regarding standards for evaluating the correctness of judicial decisions, Hart's theory is itself somewhat vague. According to the usual interpretation, Hart's theory limits the discretion of judges to those cases falling within the "penumbra of doubt", i.e., to hard cases. If a case is clear, falling within the core of certainty of a rule, a judge is bound to apply the rule. As this core of certainty is apparent to everyone, by definition, this is considered to provide a test limiting discretion. To the extent of the clear meaning of the valid legal rules, legal reasoning is, according to this view of Hart, deductive.

However there are problems with this simple interpretation of Hart, if one considers deduction to mean reasoning using a standard, monotonic logic. As we have seen, Hart recognized that rules may conflict, and that some secondary rule would be necessary to resolve such conflicts. It is unclear whether he thought these conflict resolution rules would always be sufficient to dictate a single solution, or whether here too judicial discretion would sometimes be necessary. Conflicting rules may lead to multiple solutions, even when the case falls within the core of certainty of each rule.

Moreover, and this is considerably more serious, there are passages where Hart seems to recognize that there are cases which should be decided contrary to the (previous) clear meaning of some valid rule. In his essay on "Jhering's Heaven of Concepts" [53], first published in 1970, Hart joins Jhering in criticizing conceptualism by saying: "... all legal rules and concepts are 'open'; and when an unenvisaged case arises we must make a fresh choice, and in doing so elaborate our legal concepts, adapting them to socially desirable ends." And, later in the same essay, "We can only *redefine* and refine our concepts to meet new situations when they arise." (Emphasis added)

Further, in his overworked example of a rule stating "no vehicle may be taken into the park", the clear, paradigm case is a "motor car". But then he goes on to write, [52, p. 126]:

... until we have put the general aim of peace in the park into conjunction with those cases which we did not, or perhaps could not, initially envisage (perhaps a toy *motor-car* electrically propelled), our aim is, in this direction, indeterminate. ... When the unenvisaged case does arise, we confront the issues at stake and can then settle the question by choosing between the competing interests in the way which best satisfies us. In doing so we shall have rendered more determinate our initial aim, and shall incidentally have settled a question as to the meaning, for the purposes of this rule, of a general word. (Emphasis added)

Is a toy motor car a vehicle? If so and the toy should nonetheless be permitted in the park, then this unanticipated case requires a decision contrary to the previous core of certainty of the general rule. If not, if toy cars are outside the prototypical meaning of vehicles in the rule, even though the case had not been imagined, then the intuition behind this idea of a prototype, or core of certainty, would not seem to be expressible in language, at least not in general statements. How useful can such an intangible notion of prototype be for publicly defending or justifying arguments?[4]

This line of reasoning, of course, brings us dangerously close to the position of the rule skeptics. However, I will avoid contradicting myself by not adopting, as the realists implicitly did, the correspondence theory of meaning. I will come back to this subject later, when discussing Alexy's discourse theory of argumentation, below. For now, my point is that Hart's form of positivism does not provide clear normative criteria for restricting discretion or evaluating the "technical correctness" [66] of judicial decisions. One the one hand, he claims that judges only have discretion when the case falls outside of the conventional, context-independent meaning of the terms used in the rule. That is, he adopts a standard of strict or literal interpretation. On the other hand, his examples show that he considers conventional meaning to be too restrictive. He recognizes that arguments using the purpose of some rule, such as peace and quiet in the park, can be necessary to reach a just decision. Although the lack of norms for restricting judicial power was one of his principal criticisms of realism, Hart's theory does not, I'm afraid, fair much better in this respect.

One might argue that these problems don't often arise, that in most cases, the general rule *will* be applied as expected. This may be true, but it would be missing the point. This argument asserts the core of certainty may be useful for predicting how a judge will decide some case; we are back to the realist's position. A minor difference would be the preferred form of representation of the descriptive theories. The realists might prefer probabilistic, statistical models; Hart followers might prefer to simulate judicial justification using a set of general rules. However, the issue here is whether Hart's theory provides the *normative*

---

[4]Perhaps your intuitions tell you that toy cars are neither cars nor vehicles. No problem. There are plenty of other examples where reasoning about the purpose of the law is required to reach the intuitively correct result, where there should be no doubt that the object in question falls within the conventional meaning of "vehicle". Consider baby carriages, or the army tank to be used as a war memorial, to mention just two other well-worn examples.

criteria he claims for deciding whether or not a judicial decision, after the fact, was within the prescribed limits of judicial discretion. If he permits teleological arguments to decide an unanticipated but clear case in a way contrary to the conventional meaning of the terms of the general rule, as the "motor car" example implies, then it would appear that other factors, unaccounted for by his theory of clear cases, are being suggested for testing whether a judicial decision has been sufficiently justified.

It might also be suggested, although I have yet to hear this argument, that it would be inconsistent to demand a "bright-line" rule for evaluating judicial decisions while maintaining, as Hart does, that hard cases exist. Shouldn't one expect there to be indeterminate cases where it is unclear whether a judge exceeded the limits of his discretion? This would be a straw man argument. It's easy to knock down. It is not the indeterminacy of Hart's criteria that is the object of my criticism here, but its incoherence. A proper theory of justification need not permit us to determine in every case whether or not a decision was within permissible bounds. But, a theory of justification should at least be consistent. If teleological arguments are to be permitted, this must be accounted for in the theory.

This sketch of Hart's theory will have to suffice for our purposes here. Let me now, finally, evaluate the theory with respect to the three issues of interest: the pragmatic limitations on rationality it recognizes, its notion of correctness of legal judgments, and the methods it proposes for evaluating legal decisions.

Recognized Limitations

As we have seen, Hart, borrowing primarily from Wittgenstein, did recognize certain limitations of natural language: most terms are "porous" and rules are subject to implicit exceptions. Moreover, he recognized that persons can only have imperfect knowledge about the world and about their goals. This insight was used to praise the ability of natural language to be vague and imprecise. That is, vagueness was not considered to be only, or even primarily, a limitation of natural language, but also one of its useful features.

Correctness Criteria

Hart's original theory placed the limits of judicial discretion at the border of the literal meaning of the words used in the rule. When the concrete facts of a case are not subsumed by the general terms of the rule, interpreted literally, the judge is free to decide as he or she pleases. The decision of a clear case is "correct" if and only if the decision conforms to the rule; the decision of a hard case is, by definition, always correct. Hart later retreated from this view by conceding that the purpose of the rule must also somehow be taken into account.

Methods

As the revised verion of Hart's theory does not provide a satisfactory definition of a correct or justified legal judgment, there can be little hope of deriving methods from his theory for identifying or constructing justified decisions.

To conclude this section let me reiterate the lessons from Hart's form of analytical jurisprudence. These are insights that should be taken into consideration by any theory of legal justification:

1. Hart was the first legal philosopher (to my knowledge) to draw upon Wittgenstein's insights regarding the nature of language. Language has a variety of uses beyond that of describing the world. Language is behavior. The correspondence theory of meaning was rightly called into question. However, whether or not terms have conventional meaning, Hart was wrong in thinking this distinction alone would be sufficient for defining the limits of judicial discretion.

2. He recognized that persons (and legislatures) are not omniscient; our knowledge about the facts of the world and purposes, goals, values and interests is limited.

3. One consequence of this last point is a rejection of conceptualism's ideal of a logically closed set of norms. On this point, the realists and Hart agree.

4. Rather than rejecting the concept of a rule, openness is achieved by further elaborating the structure of rules in a legal system. Secondary rules, such as the "rule of recognition", regulate the development, modification and application of primary rules. They may also rank conflicting primary rules.

5. Further, some power should be delegated to judges for refining and shaping the law as cases are decided, at the point where there is more information about the benefits and costs of alternative possibilities.

6. One mechanism for delegating this power to the judiciary is to use suitably vague terms, such as "variable standards". The ability to be intentionally vague is a useful feature of natural language for expressing the law. We should avoid undue precision when expressing norms.

7. Although useful, a descriptive or predictive theory of judicial behavior, as proposed by the realists, is not sufficient. Judicial power must be balanced against other goals, such as avoiding subversion of the will of the legislature, arbitrariness, prejudice and caprice. A normative theory delimiting judicial power is required.

3.2   Rödig's Legal Logic

Starting at about 1950, when Ulrich Klug's book "Juristische Logik" (Legal Logic) [59] was first published, there has been considerable academic interest within German-language jurisprudence in the application of formal logic, usually first-order predicate logic, to problems of legal reasoning, argumentation, and legislation.[5] Schreiber, for example, as early as 1962 represented sections of the German Civil Code (BGB) in predicate logic [108]. Other leading figures include Philipps [90], Klug's students Fiedler [34] and Rödig [104; 105], Tammelo [120], Wagner [126], and Weinberger [127; 128]. This amount of activity must be compared to Allen's lonely voice within Anglo-American jurisprudence [5; 6], until around the time of McCarty's Harvard Law Review article on Artificial Intelligence and Law, in 1977 [77].

It might be asked whether it makes sense to speak of a "legal logic". Does each domain or field have its own logic? Is there a "logic of biology", for example? I am not aware of any of these authors making this claim; on the contrary, some have specifically explained that they simply mean the application of some general purpose formal logic to legal problems [59, pp. 5] [121, pp. 120] [128, p. 9]. And by "formal logic" they do mean "modern" logic, as developed by Frege, Russell, Whitehead, Carnap, Hilbert and many others [59, p. 13], which they contrast with the "classical" logic of Aristotle. However, despite an emphasis on "classical" (here in the sense of Tarskian semantics), two-valued, predicate logic, there is less consensus about which logics are useful for legal reasoning. Philipps, for example, was an early proponent of intuitionism [58, p. 147]. There has also been a continuing debate about whether or not a special deontic logic, such as von Wright's early proposal [125], is required for expressing legal norms. Rödig, for example, has argued at length that this is *not* necessary [105, pp. 185-207]. Weinberger's latest edition of his "Rechtslogik" stretches the concept of logic to its limits; in addition to the usual material on propositional and predicate logic, it includes chapters on modal logic, deontic logic, teleology and action theory, value and preference logic, the logic of questions (Fragenlogik), induction, causality and probability, among others.

These legal logicians, strictly speaking, do not form a *school* of jurisprudence. A common conviction in the value of formal logic for a variety of legal tasks does not entail a particular stance on any of the (other) big issues in legal philosophy, such as the relationship between law and morality, the ultimate source of authority of a state, or structural questions such as the appropriate division of power between legislative, judicial and executive branches of government. Perhaps one could say that they form a school of thought with respect to claims about the value and limits of logic for various purposes in the law, but these purposes and claims are quite varied, and it is unclear whether there is much consensus even among these few authors. Here is just a sample of some of these claims:

---

[5]Tammelo claims to have published the first articles on the subject, in 1948 [58, pp. 123]. Klug claims his book had been completed by 1939, but was prevented from being published for political reasons [59, preface].

- Klug [59, pp. 1-3]: "Formal logic is that part of the philosophy of science which delivers the inference rules necessary for the development of any scientific field. ... It is appropriate to call this logic formal, because it states how to derive the consequences of assertions ... It is the study of the correctness of inference and offers a system of rules for distinguishing between valid and invalid arguments. ... From this it follows that logic is naturally also of great importance for legal science, unless one is willing to do without the possibility of discussion, the representation of reasons and proofs, and the development of theories. ..."

- Weinberger [128, p. 23]: "On the one hand, Logic provides lawyers with a tool for arguing more precisely, and for critically examining proofs and reasons (Gründe). One the other hand, logical analysis defines its own limits: it shows where pure logical argumentation ends, where plausibility takes its place, and finally where pure arbitrariness is decisive."

- Tammelo [121, p. 120]: "In the field of legal theory, legal logic has a central role, as it is its task to dictate (bestimmen) the requirements and process of correct thinking."

Just these few claims for logic are already quite diverse, and this is but a small subset of the kinds of claims which have been made. Klug seems to adhere to a very restrictive conception of "science", and desires jurisprudence to meet the requirements of such a science. He claims that science without formal logic is impossible. Weinberger seems to be more interested in tools for working lawyers. He also stresses logic's limitations. Tammelo, on the other hand, does not appear to recognize these limits, or at least does not emphasize them. For him, logic establishes norms for correct thinking.

Of course, one should be careful about over interpreting these isolated passages. Rather than risk misrepresenting the views of any of these leading legal logicians by trying to present some composite view, I have chosen instead to focus on the arguments presented in an article by Rödig, written in 1973, in which he presents and defends the goals of formalization and "axiomatization" of the law [105, pp. 65-109]. The alternative would have been a comparative study of each of the main authors in the field, but I suspect that such depth would be unwarranted for my purposes here. However I should say that there is no consensus about the value of axiomatization. Tammelo writes, for example [58, p. 125]:

Whether or not the law can be axiomatized is a technical question; whether is should be axiomatized is a political question. If axiomatization of the law is possible and desirable, then legal logic can offer appropriate methods. *But just what the purpose of such an undertaking would be, is very difficult to recognize.* There is hardly anyone knowledgeable about the law who considers it possible to reduce the total, huge mass of law to a handful of axioms, from which it would be possible to deduce all possible legal decisions. ... It is true that formal systems of legal logic can be constructed axiomatically. But that has nothing to do with the axiomatization of the law. The methods and standards of logic itself in no way need to be the methods and standards of the law. Logic is a tool. A tool, and the object it is applied to, do not need to be structurally equivalent. (Emphasis added)

Klug was the original proponent of axiomatization [59, pp. 194-197]. But let us end our comparative remarks here and turn to Rödig's article. As we will see, Rödig consider's some of the misgivings expressed here to be the result of a misunderstanding about the goals of axiomatization. Let us begin with a summary of his description of the process:

1. Axiomatization should not be confused with formalization. Axiomatization is possible and desirable, indeed *necessary*, whether or not formal methods are used. Formal logic is a powerful tool for maximizing the benefits of axiomatization.

2. The purpose of axiomatization is to concisely express the infinite number of sentences making up a legal "theory". The "axioms" are a finite subset of the theory. The "theorems" are the logical consequences of the axioms.

3. The axiomatization is successful if the set of axioms is correct and complete. It is correct if all of the theorems are members of the legal theory. It is (materially) complete if every member of the theory is an axiom or a theorem.

4. The choice of axioms from the theory is arbitrary, so long as the set is finite, correct and complete. In particular, despite the common sense meaning of "axiomatic", the axioms do not have greater weight, authority, validity or reliability than any other member of the theory.

I can agree entirely with Rödig's point that axiomatization and formalization are separate issues. Unfortunately it is not always clear in his article whether certain arguments regard one or the other, or both. Despite his initial caveat that axiomatization *need* not imply formalization, he sometimes uses "axiomatization" to mean both axiomatization and formalization. Nonetheless, I will try to untangle things here, and discuss his view of the pros and cons of axiomatization and formalization separately.

3.2.1 Axiomatization

Between formalization and axiomatization, Rödig seems to think that formalization is the more controversial of the two. Perhaps more authors have expressed doubts about formalization, I am not sure, but my own intuitions are just the opposite: the idea of axiomatizing a legal domain is, as I will argue in the course of this section, somewhat mistaken.

Roughly speaking, the task of axiomatization is to represent a theory by a finite set of propositions having certain desirable properties, such as completeness and correctness. By "theory" here, we simply mean any set of propositions. This purely formal notion of theory is sufficient for defining axiomatization and discussing its supposed benefits.

Rödig's first argument is that axiomatization is not only desirable, but necessary [105, p. 79]. Any theory of law is necessarily infinite. If it contains any sentence, such as p, then it contains infinitely many, such as: $p \wedge p, p \wedge p \wedge p$ and so on.[6] Thus, as all texts are finite, a legislature *must* express its intent as a finite set of axioms when it codifies some field of law.

Ignoring the question of the role and power of the judiciary for the moment, there is a fallacy here. Rödig appears to identify the will of a legislative body, as expressed in a set of statutes, with a "theory" of law, in the sense here of an infinite set of norms exhaustively defining some field of law. This is quite doubtful. It ignores the insight, found in Hart's theory, that persons do not have complete knowledge about the world or their goals. Legislatures are not omniscient. If this is not Rödig's intention, then it is difficult to guess what he could mean by axiomatization. He describes it as a process of selecting axioms from a theory, which presupposes that there is such a theory. But let us continue.

Rödig next argues that, if axiomatization is inevitable, then we might as well do the job "exactly". He starts by citing Friederich Carl v. Savigny, writing about Roman law [105, p. 80] :

> [the statutes] form an entity which is intended to solve all possible legal questions. To be suitable for this purpose, it has to satisfy two requirements: unity and completeness.

Well, as Savigny at this time believed the law to be a closed system, and would have been entitled to full membership in Jhering's *Begriffshimmel*, Rödig's use of this excerpt does little to bolster his argument in favor of axiomatization. Is he proposing a return to conceptualism? He later makes it clear that this is not his intention [105, pp. 104-105]: "When axiomatizing a theory, one need not admit the theory is right (richtig)." He also writes: "Let us remember that the use of the axiomatic method does not hinder the flexibility (Beweglichkeit) of a legal system." Indeed, he goes on to argue that an exact logical analysis of legal arguments, by bringing hidden premises to light, subjects a legal

---

[6]Notice that these sentences are not tautologies. They are not true in every world, as is for example $p \rightarrow p$.

theory to criticism which may have otherwise gone unnoticed. So even if, as Savigny writes, a code is "intended" to be applicable to all legal problems, logical analysis opens this intention up to public criticism.

However, since the theory remains intangible, how can we distinguish criticism of the theory from criticism of the axiomatization? Perhaps the (intended) theory is beyond reproach, but the axiomatization lacks "unity" or "completeness". Thus, it is not at all clear that an axiomatization can help subject some legal theory to public criticism. One can always blame the axiomatization.

What are "unity" and "completeness"? Savigny writes [105, p. 80]: "If unity is missing, then there is a contradiction to be removed; if the statutes are incomplete, then there is a hole to be filled." Rödig then notices the similarity between this and the requirements of correctness and completeness of axiomatic systems.[7] But, other than Savigny's questionable authority, are there good reasons for demanding that laws be correct and complete, in the restricted sense of axiomatic systems?

An axiomatic system is correct just when the axioms and every theorem, i.e., every sentence entailed by the axioms, is a member of the theory to be axiomatized. Normally, a contradictory set of axioms is not correct, as every sentence is implied by a set of contradictory sentences. However, Rödig points out that this is true only if the theory to be axiomatized is itself consistent. If the theory is inconsistent, then not only is an inconsistent set of axioms correct, inconsistency is required for the axiomatization to be complete. It is not the job of axiomatization to remove contradictions in the theory. Nonetheless, Rödig argues [105, p. 81]: "An axiomatic system in which every sentence is derivable is both trivial and, from a practical perspective, useless." However, this is not at all obvious to me. It presupposes that logical reasoning from a set of premises is limited to deductive reasoning in a monotonic logic. Moreover, it assumes that *any* legal decision can be justified from an inconsistent set of laws. Rödig mistakes derivability for justifiability. Perhaps an example will make these claims more comprehensible.

A9W § 1-103 states that "Unless displaced by the particular provisions of this Act, the principles of law and equity, including ... fraud, misrepresentation ... shall supplement its provisions". A9W § 9-312 (5) (a) states "Conflicting security interests rank according to priority in time of filing or perfection, whichever is earlier". Now suppose one creditor, x, promises another creditor, y, to wait until y has filed, but then goes ahead and files first. Who has priority? According to § 9-312, x. But, assuming this was an act of fraud, § 1-103 would give y priority. Both conclusions are derivable, but are they equally justifiable? If nothing else where known about the relevant law, perhaps. Let us suppose, however, that there is an established secondary rule which ranks § 1-103 higher than than § 9-312. Such a rule would resolve this conflict in favor of y. Here we have an example of a rule subject to an implicit exception.

For the sake of argument, however, let us suppose that there is no such secondary rule and that "x has priority over y" and "x does not have priority over y" are both defensible

---

[7]For legal theories, Rödig argues the axioms need not be "independent". They are independent only if no axiom is a logical consequence of the others.

decisions. Would this state of affairs be sufficient justification for any decision? Could a third creditor, z, claim that *he* has priority over both x and y by simply pointing to the conflict between § 1-103 and § 9-312? Plainly not. Further, supposing that z had filed before both x and y, would it make sense for them to argue that it was unclear whether or not z had priority, merely because of the supposed conflict between § 1-103 and § 9-312? Again, clearly not. Even though z's argument uses one of the sections involved in the conflict, unless x or y were to claim priority because of some inequitable action by z, the conflict between these two sections is irrelevant.

Now, my arguments here have been informal, but hopefully clear nonetheless. After all, we are still discussing the supposed benefits of axiomatization, independently of the merits of formalization. My argument depends on the usual predicate logic meaning of the term "contradiction". Rödig insists on restricting its meaning in just this way [105, p. 82]:

> The term "contradiction" is often used in the literature on legal methods in ways other than in mathematical logic. The differences are sometimes especially confusing.

He complains, for example, about the idea of "contradictory concepts", asserting that only propositions about concepts can be contradictory. As we have seen, contradictory laws, in this logical sense, need not be useless. They do not permit arbitrary decisions to be justified, and they prohibit some arguments from being defensible. Rödig is mistaken, I believe, to identify Savigny's notion of "unity" with this narrow sense of "noncontradictory".

The counter-example given here is based on a general rule subject to an exception. As Hart has pointed out, all legal rules are subject to an indefinite number of implicit exceptions [51]. But the example here is a bit different. It has been constructed so that the "axiomatization" includes an explicit conflict between two sections.

Rödig has addressed this problem of the "rule-exception principle" a number of times [105, pp. 51, 98, 329]. He points out that "The drafters of older as well as newer statutes make extensive use of the technique of general rules subject to exceptions." (As we have seen, this "technique" is also used widely in the Uniform Commercial Code.) He then asserts that the use of this method leads to contradictory laws. But it is difficult to understand how this drafting method can have had such a long tradition if it allows arbitrary legal arguments to be defensible. Rather than trying to understand how the law has been able to serve its normative function despite this stubborn refusal to use the axiomatic method, Rödig suggests abandoning the technique. He shows how to collapse the rule-exception structure into a flat set of exceptionless rules.[8] If one has the misfortune to have to construct or criticize a legal argument using laws structured as general rules and exceptions, Rödig recommends [105, p. 99] :

---

[8] The method proposed is as follows. If there is a rule $p \to q$ and an exception $r \to \neg q$ then add a negative condition to the first rule, $p \wedge \neg ab \to q$, and replace the exception with the definition of ab as follows: $r \leftrightarrow ab$. This definition would need to be modified to add further exceptions.

[Such statutes] do not mean what they say. ... The application of statutes written using the rule-exception principle requires conflicts among the statutes to first be resolved. The statutes must, in other words, first be transformed into statements expressing the actually intended norms; it is these transformed sentences which must then be refined in the direction of the facts of the case.

There are a number of problems with these recommendations. The transformation process is likely to be tricky, tedious and error prone [106]. Moreover, to do the job correctly, one must resolve the conflicts between general rules and exceptions somehow, presumably using secondary rules. If this can be done, why not construct (or criticize) legal arguments using the conflicting rules and these secondary rules directly, rather than expending the extra effort to first transform them into a consistent set of sentences? Finally, although it may be easy to demonstrate that some decision is (or is not) a logical consequence of these consistent sentences, such a demonstration would not be sufficient *legal* justification for the decision. The transformed version of the law would consist of, in Susskind's terms, law-statements but, unlike the original version, not *authoritative* law-formulations. Each sentence must be shown to be backed by appropriate legal authority. In effect, the justification of the decision must include an argument defending the transformation. This task is made especially difficult if there is no simple mapping of the sentences in the transformation back into the original sentences of the statutes and other authoritative statements of law.

Of course, these last problems may be avoided if, as Rödig proposes, codified laws would be organized as consistent sets of statutes, rather than using the traditional method of general rules and exceptions. In "The Importance of Nonmonotonicity for Legal Reasoning" [45], I argued that there are compelling reasons for preserving this traditional structure of the law. Let me reiterate these arguments here.

As Hart recognized, we are not omniscient. We do not have complete knowledge of either our world or our goals. Legal reasoning is a form of *practical* reasoning. Whether one is planning an estate, drafting a contract or resolving a controversy, decisions must be made despite these limitations.

The law as a system of rules has at least two purposes: the guidance of behavior so as to avoid conflicts and provide the means for achieving socially desirable goals and the settlement of disputes after they have arisen. This second purpose is an admission that the law is incapable of completely accomplishing the first. The normative and conflict resolution roles of the law set it apart from the problem of common sense reasoning in general.

Structuring the law as general rules with exceptions supports these two goals, but for different reasons in each case. In order to promote the normative purpose of the law, persons who are not particularly knowledgeable of the law must be capable of learning and applying the law when planning their affairs. The settlement of disputes according to law, the second goal, is possible only to the extent that the legal system provides a means of resolving legal issues which is sensitive to the value of a decision to the parties involved. Let me explore these considerations in somewhat more detail.

The law can serve its normative function only if ordinary persons are able to learn and apply the law with some success.[9] Given the complexity of modern legal systems, systems which even lawyers have great difficulty in learning, it is reasonable to ask how we can fairly expect ordinary citizens to know the law. The difficulty is reduced significantly by the observation that no one needs to know all of the law, at least not all at once. The problem is finding a way of expressing the law which allows persons to quickly find that portion of the law which is relevant to the problem at hand. It should be possible to quickly acquire a rough sketch of some area of law, an overview, and to fill in the details as the need arises. That is, the law should support various depths of understanding. A useful, if shallow, understanding of legal rules and principles should be easy to learn. This shallow knowledge should then be able to be deepened, on an incremental basis.

There are a number of techniques which can be used for the purpose of managing complexity in the law, but I will discuss just two, abstraction and general rules subject to exceptions, both of which have been traditionally used to draft legislation. By using "top-down refinement", laws can be described in terms of very high-level concepts. These concepts can be given more precise, and perhaps technical meaning at the next, lower, level of abstraction. Terms at that level can be refined still further at the next level, and so on. Thus, the same law can be described at various levels of detail. One runs the risk, when restricting his attention to some level of description, of misunderstanding the law. It may be, for example, that a term used at one level of description is defined in a technical, nonintuitive way at the next level. But this risk is more than balanced by the possibility of getting a rough picture of the law.

Abstraction, however, is not enough. No matter how abstractly rules are stated, if the law is not structured as general rules with exceptions, then each rule must state sufficient conditions for its conclusion. If intuitive terms are used at the most abstract level of description, then the logical structure of these conditions is in general much too complex to be quickly grasped and applied. Of course, as Rödig has pointed out [105, pp. 329-333], any complex set of conditions can be represented abstractly by a single technical term or symbol, such as "A contract is valid if it is enforceable", where enforceability is a complex technical concept defined at lower levels, or worse "A contract is valid if the conditions of § 978 are satisfied". Although Rödig is right about this, I must object that such rules are of limited use, as they define unknown, complex concepts in terms of equally unknown and complex concepts.

A better approach is to use general rules subject to exceptions to supplement abstraction. As with abstraction, this technique introduces a kind of risk, in this case that a relevant exception will be overlooked. But when the laws are even slightly complex, this risk is outweighed by the advantage of being able to remember and apply general rules. Knowing a general rule is better than knowing none at all.

---

[9]Rödig also made this observation [105, p. 57] but came to the conclusion that "the more precisely a legal decision can be explained in terms of general norms, the easier it is to learn the law." I can only speculate whether or not he considered exceptions to violate this principle. He has criticized the use of exceptions in other places, but has not, so far as I am aware, discussed the connection between exceptions and learnability.

Implicit in our discussion so far is the conviction that a law must not only be understandable when we have the text of some statute in front of us, it must also be possible to remember the law. Persons must be able to make legal judgments and plan their affairs without having to consult their law books (or computers). When someone needs to decide whether and how long he has a legal obligation to remain at the scene of a traffic accident, for example, his only source of legal advice will be his recollection.

When the efforts of the law to guide behavior break down and conflicts do arise, then we turn to the law to determine liability. In civil cases, at least, the parties involved decide, effectively, whether or not to bring their dispute to the courts. There is usually the possibility of settling the case out of court, and indeed most cases, I believe, do not proceed to judgment. Such settlements are not usually reached because one party finally acknowledges the validity of the legal argument made by his adversary, but because the parties have weighed the costs of pursuing the case further against the gains to be expected from a favorable judgment, taking into consideration the risk of an unfavorable judgment, and have determined that settlement is the least expensive alternative. Other factors do play a role here (we are not always as rational as economists would like us to be); but this is nonetheless a fair first approximation of the process.

Whether or not out of court settlements are socially desirable or not is irrelevant for our purposes here. The point is only that parties do take the costs and risks of litigation into consideration, and that the courts will be used only if procedures are available for reaching a decision which is sufficiently inexpensive. The substantive law on some matter does play a role in deciding whether or not to settle, so it is not necessarily true that the law is ineffective when cases are not brought to the courts. But if it is difficult for the parties to estimate their rights under the relevant law, or even to determine which laws are relevant, then the role of the law here may be limited to a simple decision to ignore it.

How do general rules with exceptions effect the cost of reaching legal decisions? They are one way of dividing up the burden of proof. The party interested in showing that some legal conclusion is satisfied need only show that the conditions of the general rule are satisfied. It is the burden of the opposing party to show that one of the exceptions to the rule is applicable. If the opposing party does not care, or remember, to make an issue out of one of the exceptions, then the question is decided without having to consider the exceptions.

To show that some condition of a legal rule is satisfied, evidence must be discovered and introduced. Such "discovery" is a major expense of trials. It should be remembered that neither the courts nor attorneys involved usually have first-hand information about the facts of the case. By dividing up the burden of proof, the costs of discovery can be distributed among the parties. Each party can decide, based on whatever partial information is available, whether to make an issue out of some exception. By allowing certain "facts" to be assumed unless put at issue by an interested party, the costs of resolving some issues can be avoided altogether.

Without exceptions, every necessary condition of a rule would become an issue. It may not be necessary to introduce evidence with respect to each issue, the parties may be permitted to agree to the facts, but every possible issue would at least have to be brought to the attention of the parties and the courts. No stone could be left unturned. It may be thought, in the interest of justice, that such thoroughness is necessary. Justice can be served, however, at lower cost. A system with exceptions permits the parties to decide which issues to raise, without having to suffer the costs of a formal checklist.

Let us return now to Rödig's claim that the correctness and completeness requirements of an axiomatic system should also be applied to legal systems. As we have seen, Rödig views the law as a theory, and argues that, assuming such a theory is consistent, an axiomatization of the law is correct only if it too is consistent. Moreover, he went on to claim that an inconsistent axiomatization is useless, as every sentence is a logical consequence of such an axiomatization. This led to the above discussion on the utility of structuring laws as general rules with exceptions, in the usual way. I have argued that although exceptions do lead to inconsistency, laws structured in this way are obviously not useless. On the contrary, I have identified a number of reasons why it makes good sense to organize legal rules in just this way. Thus, as we should not demand laws to be consistent in this sense, further doubt is cast on the appropriateness of viewing the law as an axiomatic system.

Nonetheless, there is certainly an intuitive notion of correctness or "unity", as Savigny calls it, that should be required of the law. Rödig's mistake was to identify this common sense meaning of correctness with its technical meaning in predicate logic. A fundamental goal of the law is regulate and constrain action. Its purpose is to set limits within which persons may plan and act. If every decision or action were permissible, then there would be no need for law, let alone courts. The purpose of correctness is to draw a line between that which is legal and that which is not. But the bright line drawn by the predicate logic meaning of correctness is too restrictive here. There is not a "theory" of law in which all cases have been decided in advance. As Hart points out, there are hard cases. The basic regulatory function of the law is not offended by indeterminacy. In each case, there may be alternative defensible arguments, so long as all arguments are not equally well founded.

Enough has been said about correctness; let us now turn to completeness. A set of axioms is complete only if every sentence of the theory to be axiomatized is entailed by the axioms.[10] Together, correctness and completeness demand that exactly the sentences of the theory be entailed by the axioms; no more, no fewer.

In what sense can a set of norms be complete, and does it make a difference whether these norms are expressed as authoritative law-formulations or only as law-statements? Rödig distinguishes between three types of completeness, which he calls *horizontal*, *vertical* and *proof* completeness. These can all be viewed as applications of the general definition of completeness for axiomatic systems just given. They differ only with respect to what is taken to be the theory against which an axiomatization is measured.

In the case of horizontal completeness, the theory is taken to be some set of authoritative statements of law, as stated in the paragraphs of some statutory code, for example. An axiomatization in this case, then, is a nonauthoritative reconstruction of some area of law, and completeness is to be measured by the comprehensiveness of the

---

[10]Notice that this conception of completeness does *not* require that either p or $\neg p$ be entailed by the axioms, for an arbitrary sentence of the language, p.

reconstruction. For example, my model of Article 9 of the Uniform Commercial Code, in Appendix A, is an incomplete reconstruction, in this sense. It is a simplification which intentionally ignores aspects of the original code. However, even a complete reconstruction of UCC Article 9, if possible, would be an incomplete representation of the law of secured transactions, as Article 9 itself does not exhaust the law on this subject.

This is not the kind of completeness, however, that Savigny demands of a legal system. He was concerned not with the adequacy of some reconstruction of the law, but with the law itself. In Savigny's sense, the authoritative formulation of the law of some field is complete only if determines the result of every potential legal question. Interestingly, Rödig does not want to equate this kind of completeness with completeness in the sense of axiomatic systems. He writes that a legal decision which extends the law of some field by "filling a hole", as Savigny might say, does not repair a weakness in some axiomatization of the field, but [105, p. 88] "is a modification of the sentences of the field to be axiomatized." This is interesting, because it suggests a shift in Rödig's perspective. Up until this point, he appeared to be willing to view the authoritative statements of the law of some field as an axiomatization of some intangible theory. According to this perspective, the authoritative statements of law, such as statutes, can be incorrect or incomplete in the axiomatic sense. When, for example, a judge needs to go beyond the existing authoritative statements of law to decide a hard case, he does not change this theory of law, according to this view, but merely takes a step towards completing or correcting the "axiomatization". This perspective is compatible with the widely held view that judges do not, or should not, make law but merely "find" the law. But here Rödig adopts an opposing perspective; it is not the axiomatization which is repaired when deciding a hard case, but the underlying "theory" of the law. I find neither view convincing, as they both consider the law to be a theory.

Alas, in the case of "vertical completeness", the theory to be axiomatized is again the intangible set of sentences containing the solutions to all potential cases. The problem here is the *subsumption* of the particular facts of some case under the general legal terms of the authoritative statements of the law. Is a coin collection "goods" or "money" for the purposes of Article 9? Is a baby carriage a vehicle to be prohibited from the park? Here we see again that Rödig is not a believer in mechanical (or deductive) legal reasoning:

> ... the particular facts of the case need to be generalized in the direction of the legal terms of the norm, or the norm needs to be transformed in the direction of the facts. ... Also, the legal consequences of the norm may need to be specialized; ... A system of analytical sentences allowing subsumption to appear as a quasi-logical or even logical process, does not exist.
>
> It would be a mistake to expect axiomatization to satisfy requirements which the theory to be axiomatized itself does not satisfy. The notion of a computer judge ... which suggests that it is only a matter of filling a computer with general rules and the particular facts in order to decide concrete issues, is repulsive. ... The technological fantasy exceeds the logically realizable.

Although I agree with Rödig entirely here, we are left asking what is left of his goal of axiomatizing the law? Either the law is an intangible ideal, against which an "axiomatization" cannot be compared in order to establish its correctness or completeness, or the law itself is a finite set of statements to be molded, modified and extended during the process of deciding cases, as suggested in these passages, in which case axiomatization would appear redundant.

Finally, Rödig speaks of *proof completeness*, by which he means all premises of an argument have been made explicit. That is, a proof is viewed here as a set of sentences entailing the goal sentence. The "theory" to be axiomatized is the closure of the proof. Presumably, the set of axioms chosen would somehow be superior to the proof itself. Perhaps the axioms are more readily understandable for a particular audience. Also, the goal sentence itself may not be an axiom, unless one is willing to accept "proof by assumption". Rödig chose this as an example application of axiomatization to emphasize that there are no *logical* criteria dictating the depth or breadth of the theory to be axiomatized; even a "micro-axiomatization" of the proof of a single sentence can be useful.

Here again, as in the case of the vertical variety, "completeness" is used to qualify the theory to be axiomatized, rather than as an attribute of the axiomatization itself. Of the three forms of completeness identified, only horizontal completeness is a property of the axiomatization and thus the only form which can be considered completeness in the sense of axiomatic systems. As Rödig's motivation for discussing completeness was to demonstrate the relevance of axiomatization for legal reasoning, vertical and proof completeness are at best only of peripheral relevance to this goal.

Why would one be interested in axiomatizing the "proof" of a legal decision? Judging by Rödig's answer to this question, it seems that he is not so much interested in the axiomatization of an existing deductive proof as in insisting that the decision be formulated as a deductive proof in the first place [105, pp. 90-92] :

> One of the purposes of proof completion can be to discover subconscious factors taken into account by those who drafted the law, or the interpretation of the law ... There is no better way to challenge the adequacy of a legal decision than by formulating the reasons for the decision as a set of axioms and then deriving unacceptable theorems or contradictions with other rules assumed to be valid.

Here, Rödig accepts not only that legal decisions *can be* reconstructed as deductive proofs, but that this *should be* done so as to reveal hidden premises and open up the decision to public criticism. Let me emphasize that Rödig does not belong to those who claim that legal decisions are reached deductively. The concern is adequate justification or grounding of a decision, however made. Let us assume that Rödig is right about the importance of deduction for this purpose. I fail to see how this also can be construed as an argument in favor of axiomatization. We can substitute "set of sentences" for "set of axioms" in the above quotation without loss. To open up a legal decision to criticism, it need not be supposed that the set of sentences used in a deductive argument offered as justification of the decision is an axiomatization of some implicit and intangible theory containing the decision.

3.2.2 Formalization

Rödig is careful to distinguish between axiomatization and formalization [105, p. 71]: "The division of the propositions of a theory of some field into axioms and theorems does not depend on a formalization of these propositions. ... An artificial language is not necessary. As mentioned, formalization is not a necessary condition for the application of the axiomatic method; but it is an excellent instrument allowing the full value of axiomatization to be realized."

Axiomatization of the law, I have argued, is a somewhat incoherent goal. Can formalization of the law be useful absent axiomatization? To help answer this question, let us first examine Rödig's arguments in favor of formalization, to identify the interests which formalization is expected to serve. There are just two:

1.   To avoid the risks of "substantial reasoning" (inhaltlichen Schließens);

2.   To improve efficiency, especially with the aid of automated theorem proving, using computers.

By "substantial reasoning", Rödig is referring to the use of concepts, i.e., the *meaning* of terms, to infer sentences. For example, if you are told that John has a security interest in a video recorder, you might infer his interest is in goods, simply using the common sense meaning of the term "goods". If you believe that thinking is the manipulation of symbolic expressions, then you might object here that one cannot reason directly with concepts, and that this conclusion must have been reached by manipulating some cognitive *representation* of the concepts of video recorder and goods. Rödig does not consider this argument, presumably because he is less concerned with how the conclusion is reached than with how it is publicly justified. As discussed above, in the section on "proof completion", Rödig is convinced that legal arguments should be formulated publicly as deductive proofs, revealing all of the premises used to infer the decision:

> When one acts as if one has reasoned directly with concepts, in fact the conclusions are derived from undefined, and usually not discussed, sentences associated with the concepts. These sentences ... are not infrequently worthy of discussion. However, precisely because one supposedly is reasoning with concepts, they are withheld from an impartial debate.
>
> One purpose of formalization is to attempt, if only to attempt, to master this danger of substantial reasoning. ... [105, p. 71]

At least two issues are raised here. Firstly, if the purpose of formalization is to promote the reconstruction of legal arguments as deductive proofs, then we should ask what interests are served by such a reconstruction. Secondly, should this indeed be a worthy goal, just how can formalization be expected to promote it? As Rödig has noted, deductive arguments need not be formalized. Why is it not enough to simply require premises to be made explicit, without recommending formal notation?

Let me begin with the second issue first, as it is the easier of the two. Most arguments are *elliptical*; many premises are left implicit. Suppose I tell you that my bicycle has a flat tire and that my wife will *therefore* pick me up at the office. I suppose this conclusion is perfectly understandable. It would be considered irritating and laborious if I in addition went on to explain that one shouldn't ride a bicycle when it has a flat tire, that I do not have the means to repair the tire here, that I live too far from home to walk, and so on. Indeed, the number of premises which would have to be made explicit to make my wife picking me up in such circumstances a *logical necessity* of the flat tire might be enormous. Thankfully, normal communication apparently does not demand this degree of explicitness, at least so long as the participants share the same language, culture and experience to an extent sufficient given the context of the message.

As it is both unnatural and awkward to make all premises explicit, it is easy to not notice that some premise has been left implicit when arguments are stated in natural language. Formalization imposes a discipline which reduces the risk of failing to uncover some premise. Moreover, in the case of automated theorem proving, this risk is eliminated entirely. The key feature of formalization which makes this possible is the complete disassociation of symbols from their meaning. Rödig explains this as follows [105, p. 73]:

> The basic idea is simple. The distinguishing feature of a formalized axiomatic system is the use of a *characteristica universalis*, as formulated by Leibniz. This is the use of an artificial language, meaning that operations of thought are replaced by rule-governed operations on elements of language. This language is, if one may say so, divorced from its "actual" purpose, namely communication. The symbol is reduced to an object of rule-governed operations, and no longer designates anything other than itself. ... The symbol acquires the solidity of a piece of chalk.[11]

By divorcing language from meaning, formalization prevents meaning from being used to infer conclusions not deductively entailed by the explicit statements of the argument. Thus, the main purpose of formalization is to intentionally restrict language, robbing it of one of its principle functions and preventing a natural form of reasoning in contexts where a higher degree of explicitness is deemed warranted.

Regarding efficiency, as the formalization of legal arguments is a tedious and time-consuming task, it must be asked whether efficient proof checking alone would be a sufficiently valuable service to warrant this extraordinary effort. This is questionable.

---

[11]Thus Leibniz's choice of the term "calculus", whose root is the Latin word for chalk.

Although the procedure of checking the proof would be efficient, once the formalization has been completed, total efficiency must also account for the overhead incurred by the formalization. Nonetheless, perhaps there are contexts where this would be the case, at least once suitable software tools for managing the more tedious chores are widely available. Presumably, the domain must at least allow the same formalization, or large parts of it, to be reused to check multiple arguments. The potential utility of formalization would certainly be much greater if it would also support the construction and generation of arguments. In Rödig's view, at least, logic is of limited assistance for this task.

Again, Rödig's main argument in favor of formalization hinges on the desirability of ensuring that legal arguments be publicly reconstructed in the form of deductive proofs. For Rödig, the advantages of this are self-evident; other than pointing out that premises are made explicit by doing so, he makes no effort to justify this claim. Let us subject this assertion to a brief critical examination. Chaim Perelman is of some help here. In [89, pp. 24-35], he describes the development of the doctrine of a separation of powers between the legislative, judicial and executive branches of government, by Hobbes, Montesquieu and Rousseau.

Hobbes originated the idea of law separate from morality or reason. For Hobbes, law was the will of the sovereign, whose interests were assumed to be identical to those of his subjects. Hobbes theory was a reaction to natural law philosophers of the early 17th century who, inspired by progress in mathematics and natural science, believed law to be a system of universal morals founded on reason and rationality.[12] But Hobbes considered natural law to be the "law of the jungle". To avoid a constant state of war, and to provide a nonviolent means of settling disputes, Hobbes postulated a *social contract* in which the people of a nation empower a sovereign to enact and enforce laws regulating action.

Hobbes had concentrated the powers of sovereignty in a single person, the king. Montesquieu challenged Hobbes' claim that the interests of an individual sovereign can be identical to those of the people. To avoid abuses of power, he originated the idea of a separation of powers between different branches of government. Let us ignore the executive branch here. The abuse to be prevented by separating the legislative and judicial powers is the modification of the law in the course of resolving particular conflicts, for the purpose of obtaining a decision motivated by illegitimate factors, such as prejudice or the private interests of the judge. *Equality* under the law demands that the courts be "blind" to irrelevant factors. Denying judges legislative powers, while not restricting their powers of vision, does limit their ability to respond to prejudice when deciding cases. Judges should only be [89, p. 30] "the mouth that speaks the words of law, that is able to change neither the force nor the strictness of the law."

Equality is the first of two interests promoted by separating judicial and legislative functions. The second is the *certainty* of the law (Rechtssicherheit). Certainty requires legal rights and obligations to be predictable. This leads Montesquieu to conclude that the

---

[12]Modern variants of this rationalist tradition include economic theories of law, such as Posner's [95]. Presumably, Dworkin's notion of universal "principles" which converge to determine a single, correct legal decision, is also an expression of this ideal.

law applied by judges when deciding cases should be the same as the law at the time of the actions giving rise to the conflict [89, pp. 30-31] :

> ... the decisions of courts should be so limited that they are nothing more than a specialization of a statute. If court decisions were only the opinions of individual judges, then one would live in a state where it cannot be precisely known what responsibilities one assumes by living in this state.

Rousseau added a further argument in favor of this separation of powers. Like Hobbes, he associated law with the will of the sovereign. Unlike Hobbes, Rousseau was a democrat: the sovereign power is not a monarch, but the people. The general will of the people determines justice and injustice. In a representative democracy, it is the legislature, and not the judiciary, which embodies the will of the people. Judges lack the necessary authority for making law.

These views of Hobbes, Montesquieu and Rousseau played a central role in the division of powers in France after the revolution. According to Perelman [89, p. 32], it was here that the power of the courts was, as a matter of law, restricted to "correct deduction, without interpretation. Interpretation brings with it the danger that the will of the legislature be subverted." A law was enacted which required the judiciary to consult the legislature should the applicability of some law to a particular case not be clear. This turned out to be unworkable. As the courts frequently invoked the procedure, they became bogged down. More seriously, the rule itself violated the doctrine of the separation of powers, contrary to its very purpose. Not only should the courts not exercise legislative powers, the legislature should not be in the business of deciding particular cases. When this occurs, there is a danger the principle of equality will be violated by a specific law enacted solely to decide the particular case. Thus, the later Code Napoleon was modified so as to *oblige* judges to decide every case, even when the law is unclear or incomplete. This change was explained in an introduction to a draft of the Code, by Portalis, who wrote [89, p. 34] :

> The legislature cannot foresee everything. ... When the law is clear and meaningful, it must be followed; when it is unclear, then the policies and purpose of the law should be clarified. If there is no relevant law, then the case must be judged according to conventional practices and general principles of justice. This is a return to natural law, when positive law has nothing to say, or is contradictory or unclear.

Notice that Portalis here, at this earlier date, is already in full agreement with several core points of Hart's form of analytical jurisprudence, as discussed above. It is recognized that natural language is often imprecise and that the intent and purpose of legislation is less than complete. Moreover, there are seeds here of the distinction between hard and clear cases.[13]

Now, what does this short history of the separation of powers doctrine have to tell us about the soundness of Rödig's claim that judicial decisions should be formulated as deductive proofs? The deductive view of legal reasoning provided a convenient dividing line between the powers of the judiciary and legislature, as proposed by Montesquieu. Had it not been considered possible to decide cases deductively, by merely applying the law to the facts, then the feasibility of Montesquieu's proposal to completely deny the judiciary legislative power's may have been seriously doubted. In order to assure that indeed judges did not exceed the limits of their authority, court decisions were required to be explained or justified in writing. This requirement in turn, according to Perelman [89, p. 39], provided additional impetus to those 19th century schools of jurisprudence, such as Begriffsjurisprudenz, whose focus was on refining methods for deductively deciding cases.[14]

However, as it became clear that deduction alone was insufficient for deciding cases, for the reasons recognized by Portalis, one might have thought the expectation that decisions should be justified in the form of deductive proofs, applying the law to the facts, would be revised accordingly. It seems, however, that this did not occur, and I can only speculate here as to the reasons. Presumably, although it was necessary to retreat from the purely deductive view of legal reasoning, this was still considered the ideal to be achieved to the extent possible. We see this conviction for example in Hart's analytical jurisprudence, where hard cases are considered to be exceptional and infrequent.

Although Rödig argues that legal decisions should be justified in the form of deductive proofs, he has stressed that deduction is not sufficient for reaching the decision. Rödig is in agreement with Engisch and Fiedler on this point. Engisch spoke of "the focus of attention wandering back and forth" between the law and the facts, in the process of searching for an understanding of both which allows the facts to be subsumed under the general terms of the law [36, p. 61]. Because of this, Engisch was skeptical about the value of modern logic for legal reasoning. Fiedler was one of the first to respond to this observation with the argument that deduction is still useful as a constraint on the form of the decision, however it is found or made [36], which is also Rödig's position. According to Fiedler, legal reasoning is a process of modeling, or design, in which the argument being drafted *should be* a deductive proof of the decision [36; 37].

Notice that Fiedler's claim is normative. He does not assert that court decisions are in fact formulated as deductive proofs, but that they should be. Indeed, it is unlikely that one could find a single published court decision fully meeting this stringent requirement. The arguments in these decisions are elliptical, just as in everyday argumentation. Many premises which would be necessary to transform the argument into a deductive proof are left implicit.

I suspect there are good reasons for not insisting that legal arguments be formulated as

---

[13]However, Portalis' assertion that natural law principles should be resorted to in hard cases sounds more like Dworkin than Hart.

[14]Fiedler points out, however, that the terms "logic" and "deduction" did not then have the narrow, technical meanings they have acquired in this century, with the development of mathematical logic. "Logical" was little more than a synonym for "rational" or "reasonable". Savigny, for example, spoke of the "logical interpretation" of statutes [35]. Even today, the common sense, conventional meaning of "logical" is just as broad.

deductive proofs. Current and traditional practice is not arbitrary, but presumably persists and survives because of its utility. The goal of subjecting judicial decisions to review, to maintain a satisfactory balance of power between the legislative and judicial branches of government, is but one among a number of interests to be taken into consideration. Moreover, I claim deductive proof alone is neither necessary nor sufficient for even this purpose.

Competing with the interest of subjecting judgments to review by requiring all premises to be made explicit is the interest of resolving conflicts at least cost, by avoiding nonessential issues. Let me make this clear with an example. Suppose one party, say the plaintiff, interprets some statute to mean $p \rightarrow q$, whereas the defendant believes the same paragraph to mean $r \rightarrow q$. Although they disagree about the proper interpretation of the statute, let us suppose they agree that both p and r took place. Thus, no matter which interpretation is accepted, they both must agree that q also holds. The question as to which interpretation to prefer is simply irrelevant if the issue is whether or not q holds. Now, requiring the court to make a choice between these two interpretations, just for the purpose of constructing a deductive justification of its decision, would make poor use of the court's limited resources. Moreover, a decision on this point would be premature; it would be better to wait for a case in which the outcome turns on a choice between these interpretations, as such a case would presumably place the issues, the pros and cons of each choice, in sharper relief.

It might be objected at this point that the decision can be reconstructed as a deductive proof without making a choice between the competing interpretations. The premise would be $(p \rightarrow q) \vee (r \rightarrow q)$. That is, the alternative interpretations could be joined in a disjunctive proposition. But what would be the backing for this proposition? To show that this disjunction holds, one would have to show that at least one of the disjuncts is the proper interpretation of the contested statute, which raises the very issue we are trying to avoid. An alternative would be to allow some premises to remain unbacked, but then this would risk making a farce of deductive proof. Why not then simply assume that which one wants to prove? Every proposition is a logical consequence of itself.

Instead, permitting an elliptical argument here would be preferable. q would be justified directly in terms of the facts, $\{p, r\}$, without stating a general rule. Presumably, both p and r are properly backed by evidence, so this proposal does not suffer from the problem just mentioned of assuming propositions without backing.

Although q is not a logical consequence of $\{p, r\}$, a decision supported with this kind of argument is nonetheless sufficient to subject it to critical review, should it be doubted that it complies with the law. Had the decision been formulated as a deductive proof, review would have consisted of two tasks: 1) checking that the conclusion is indeed a logical consequence of the stated premises; 2) confirming that the premises are not inconsistent; and 3) checking that each premise is sufficiently backed by legal sources or evidence.[15]

---

[15]The *factual* premises are usually not questioned by appellate courts, unless there is insufficient evidence as a "matter of law". I suppose there are two reasons for this. It would be prohibitively expense to do so, at worst requiring the case to be retried, and there is no reason to suppose that appellate judges are better qualified than

The procedure for checking an elliptical argument is different, but not necessarily more difficult. It is an *abductive* process of finding an acceptable explanation for the decision. That is, additional propositions must be found which, together with those stated in the judgment, allow the decision to be deduced. In other words, responsibility for creating a deductive proof of the decision is shifted from the judge deciding the case, to those trying to understand or confirm it.

This is almost but not quite right. It is a fair characterization of the process of understanding the decision. But on review, the task is not to understand or *confirm* the judgment, but to *challenge* it. The problem is to find an interpretation of the law which is inconsistent with the judgment. More precisely, to continue with our abstract example, the task is to find a proposition, d, backed by the authorities, such that $\{p, q, r, d\} \models \perp$. (Here $\perp$ denotes inconsistency or falsity.) Presumably, the losing party will only bother to appeal if it has been able to find one or more such d for the appellate court to consider.

I have been arguing that there good reasons for permitting judicial decisions to use elliptical arguments. However, it should be emphasized that this is not an argument in favor of never requiring judges to state general rules in their decisions. The example was somewhat artificial, as the premises of the argument consisted solely of facts. Thus, one may have had the impression that all decisions could be justified in this way, solely in terms of the facts. But that is not my position. Rather, general rules should be included in the argument justifying the decision to the extent necessary to address the arguments made by the parties. Here is a simple example. Suppose, as before, that the issue is q and the parties agree as to the facts, $\{p, r\}$. However, this time one party claims that the proper interpretation of some statute is $p \rightarrow q$ and the other party disagrees, claiming the same statute means $p \rightarrow \neg q$. Here, I think, the judge should be required to make an explicit choice between these alternatives, or explain why he thinks yet another interpretation is correct. To permit an elliptical argument regarding this issue would allow the judge to simply ignore arguments made by the parties.

Above, I claimed that the formulation of legal argument as a deductive proof is neither necessary nor sufficient for the purpose of opening up the judgment to public review, to ascertain whether or not it was made in accordance with applicable law. Perhaps the reasons for this claim are now clear. We have already seen why an elliptical argument, leaving some premises implicit, can still serve this purpose. Thus, a purely deductive argument is not necessary. Moreover, it has already been noted that a deductive argument can be trivially constructed by simply assuming the conclusion, as all propositions are logical consequences of themselves. Surely this would not be acceptable, and so quite obviously entailment of the conclusion from some *arbitrary* set of premises is not sufficient. Rather, the premises must be demonstrated to bear an appropriate relationship to the legal sources and the evidence; they must themselves be backed or justified. To avoid an infinite regress, we cannot demand that the connection between each premise and its backing be justified by the same stringent kind of deductive argument. As nondeductive

---

the trial courts for this job. Indeed, in Anglo-American jurisdictions, the facts are found by lay juries, rather than legal experts such as judges.

forms of argument must be accepted at some point, relying on common sense knowledge and shared cultural experience, we may as well permit some elliptical arguments in the first place.

Rödig's arguments in favor of formalization were based on the assumption that legal arguments should be formulated as deductive proofs. Now that doubt has been cast on the appropriateness of such a requirement, let us return to formalization. Do my arguments against deductive justification reduce the potential utility of formalization? Not necessarily. Although legal reasoning is not completely, or even primarily, deductive, deduction stills retains a central and important role, both in generating and justifying arguments. Elliptical arguments are understood and criticized using abduction, which in turn relies on deduction as a subprocess. In relatively stable legal areas, where the initial expense of formalization can be amortized over a sufficiently long period of time, or in areas of great technical complexity, such as tax law, where it is difficult to even express the applicable legal rules precisely without resorting to formal, or quasi-formal, languages, formalization may be of great assistance. At the risk of excess rigidity, formalization can further the goals of equality and certainty of the law. Also, formalization should not be identified with deduction. Relationships between sentences other than that of monotonic entailment can be usefully formalized. Examples here include probabilistic, associative, nonmonotonic, inductive and abductive reasoning. Each of these modes of reasoning can be formalized and, to some extent, automated.

A central goal of this book is to demonstrate that formalization *can be* useful for legal argumentation even though legal decisions are not generated deductively and need not be justified deductively. This work may be considered to belong to the tradition of legal logic, in that I too claim that logic and formalization are of great significance and utility for legal reasoning. But, as the discussion in this section hopefully demonstrates, the reasons for my believing this are considerably different than Rödig's, as are the sorts of uses for logic that I envision, as will become clearer later.

3.2.3   Evaluation of Rödig's Theory

My discussion of Rödig and legal logic is just about complete. It remains only to reiterate Rödig's view of the importance of logic with respect to my catalog of issues and to summarize the lessons learned. First, Rödig's view of the issues:

Recognized Limitations.
> Following Fiedler, he stresses that legal reasoning is not purely deductive. Rather, it is a "modeling" process requiring both the facts and the law to be molded and shaped. Rödig considers this to be a pragmatic limitation on our ability to formalize and automate legal argumentation, as his view of formalization is limited to deduction.

Correctness Criteria.
Correct legal decisions are formulated as deductive proofs, in which the conclusion
is logically entailed by some explicit set of premises. Although the discovery or
creation of the judgment is not purely deductive, it must at least be justified by a
deductive reconstruction of an argument. However, no other restrictions are placed
on judgments. Rödig does not discuss, for example, the importance of backing each
premise with legal authority or evidence.

Methods.
Although formalization is of little use for generating arguments, it can be useful for
checking the correctness of an argument, and help ensure that all premises have been
made explicit.

Here the main points to be remember from our discussion of Rödig's work:

1. The issues surrounding the pros and cons of formalization are separate from those of
    axiomatization, or indeed deduction.

2. Axiomatization of the law is not a sound idea; it presumes the existence of a theory
    of law capable of deciding all future cases, ignoring Hart's insight that legislatures
    are not omniscient, even about their own goals. As evidenced by such properties as
    correctness and completeness, the idea of axiomatization depends on a distinction
    between such a theory and the axioms representing it. As the law is refined in the
    process of deciding cases, this distinction breaks down. It cannot be determined
    whether the axiomatization has been corrected, or the "theory" revised.

3. It is not clear that judgments should be formulated as deductive proofs. This ideal
    has its roots in mechanical jurisprudence, which Rödig himself does not accept.
    For the purpose of maintaining a suitable balance of power between the legislative
    and judicial branches of government, formulating judgments as deductive proofs is
    neither sufficient nor necessary. Moreover, there are interests, such as delaying the
    decision of irrelevant issues, which are better served by elliptical arguments.

4. Formalization should not be identified with deduction. The limited role of deduction
    for generating and justifying legal decisions does not imply similar limitations for
    formalization. There are numerous reasoning processes in addition to deduction, such
    as abduction, which can be formalized and perhaps automated.

5. Rödig considers the traditional structure of legal codes, as general rules with
    exceptions, to fail to make full use of contemporary knowledge about logic. However,
    this traditional structure should be preserved, as it serves well both the normative and
    conflict resolution roles of the law.

3.3 Alexy's Theory of Legal Argumentation

In the previous two sections I came to the conclusion that neither Hart's nor Rödig's theories of legal reasoning provide adequate criteria for delimiting judicial discretion. Hart first adopts a strict theory of interpretation. According to this approach, judges are required to apply the *literal* meaning of statutes and other authoritative legal sources. Discretion is permitted, indeed required, only if this literal meaning does not determine a decision. These are the "hard" cases. However, he later retreats from this position and admits that justice may require a decision contrary to the literal meaning of the law. Arguments resorting to the *purpose* of the law, for example, may be required. In the end, Hart abandons the criteria he had proposed for limiting discretion without finding a suitable alternative.

Rödig on the other hand claims only that judgments should be expressed as a deductive proof of the decision from explicit premises. I have argued that this kind of logical constraint is neither necessary nor sufficient to justify a judgment. It is unnecessary, indeed too restrictive, as it causes issues to be raised and addressed which are not in dispute. Deduction alone is insufficient as no restrictions are placed on the premises. They need not be shown to bear any particular relationship to either law or evidence.

Despite these failed attempts, it would be premature to give up hope of finding a solution to the problem of delimiting judicial discretion. In this section, we examine a third approach, Robert Alexy's theory of legal argumentation [4]. The main tenets of this theory are:

- Legal argumentation is a specialization of general *practical discourse.*

- Practical discourse is a kind of language "game", involving a number of participants. The rules of the game are designed to assure that each participant has a fair and equal opportunity to express his views and opinions.

- The decision made after such a discussion is right or correct, and in the case of legal discourse *just*, if and only if these procedural rules have been obeyed.

- The procedural rules are not limited to *a priori*, analytical constraints on rationality, such as logical consistency, but may take practical constraints of the context into consideration, such as particular resource limitations.

- Moreover, these rules may themselves be made the subject of debate and revised, if necessary.

For the purpose of delimiting judicial discretion, Alexy's theory shifts the focus of our attention from the properties of the argument justifying the judgment to the process by which the judgment was reached. The limits of discretion are respected so long as the procedural rules have been obeyed. The correctness of a judicial decision is made dependent on the events leading up to it, in particular the actions of the parties involved in the dispute. Notice also that the theory imposes obligations not only on the judge, but also on the parties. The discourse rules regulate the behavior of all participants, of which the judge is but a distinguished member with a particular role.

Just what kinds of procedural rules does Alexy propose? His book contains a seven page appendix listing all of them. It is tempting to restate them here, but instead let me just give a few examples, below. Alexy emphasizes that the particular rules he proposes are not the central contribution of his theory, but merely a draft of general rules proposed for discussion [4, p. 17] :

> ... The explicit formulation of these rules and forms of argument may seem pedantic, redundant, or even presumptuous. Perhaps its most important function is to reveal their shortcomings the more plainly. These deficiencies may relate to the content of the rules, their incomplete enumeration, the redundancy of particular rules and forms of argument, as well as the lack of precision in their formulation. Insofar as shortcomings of this kind do not render the rules and forms of argument entirely pointless, they present something akin to a code of practical reason.
>
> The efficacy of these rules and forms of argument should be neither overestimated nor undervalued. They are not axioms from which certain normative propositions can be deduced, but rather a group of rules and forms of various logical rankings which an argument must satisfy if the conclusion it establishes is to have the correctness it purports to have. ...

Here are several general purpose discourse rules:

- No speaker may contradict himself.

- A speaker may assert only statements which he believes.

- Each speaker must, on demand, justify an assertion, unless he can justify withholding the justification.

- A participant may make an issue out of any assertion.

And here are some rules particular to legal argumentation:

- Every judgment must be justified by at least one general legal rule.

- The judgment must be logically entailed by the general legal rule and the other propositions of the argument.

- If it is unclear whether or not a condition of some rule of law is satisfied by the facts of the case, a rule must be asserted which decides the issue.

- Every canon of interpretation that is possibly relevant shall be taken into consideration.

• Every relevant precedent case shall be mentioned.

It would be interesting to discuss each of these rules, as well as the others Alexy proposes, but as he admits his rules are tentative and probably suffer from various limitations, we would not be addressing the central claims of Alexy's theory by doing so. Nonetheless, I would like to make a few comments about the above rules.

Notice that logic still plays a significant role in this conception of argumentation. Speakers may not contradict themselves, and decisions must be justified by a deductive argument. I have already argued that this later condition should not be mandatory. Here, Alexy adopts the conventional point of view, and prohibits elliptical reasoning. As for the prohibition against self-contradiction, this presumably requires each argument asserted during the discourse to be consistent, but should not be construed so as to prohibit some party from making alternative, mutually inconsistent, arguments. Such a prohibition would be contrary to conventional practice in the law, where one makes as many arguments as one can think of supporting some position, even though one cannot accept all of the arguments simultaneously.

This last observation calls into question the rule that a participant may only assert statements he or she believes. Although this appears to be a reasonable requirement for assertions of fact, it surely is too restrictive in the case of statements about the law. Suppose the law is unclear regarding some issue. Should this discourse rule require each participant to only assert and defend, if necessary, the interpretation he believes to be proper, regardless of his own interests? This would be somewhat idealistic. Rather, we must expect that each party will support and defend the interpretation which best promotes its own interests, regardless of his subjective beliefs about which side has the better arguments. One should also question the utility of a rule as difficult to enforce as this one. The beliefs of the participants are not subject to direct inspection. More to the point, why should a party's mistaken belief about the significance of a good argument be held against him?

The next point to notice about these rules is that they make the participants responsible for raising issues. Assertions can be made without justification, so long as another participant does not question the assertion. More importantly, issues which could have been raised, but were not, cannot affect the justice or correctness of the resulting decision. It is this property of Alexy's theory which avoids the limitations of Hart's analytical jurisprudence. The clearness of a case does not depend on an objective or literal theory of meaning, but on the subjective views of the actual participants. That is, a term is clearly applicable to the facts if the parties do not make an issue out of its applicability. Consensus determines clarity.

Finally, notice that these rules *do* place requirements on the premises of arguments, unlike Rödig's form of legal logic. Each legal argument must include at least one general legal rule which, together with the facts, entails the decision. When there is disagreement about the applicability of some legal rule to the facts, the judgment must include a general rule resolving the issue. That is, the rules require a *ratio decidendi* for the decision to be formulated. Along the same lines, the argument justifying the decision may not ignore relevant precedents.

It may be that Rödig and other legal logicians would agree to these extra-logical constraints. Perhaps such constraints on the premises were considered to be self-evident. But this is speculation. Alexy's theory makes them explicit.

This brief discussion of some discourse rules will have to suffice for our purposes here. It would lead me too far astray to even mention all of the discourse rules Alexy proposes, let alone try to evaluate them or develop alternatives. Instead, I would prefer to survey the philosophical works upon which Alexy bases his theory. These Alexy divides into four sections: 1) analytical theories of practical discourse and argumentation, including the theories of Hare, Toulmin and Baier; 2) Habermas' consensus theory of truth; 3) the Erlangen school's attempt to apply constructive mathematics, especially Lorenzen's dialogue logic, to the field of ethics; and 4) Perelman's theory of argumentation, called the "new rhetoric". Of course, I will not be able to say much about any of these, given space limitations and the general goals of this book. The discussion will be focused, as before, on the issues of which limitations on rationality are recognized, correctness criteria for decisions, and methods for constructing or evaluating arguments. The main purpose of this survey will be to support Alexy's claim that procedural discourse rules of the kind shown above can sensibly be used to define when a judgment is justified.

Legal decisions are normative judgments. For this reason, Alexy begins with a comparison of three positions regarding the ontological status of normative expressions: naturalism, intuitionism and emotionalism. The naturalistic position is that normative statements, often called "value judgments", can be reduced to empirical statements, which can then be evaluated using the methods of natural science. Thus naturalism here appears to be a form of utilitarianism. Alexy mentions Moore's "open-question" argument against this position, which claims that, no matter how some value is operationalized, one can always question the value of the standard adopted [4, pp. 35-37]. For example, if the abstract value "good" is defined as "desired by most people", one can legitimately ask why this particular measure of goodness is better than other possibilities. Although there are a number of responses to this argument, Alexy concludes that it at least demonstrates that factual, empirical statements cannot completely replace normative ones.

The intuitionistic position, which should not be confused with intuitionism in the sense of constructive mathematics, claims that all persons have the ability to order events or situations according to an innate hierarchy of preexisting values. Theorists disagree about the number and order of these values. Ross, for example, claims there are just two basic values, "right" and "good" [4, p. 38]. Alexy complains that this very inability to agree as to what values there are, or their relative importance, causes intuitionism to fail as an objective theory of moral truth suitable for resolving disputes.

According to emotionalism, the purpose of normative statements is not to describe, but to *influence*. Alexy focuses on the Stevenson's theory [4, pp. 39-47]. According to Stevenson, to say "This is good." means no more than "I approve of this; continue doing it." Normative statements have descriptive and imperative parts. The descriptive part is about the mental state of the speaker; the imperative part points to the behavior eliciting the mental state, and demands that the behavior be continued or discontinued. The imperative part, however, is usually not a blunt command, but a subtle suggestion. The most relevant part of Stevenson's work here is his theory of moral argument. Except for prohibiting contradictory arguments, there is no logical relationship between a conclusion and its justification in Stevenson's theory [4, p. 42]:

> Any statement about any matter of fact which any speaker considers likely to alter attitudes may be adduced as a reason for or against an ethical judgment. Whether this reason will in fact support or oppose the judgment will depend on whether the hearer believes it, and upon whether, if he does, it will actually make a difference to his attitudes.

We see here that Stevenson's theory is psychological, rather than normative. It reminds me of American Realism, and fails as a basis for evaluating arguments for the same reason: it does not provide normative criteria for distinguishing valid from invalid arguments. Stevenson does distinguish between "rational" and "persuasive" arguments — rational arguments use only empirical statements as reasons for conclusions — but this distinction is orthogonal to validity. Indeed, Stevenson denies that it can make sense to speak of the validity of normative judgments [4, p. 46].

The next group of theories Alexy considers all view practical discourse as rule-governed activity. By "rules" here, we do not mean natural laws describing how arguments are in fact conducted, but norms describing the obligations and permissions of the argument's participants. The theories differ primarily in the norms they recommend for regulating arguments. They can all be better understood in the light of Wittgenstein's metaphor of a language "game" and Austin's speech act theory.

Wittgenstein was discussed briefly above, in section 3.1 on Hart's analytical jurisprudence. There I explained Wittgenstein's view that language is behavior serving a variety of functions, of which describing the world is but one. There are a variety of language games, each of which is governed by rules. Practical argumentation is one such game, with its own set of rules. For Wittgenstein, the rules are a matter of convention dependent on culture (Lebensform). A rule exists in this sense only if many people have obeyed the rule many times [4, p. 51]: "It is not possible that there should have been only one occasion on which someone obeyed a rule." Here we see a difference between Wittgenstein and positive law, where it surely is possible for rules to exist which no one has followed. But the source of the rules, be it convention or enactment by some legal authority, is not of central importance here. Wittgenstein was not so concerned with the legitimacy of rules governing language activity as their mere existence, which was a novel idea at his time.

Wittgenstein recognized that there are various uses of language, but he did not attempt to develop a theoretical framework categorizing them. J. L. Austin developed just such a framework, in which he distinguishes between *locutionary, illocutionary* and *perlocutionary* acts [4, pp. 53-58]. Actually, as we will see, these are not so much different sorts of acts, as various properties of each speech act. Suppose John asks his friend Peter, "Shall I pick you up at the airport?" The locutionary part of an expression is its literal meaning. In the example, this meaning is something like "Do I have an obligation to pick you up at the airport?", which we can suppose is not the case. The illocutionary part of the expression is its *conventional* effect. The illocutionary effect here, at least after Peter agrees, is to create a moral obligation to pick Peter up. The perlocutionary effect of the speech act are any nonconventional side effects of the act. If Peter and John have recently had a fight, Peter may be surprised at John's kind offer to pick him up. Indeed John may have made the offer for the very purpose of patching up his relationship with Peter. The illocutionary force of the message need not be the primary effect intended by the particular speaker.

Like Wittgenstein, Austin recognizes that pragmatic rules governing language use exist alongside the rules of grammar and logic. One of his examples is "The cat is on the mat, but I don't believe it." Although the sentence is both grammatically correct and logically consistent, it violates the conventional rule that a speaker may only assert something he believes.

Finally, Austin develops a notion of truth which is dependent on the context of the utterance, and not merely on the conventional meaning of the terms of the sentence uttered. According to this theory, a sentence is "true" just when its expression is appropriate in the context, including the facts, the intentions of the speaker and other pragmatic aspects of the situation. He denies that a context independent interpretation of truth is sensible. He claims, for example, that the truth of "France is a hexagon." cannot be determined without knowing the context in which it was stated. Austin goes on to claim that the criteria establishing the truth of normative expressions is not significantly different from those for descriptive statements.

3.3.1 Normative Theories of Practical Discourse

Wittgenstein and Austin were concerned with general problems of language, and both recognized that norms regulating discourse exist. However, they did not make an effort to develop particular rules for rational discourse or argument. Hare's theory of moral argumentation is the first of this kind which Alexy considers [4, pp. 58-79]. It is based on Hare's theory of the language of morals, which can be viewed as a variant of Austin's speech act theory. There are two main rules: 1) the principle of "universalizability" and 2) the principle of "prescriptivity". If a speaker applies a predicate p to some object x, the principle of universalizability requires that speaker to apply the same predicate to every object which is similar to x in "all relevant aspects". These relevant aspects are the "reason" for using the predicate to describe the object. Hare does not explain the concept of relevance, or provide a clue as to how to determine whether two objects are similar or not. Rather, Hare supposes that the speaker admits that the two objects are similar in every relevant aspect and then asks whether it would make sense to permit him to apply the predicate to one object without obligating him to apply it to the other.

Alexy suggests that the principle of universalizability implies that there is a general rule implicit in every moral judgment [4, p. 66]. The conditions of such a rule are satisfied just by the objects which are similar "in all relevant aspects"; the conclusion of the rule applies the predicate to the particular individual. Notice that these rules do not regulate moral discourse, such as the two principles discussed here, but are particular moral rules.

At points, Alexy seems to suggest Hare's theory requires the speaker to state such a general rule when making the moral statement [4, p. 79]. But I am not convinced this is necessary. The universalizability principle could be applied in a "case-based" fashion, comparing a previous case with the current one to decide if they are sufficiently similar, without ever explicitly stating a general rule.

The principle of prescriptivity permits a speaker to assert that another person is subject to an obligation only if the speaker would be willing to accept the obligation if he were in the other person's position. The rule requires the speaker to imagine himself to be in the position of the other person. This is Hare's version of the so-called "golden rule".

Hare claims his theory provides a "logic of normative language" capable of determining the correctness of a moral judgment, given sufficient information about the relevant facts, the inclinations and interests of the speakers and their imagination of the situations of others, where required to apply the principle of prescriptivity [4, p. 71]. One suspects, however, that this precondition is so difficult to satisfy that Hare's theory cannot be useful for this purpose in practice. An interesting feature of Hare's theory is that the correctness of a moral decision does not depend on a particular set of moral rules. The speakers remain solely responsible for deciding which morals to accept. This feature is also a source of criticism. If the speaker is a judge, Hare's theory does not limit sufficiently his discretion; indeed it leaves him completely free to choose norms according to his personal wishes and inclinations. Hare developed an alternative version of his theory in response to this criticism, in which the combined effects of the rule under consideration on *all* persons must be taken into consideration. But this solution requires a moral rule for combining these interests, which itself must be justified. Hare does not provide one.

Hare's two principles of moral discourse are not themselves justified. Instead, Hare views them as the procedural rules of a particular language game, the "moral game". One can choose to participate or not, but it only makes sense to speak of justification once one has accepted the rules of this particular game. Alexy objects to this and argues that the rules of the moral game should themselves be open to discussion and criticism.

Next, Alexy discusses Toulmin's theory of argumentation [4, pp. 79-93]. There are two versions. The first, published in 1950 in "The Place of Reason in Ethics" [122], focussed on the problem of justifying *moral* decisions. It distinguishes between two kinds of justification. Moral decisions are justified "deontically", by reference to some moral rule which, together with other facts assumed to be true, logically entail the decision. Should this moral rule be doubted then the rule itself must be justified. This is to be done "teleologically", by determining whether the rule (best) furthers the goal of reducing human suffering to a minimum. Thus, this is a utilitarian theory, with minimum suffering being the ultimate moral value. A set of moral rules are presumed to exist, but these are not fixed. The theory has several weaknesses: 1) it underestimates the problem of determining whether the preconditions of some moral rule are satisfied; 2) it fails to explain how to measure human suffering, and 3) the choice of minimizing human suffering as the ultimate moral value seems arbitrary. Why not prefer least harm to the environment, for example, or maximum wealth? This latter problem is shared by all versions of utilitarianism.

Toulmin's second theory of argumentation, presented in "The Uses of Argument" in 1958 [123], does not depend on utilitarianism. Interestingly, he claims that a theory of practical reasoning and argumentation should be measured by the ideals of jurisprudence, rather than mathematics. Legal reasoning is institutionalized practical reasoning. Conversely, Toulmin writes [123, p. 7], "Logic (we may say) is generalized jurisprudence." Toulmin insists that he means this literally, and not merely metaphorically. He argues that the mathematical orientation, beginning with Aristotle's theory of syllogism, has lead to an overemphasis on the relationship of logical necessity (entailment), at the expense of other norms for argumentation of greater practical significance. For Toulmin, a "logic" is a set of norms regulating practical discourse. The inference rules of a deductive logic refine the more abstract norm prohibiting contradictory arguments. Such rules are necessary, but not sufficient, for resolving disputes. The legitimate subject matter of logic encompasses all norms required for regulating practical discourse, and not just the subset concerning logical necessity and contradiction. Logic is a normative science, like law, rather than primarily analytic, like pure mathematics.

My thesis compliments Toulmin's. He looked to jurisprudence for insight into practical argumentation, whereas I, following Alexy, hope to draw insight from general theories of practical discourse for my theory of legal argumentation. Toulmin shifted attention from mathematics to jurisprudence, to broaden the scope of logic. I agree that the norms governing practical argumentation are broader than those which traditionally have been the subject matter of logic, but use mathematics to describe, analyze and apply these additional norms. Mathematics is a modeling tool. The scope of logic was not limited by the capabilities of mathematics, but by an unduly restrictive view of the object to be modeled. Although I can agree with Toulmin that the classical consequence relation, together with its notion of validity, are of limited value for judging practical arguments in domains such as the law, the use of mathematics to analyze and formalize the idea of entailment did not cause these limitations.

It is unclear whether broadening the scope of logic, as Toulmin suggests, is to be recommended. Perhaps argumentation should be a field of its own, in which logic plays a role, and the scope of logic should remain restricted to the problems of consequence and entailment. Logic in this narrow sense has uses outside of practical argumentation. On the other hand, within Artificial Intelligence at least, there is a trend toward broadening the meaning of logic, as in the case of nonmonotonic logic. Is Toulmin's view of logic a possible conclusion of this development?

The aspect of Toulmin's theory which has attracted the most attention is his analysis of the structure of arguments. (See Figure 3.1.) He arrived at this structure by examining arguments in several fields, including physics and ethics, in addition to law. The purpose of argument is to defend *claims*. A claim is the assertion of a statement by some proponent. If another person challenges the claim, the proponent must bring forward some fact, which Toulmin calls a *datum*, as a reason for the claim. For example, suppose I claim that you should take an umbrella with you. If you ask me why, I could respond by saying that it is raining. Interestingly, Toulmin does not require the proponent at this point to prove the claim by stating and applying a rule. This is not a deductive theory of justification. The opponent can challenge this argument by questioning the truth of the datum (It isn't raining), or by doubting that the datum supports the conclusion (What do umbrellas have to do with rain?). Only in the latter case is the proponent called upon to present a rule, which

Toulmin calls a *warrant*. However, the conclusion need not be necessarily true given the warrant and datum. Warrants can provide various kinds of support. It may be a defeasible rule subject to exceptions, for example, or state that the conclusion is merely probable given the datum. Should the opponent challenge the warrant, the proponent is required to support it with what Toulmin calls *backing*. If the warrant is an interpretation of a statute, for example, the backing might be a reference to the statute. If the warrant is a moral rule, its backing might be an argument that it furthers some moral goal.

Here we see the same two-tiered structure apparent in Toulmin's initial theory. At the first tier claims are supported by data; at the second tier warrants are supported by backing. The assertion of a warrant can be viewed as another claim, in which backing is a datum supporting the warrant. This opens up the possibility of challenging the backing, requiring the proponent to present still another warrant demonstrating that the backing indeed supports the original warrant, and so on. According to Toulmin, this process ends when the discourse partners find a level at which they agree. He claims that argumentation is not possible unless some rules are accepted without challenge. It seems to me that the issue is not so much whether argumentation is possible or not, but whether such an argument will be *resolved* without resort to means falling outside the normative rules of argument, such as brute force. Toulmin addresses here only a particular kind of argument, those between two parties, without the assistance of a judge or arbitrator. In this special case, agreement is only possible if there is a certain willingness by both parties to agree. Such an argument will not be resolved, as a matter of fact, if one party stubbornly challenges every claim, datum or warrant.

Toulmin distinguishes between "substantial" and "analytic" arguments.[16] An argument is analytic if and only if 1) the claim is necessarily true if both the datum and warrant are true; and 2) the datum and the warrant are both necessarily true. This latter condition prevents almost all practical arguments of any significance from being analytic. Toulmin does not permit the datum and warrant to be merely assumed. He gives the following example [123, p. 123]:

Claim. Anne has red hair.

Datum. Anne is one of Jack's sisters.

Warrant. All of Jack's sisters have red hair.

Here, although Anne necessarily has red hair if Anne is one of Jack's sisters and they all have red hair, the argument is not analytic: Neither the datum nor warrant are necessarily true. If we have seen each sister to have red hair, including Anne, then the warrant here does not provide additional support to the claim. On the contrary, the warrant is supported by the claim. If the warrant was derived inductively, from having seen some of Jack's sister, then the claim is at best probable. Notice that arguments supported by natural science theories are also substantial, rather than analytic. Scientific theories are not necessarily true, but

---

[16]Presumably, this is the same as Kant's distinction between "synthetic" and analytic judgments [57].

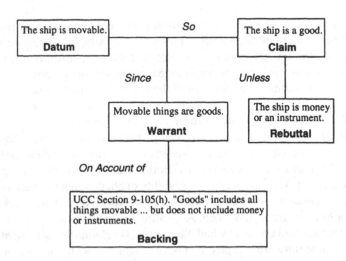

Figure 3.1. Toulmin's Argument Layout

generalizations of experimental results.

Toulmin's contribution is significant for several reasons. He convincingly demonstrated that "substantial" arguments make use of several different kinds of inference — classical, defeasible and probabilistic — as well as arguments about purpose. Conveniently, his theory lends support to my claim that decisions need not be justified by deductive arguments. Typically, facts alone are asserted as reasons for conclusions. Rules (i.e., warrants) are stated only on demand. Finally, Toulmin recognized that arguments are goal-directed. Arguments begin with the unsupported assertion of claims. Premises are added only as required to support challenged claims.

Alexy criticizes Toulmin's theory by arguing that it is not a *normative* theory of practical discourse. The discourse rules Toulmin describes were arrived at by observing actual arguments in a number of fields. Alexy calls this an "empirical-definitional" theory of argumentation [4, p. 90]. It is empirical because it claims to describe actual practice and definitional because Toulmin then labels this particular practice correct, without further justification. Although it is not unreasonable to first investigate actual practice, a normative theory requires arguments defending the practice. I have a few points of criticism to add. Toulmin's premature rejection of mathematics was mentioned above. A theory of argumentation can profit from insights from jurisprudence as well as mathematics. More importantly, Toulmin's theory does not prescribe how to order competing arguments, although it recognizes they exist. What if, for example, a defeasible rule conflicts with a probabilistic rule? I already mentioned that the theory is restricted to cooperative arguments, or discussions, between two parties. It doesn't prescribe how to resolve arguments when the interests of the parties are opposed. Finally, the theory fails to fairly balance the interests of the proponent and opponent. It obliges the proponent to defend all objections by the opponent, but places no limits on the opponent's right to challenge claims.

Baier also developed a theory of argumentation [4, pp. 93-99]. It is quite similar to Toulmin's and will not be dealt with in any detail here. The only feature of the theory I would like to mention is Baier's idea of using *priority rules* for ordering competing arguments. Judging by Alexy's treatment of the theory, however, Baier does not appear to propose any particular priority rules. Also, it is unclear how priority rules are to be used. On the one hand, Baier speaks of "the weighing of the reasons" for and against some claim. But he also says that a claim is valid when the "best" reasons support it. The idea of weighing suggests combining the factors into weighted sums for and against the claim. This approach would permit a number of poor warrants to combine to defeat a better warrant. Another possibility would be to prefer the claim supported by the best warrants. Neither alternative eliminates the possibility of leaving the decision undetermined. No matter which of these two methods is used, there may be equally good reasons for either decision. A normative theory of argumentation should address these issues. Baier points out the problem, but fails to solve it.

3.3.2 Habermas' Logic of Discourse

The next theory Alexy considers is Jürgen Habermas' Logic of Discourse [4, pp. 101-137]. Although Habermas is certainly one of the most significant contemporary German philosophers, it would lead us too far astray to discuss his theory in any depth. Instead, I will confine myself to a short summary of Alexy's analysis of Habermas' theory. My own critical remarks will be based solely on Alexy's treatment and should be weighted accordingly.

Habermas too builds on speech act theory, in particular the distinction between the illocutionary and locutionary aspects of speech, that is, between the act of asserting some statement and the meaning of the statement. According to Habermas, the assertion of some moral statement is justified just when the following conditions are satisfied:

- The statement is *comprehensible* to the other participants of the discussion. This could prohibit, for example, using technical jargon when the other parties are not members of the same profession.

- The assertion of the statement is *appropriate*. This prohibits, for example, irrelevant assertions unrelated to the subject of the discussion.

- The statement is *true*. Habermas' conception of truth is somewhat unconventional. It is discussed below.

- *Honesty*. The speaker must believe the statement asserted.

All of these conditions must be fulfilled. So, for example, a true statement not believed by the speaker would not be justified, even if it were appropriate. Again, justification depends not only on the propositional content of the statement, but also on pragmatic aspects of the discussion.

At this level of abstraction, each of these requirements may seem reasonable enough. A full treatment of Habermas' theory would require us to discuss each of them in depth. Instead, I would like to focus on Habermas' notion of truth. He rejects the conventional *correspondence theory of truth*. In the correspondence theory, a statement is true just when it accurately describes the world of interest. We say the statement is "satisfied" by the world. This theory suffers from several problems. As was discussed above in section 3.1 on Hart's analytical jurisprudence, language is indefinite for a variety of reasons, of which "open-texture" is but an example. Secondly, we are concerned here with the justification of normative statements. What objects in the world can be said to correspond to norms?

Rather than merely accepting these problems as limitations of natural language, Habermas attempts to avoid them by developing an alternative conception of truth, his *consensus theory of truth*. Habermas writes [4, p. 102]:

> I may predicate something of an object, if and only if every individual who *could* enter into a conversation with me *would* predicate the same thing of the named object. In order to distinguish true from false statements, I refer to the judgment of others—indeed to the judgment of all others with whom I might ever engage in conversation (here I include, counterfactually, all speech-partners whom I might encounter if my life history were co-extensive with that of humankind). The condition for the truth of statements is the potential agreement of *everyone* else. (Emphasis in original)

This approach indeed effectively circumvents the issue about the truth value of norms. It is true that Fred shall not covet his neighbor's wife if we all agree that he shall not. It is true that this apple is red if everyone agrees it is red. The same test applies whether the proposition is descriptive or normative. However, this truth criterion is handicapped by at least two shortcomings: 1) It can never in fact be satisfied; and 2) even its satisfaction would be insufficient. It is not practical to obtain the agreement of all living persons, and impossible to obtain the agreement of those dead or not yet born. Moreover, even if this were possible, the actual agreement of some person may have been based on error or misconception, or have been the result of some undue external pressure, such as coercion.

Habermas responds to this criticism by clarifying his intentions. He agrees that mere factual consensus is insufficient and replaces this with the stricter requirement of *reasoned consensus*. At first glance, this modification seems only to address the second shortcoming. However, reasons are not only an *additional* requirement, but weaken the previous requirement, so emphatically stated in the above quotation, that *everyone* would agree to the statement. Now, the agreement of everyone is *presumed* if the statement rests on "the strength of the better argument" [4, p. 112]. We need no longer conduct a survey of those living and dead; it is enough to examine the arguments for and against the proposition

Thus, the problem of determining the truth of a proposition has been reduced to the problem of gathering and ranking the arguments for and against the proposition. Habermas uses Toulmin's argument schema. As before, claims are supported by data and warrants.

Warrants are supported by backing. In the case of warrants expressing moral norms, rather than empirical relationships, another consensus test applies: A norm is backed if and only if its social consequences can be accepted by everyone. This is Habermas' version of Hare's principle of prescriptivity, discussed in section 3.3.1.[17]

The best arguments have the best warrants. Which warrants are best? The consensus test just discussed only establishes the existence of a norm, but does not provide criteria for evaluating the relative merits of competing norms. For this task Habermas suggests the purposes of the norms need to be identified and weighed. Which arguments are best, then, depends in the end on the judged relative merits of competing social values. Habermas does not suggest how this should be determined. He only claims that this issue must also be subject to debate. As in Toulmin's theory, an infinite regress is avoided by allowing discourse participant's to agree. There is no obligation to challenge assertions.

From these discourse norms, Habermas' derives a number of preconditions which any discourse must satisfy if there is to be the *possibility* of arriving at reasoned consensus. These preconditions are not discourse norms, as they do not state obligations or permissions. Rather, they describe conditions of the discourse setting, independent of the behavior of the speakers, which *enable* the actions obligated or permitted to be performed. That is, they are necessary but not sufficient conditions of what Habermas calls the *ideal speech situation* (ideale Sprachsituation). Two preconditions which Alexy considers to be especially significant are described by Habermas as follows [4, pp. 119-120] :

> 1. All potential participants in a discourse must have an equal opportunity of contributing communicative speech-acts, so that they may at any time initiate discourses and carry them on through dialogue and a process of question and answer.
>
> 2. All participants in discourses must have an equal opportunity to put forward interpretations, assertions, recommendations, explanations, and justifications and to problematize, justify, or refute their respective claims to validity in such a way that no opinion can remain permanently free from thematization and criticism.

A number of potential problems with Habermas' theory, as I have described it, may come to mind. It might be objected, for example, that Habermas has reduced the problem of determining whether there is reasoned consensus for some norm to the at least as difficult problem of deciding whether there is consensus that social interests are best promoted by the norm. Further, how can we be sure that the requirement of reasoned consensus is satisfied in the case of assertions merely assumed by the actual discourse partners? Finally, how can one be sure that the conditions of the ideal speech situation are met if it remains unclear which conditions are sufficient? Habermas has stated only a few necessary

---

[17]Empirical warrants can be backed by using *induction* to generalize observations. Notice that the prescriptivity principle and induction play the same role in argumentation. Both are used to back general rules.

conditions, and it is doubtful that even these can ever be satisfied completely in actual discourse.

Habermas responds by arguing that there can be no method for determining the truth of every proposition with certainty. The truth of nonanalytic propositions always remains subject to doubt. There are many potential reasons for rejecting previously accepted propositions. For example, the interpretation of the relative merits of conflicting social goals can change, some social consequence of a norm may have failed to be taken into consideration, or some necessary condition of the ideal speech situation may be discovered to not have been met.

Although it cannot provide a procedure for determining the truth of any proposition, Habermas' theory, in particular its concept of the ideal speech situation, serves three functions [4, pp. 122]:

- It provides the basis for the expectation that the consensus actually achieved by discourse is reasonable and justified. The discourse partners *assume* that the actual discussion meets the requirements of the ideal. If this assumption is unreasonable, because there are indications that one or more of the conditions are not satisfied, then it would make little sense to initiate or carry on the discussion.

- The ideal provides the standards against which actual discussions can be measured and criticized. If it can be shown that one of the discourse norms has been violated, or that one of the conditions of the ideal speech situation was not satisfied, then the presumption of reasoned consensus is rebutted.

- Finally, it serves to back additional procedural norms designed to increase the probability that the discussion will approach the ideal.

Although in general it cannot be finally determined whether or not a statement is true, there are exceptions. Tautologies are necessarily true; contradictory statements necessarily false. Habermas also considers certain statements to be *discursively impossible*. Norms which conflict with the discourse rules or which make satisfaction of conditions of the ideal speech situation impossible are of this type. For example, the statement "It will rain tomorrow, but I don't believe it." is discursively impossible. It violates the honesty rule. This does not mean that it is impossible for someone to say something like this. It just means that it is impossible for such a statement to meaningfully contribute to a discussion. It would bring us no closer to consensus about whether or not it will rain. Alexy gives another example: a norm which prohibits someone from taking part in the discussion is also discursively impossible, he claims, as it violates a basic condition of the ideal speech situation [4, p. 132].

We are just about finished with Habermas' theory. It remains only to ask how his theory may be relevant to the problems of legal reasoning and argumentation. Habermas' focus is the justification of moral statements. Alexy's thesis is that legal argumentation is a special kind of moral discourse. In his view, the general norms of moral discourse fully apply to legal argumentation; they are merely extended with additional norms particular to the legal context. However, certain aspects of Habermas' theory make it difficult for me to completely accept this thesis. The main problem concerns the prescriptivity principle for backing normative warrants. If we accept the positivist's position about the separation of law and morals, then it is surely the wrong sort of backing for legal rules. The issue is not whether the consequences of the rule can be accepted by *every* person, but whether there is legal *authority* for the rule. Perhaps a somewhat different prescriptivity principle could be postulated for legal rules: A legal rule is backed if its consequences can be accepted by a majority of the members of the legislature. But this test is not without its problems. Should actual consensus by the majority be required? This would violate the separation of powers doctrine by requiring the legislature to decide cases. Moreover, like Habermas' original consensus test, it would be insufficient. Some legislator's consent may have been obtained by coercion or error. If however a standard of *reasoned* consensus is used, as in Habermas' revised theory, then this would take us back to where we started. It is difficult to imagine a form of reasoned consensus which does not rely on an objective standard, such as Habermas' version of the prescriptivity principle.

A related question is whether Habermas' theory is pragmatic enough for our purposes. Our main concern is determining whether a legal decision was "correct", i.e., that it was within the limits of judicial discretion. It is tempting to propose that a decision is correct just when the singular norm of the decision is "true", in Habermas' sense. However, Habermas claims there can be no general method for determining whether or not a statement is true. Two possible solutions to this problem come to mind. We could try to find a notion of correctness, different from truth, which does allow correctness to be determined. Or, we can retreat from our demand for a decision procedure. The correctness of a decision would be presumed, unless rebutted by a showing that an applicable discourse norm was violated.

Finally, it should be asked whether the ideal (moral) discussion is also the ideal situation for resolving legal disputes. For example, it is a condition of the ideal speech situation that everyone have an equal opportunity to participate in the discussion. Should this also be a condition of legal argumentation? Alexy thinks so [4, p. 297]. In the United States, anyone may petition the court for permission to file a brief about some issue of the case before the court.[18] In some jurisdictions, such a brief may be filed only with permission of all the parties. There does not seem to be a general right to file these briefs; a court need not grant permission. According to Habermas' theory, it appears these rules are discursively impossible, as they restrict the unconditional right to express an opinion. Of course, the mere existence of these rules does not justify them, but I suspect there are good reasons for their limitations on the right to participate.

3.3.3 The Erlangen School

Alexy next considers the theory of practical deliberation of the Erlangen School. This

---

[18]These are called *amicus curiae* briefs. Amicus curiae means, literally, friend of the court.

school, whose leading figures included Lorenzen and Schwemmer, attempted to adapt
Brouwer's philosophy of "intuitionism", which is also called *constructivism*, to the field
of ethics. Brouwer was primarily concerned with mathematical, rather than practical
reasoning. His philosophy is perhaps most famous for his challenge of the *law of the
excluded middle* of classical logic, which states that $p \lor \neg p$ is true, for any proposition p.
The fundamental principle of intuitionism is that each belief should be constructed on top
of other beliefs whose truth is beyond doubt. The law of the excluded middle is thought to
violate this principle, as it makes the truth of the compound statement $p \lor \neg p$ independent
of the truth of p.

Intuitionism is so named because Brouwer was motivated by the cognitive behavior of a
mathematician introspecting about the properties of some abstract mathematical structure.
Lorenzen adapted intuitionism to the social context of argumentation, where one person
tries to convince another of the truth of some proposition. One of Lorenzen's achievements
is to have developed the first formal dialogue logic, which is a game played between a
proponent and opponent of some first-order formula. Dialogue Logic, which is completely
analytic, is described in detail in the next chapter. Here, we will sketch his colleague
Schwemmer's effort to broaden the field of application of the constructive method to cover
the decision of ethical and practical questions.

According to the Erlangen School, the main purpose of ethics is the peaceful,
noncoercive resolution of conflicts. Schwemmer identifies several principles of rational
argumentation which he considers to follow from this purpose. The first is that the parties
involved must methodically build-up a common terminology, beginning with undisputed
concepts. It is claimed that this common terminology can be constructed without resorting
to explanations using terms or concepts which are not part of this accepted common basis.
The second principle is that a party must be willing to accept the statements he wants
the other party to accept. The third principle is that sentences shall be asserted in their
most general form, so that they are satisfiable by the broadest class of situations, and not
just the particular facts of the current conflict. Alexy points out that, when the sentence
concerned expresses a norm, these last two principles are comparable to Hare's principles
of prescriptivity and universalizability, respectively.

It is somewhat unclear, according to Alexy, whether Schwemmer requires a proposed
norm to be acceptable only to the parties involved in the conflict, or to everyone, as
in the naive interpretation of Habermas' consensus theory of truth. Alexy cites a few
passages which seem to support this latter interpretation. I am unconvinced, however,
as this interpretation would appear to violate the spirit of constructivism. As was pointed
out when discussing Habermas' theory, it is not possible to obtain the actual consent of
everyone. The first interpretation, on the other hand, is constructive in the sense that there
is a procedure for deciding the issue: the actual agreement of both parties is conclusive.

Schwemmer recognizes that two valid norms can conflict. His *principle of morality*
was designed to resolve these conflicts. He postulates that norms are partially ordered. This
order does not reflect their relative weight or importance, but rather their relationship to
the purposes to be promoted by them. Although the idea is not explained in much detail
by Alexy, it seems that consensus is to be achieved by the parties giving up enough of
their goals and objectives until a common *supernorm* of the conflicting norms is reached.

An example would have helped to make this idea clear. Alexy complains that this idea is not practical, as a party may not be willing to give up any of his goals. However, there is an easy response to this objection: Schwemmer's theory is normative. The principal of morality prescribes what the parties should do in order to peacefully resolve their conflict, whether they are in fact willing to do so or not.

The last aspect of the Erlangen School of ethics Alexy discusses is their method of the *critical genesis* of norms. This is a complicated methodology for identifying, criticizing and reforming the norms of a culture. Alexy only touches on this subject briefly. Empirical methods are proposed for identifying norms. Historical methods are proposed for uncovering the reasons why a norm arose. These historical reasons are then used in a critical appraisal of a norm, by asking whether they are still applicable in the changed circumstances of the current time.

Alexy considers the idea of critical genesis to be the most important contribution of the Erlangen School. However, from Alexy's description of the idea, it is not clear what role it has to play in the resolution of practical disputes in concrete cases. That this approach to critically analyzing norms is appropriate in a political or academic setting is uncontroversial. But just when arguments of this kind should be admissible to resolve legal disputes is not addressed.

One is left wondering to what extent the Erlangen School has succeeded in establishing a constructivist foundation for ethical disputes. I fail to see a close relationship between Schwemmer's ethics and Brouwer's intuitionism. The goals of intuitionism and practical dispute resolution seem to be irreconcilable. Intuitionism restricts inference to careful, deliberate steps. It places demands on proof which are even more restrictive than those of classical logic. Practical reason and dispute resolution, on the other hand, require fair procedures for reaching just decisions given severe resource limitations. There must be practical methods for deciding whether to accept or reject claims of uncertain logical or factual status.

This said, if one is willing to overlook the claimed relationship to intuitionistic mathematics, most of the ideas in Schwemmer's ethics, as they have been described here, could be retained in a comprehensive theory of legal argumentation. Although it is still unclear how this may be achieved in practice, there should be a procedure for constructing a common terminology during argument. The validity of norms put forward in arguments by the parties should be decided by the parties (and the court) alone, not by the world at large. In some quasi-legal contexts, such as arbitration, Schwemmer's morality principle may offer a practical method for achieving consensus, assuming there is some way to enforce the principle. Finally, there may be a place for the method of critical genesis in some legal proceedings, such as appeal.

3.3.4   Perelman's New Rhetoric

In 1958, the same year in which Toulmin's *The Uses of Argument* appeared, Chaim Perelman, together with L. Olbrechts-Tyteca, published *The New Rhetoric: A Treatise on Argumentation*. The work shows similarities to Toulmin's, but also to Habermas' consensus theory of truth, which appeared over a decade later. The name "New Rhetoric" may mislead one into thinking that the only goal of the theory is to explain *persuasive* argumentation. However, a distinguishing feature of Perelman's theory is his attempt to find a unifying framework for effective and correct argumentation. That is, the theory strives to be both explanatory and normative.

Perelman's theory can be divided into three main parts: 1) the structure of arguments; 2) the process of constructing arguments; and 3) the evaluation of arguments. The first two parts are analytical and descriptive. The last part encompasses his predictive theory of effective arguments as well as his normative theory of valid arguments.

Regarding the structure of arguments, Perelman distinguishes premises, presumptions, a preference relation on moral values, and *topoi* of abstract values, such as liberty and equality. Arguments are created by "associating elements" of some kind. There are also various relations between arguments, such "additive strengthening", where several arguments lend each other support. Although it would interesting to pursue some of these ideas further, in particular those of topoi and associative arguments, these few remarks will have to suffice for our purposes here.

Let's turn to the process by which arguments are constructed in Perelman's theory. Unlike mathematical logic, where theorems are implicitly contained in the axioms of some theory, the conclusions which can be supported by an argument in Perelman's theory do not depend solely on the structure of the argument. Rather, Perelman makes these conclusions dependent on the *audience* being addressed. Each inference step requires the assent of the audience. This requirement can both weaken or strengthen the inference relation relative to some consequence relation, such as classical logic, depending on the audience. It may be weaker, as a sentence which is entailed may not be accepted by the audience if, e.g., its proof is too difficult to understand. It may be stronger, as the audience may accept a conclusion which is not entailed. Some of the premises required, for example, may be tacitly assumed by both the speaker and the audience. This aspect of Perelman's theory is similar to Toulmin's, where data, warrants and backing need only be brought forward by the proponent on demand. Perelman and Toulmin both reject deductive theories of justification.

A particular audience may very well accept some claim for reasons of questionable legitimacy, from a normative point of view. Perelman devotes a large part of his theory to the analysis of the effectiveness of such rhetorical tricks as flattery and character attacks. But again, Perelman strives for a theory which subsumes both the descriptive and prescriptive views of argumentation. He distinguishes effective argumentation from correct or valid argumentation by attempting to characterize the ideal audience, called the "universal audience". Arguments which effectively persuade this universal audience are not only effective, but correct. Thus, a novelty of Perelman's theory is that it views correct argumentation as a particular kind of effective argumentation.

Perelman derives a few discourse norms from this notion of the universal audience. For example, as the speaker himself is a member of the universal audience, only sincere claims are permitted, and there is an obligation to reveal any known, relevant counterarguments.

Perelman's concept of the universal audience may have been the seed for Habermas' consensus theory of truth, which came later. As in Habermas' more fully developed theory,

Perelman does not require correct arguments to actually persuade every possible person, but only "enlightened humanity", which consists only of those fictional persons who can be convinced only by rational arguments. Thus, Perelman's theory suffers from the same difficulty faced by Habermas: the problem of characterizing the ideal audience is reduced to the problem of defining rational arguments, which takes us back to where we started. Habermas, however, goes farther than Perelman in circumventing these problems, with his theory of the ideal speech situation.

To sum up, Perelman's theory is an interesting attempt to find a unifying view of effective and valid argument. I am not aware of any other author who has tried to achieve this goal. However, as a normative theory of practical argumentation, Perelman's New Rhetoric appears rather weak compared to some of the other approaches Alexy describes.

3.3.5 Evaluation of Alexy's Theory

As we have done for Hart's and Rödig's theories of legal reasoning, let us now try to summarize and evaluate Alexy's contribution in terms of the catalogue of issues identified at the beginning of this chapter.

Recognized Limitations.
Alexy views legal decision-making as a special kind of "general practical discourse" guided by norms adapted from moral philosophy. The theory insists that no method is possible for identifying with certainty valid rules or the relative priority or weight of conflicting rules. This insight applies equally to the discourse norms themselves.

Legal reasoning is limited not only by the lack of perfect knowledge about the law and facts, but also by finite resources, such as time and money.

Correctness Criteria.
A legal decision is presumably correct or just when it is the result of a fair procedure.

Methods.
A correct decision is constructed by "playing" a fair "game". Burden of proof rules are used to divide up limited resources among the players, which in the case of court proceedings includes the judge as well as the parties. A decision is tested for correctness, for example on appeal, by examining the protocol or record of the game to confirm that none of its procedural rules have been violated.

At this level of abstraction, I find myself in agreement with Alexy's general thesis. Its limitations only become apparent when trying to apply the theory to a concrete type of legal proceeding. Alexy's work would have benefited greatly from an extended legal example, showing how the various discourse rules he proposes may actually be used in the context of deciding some legal case.

As mentioned in the introduction to this section on Alexy's theory, he invites criticism of the particular set of discourse norms he proposes. Their acceptability is not critical to his thesis. This is fortunate, as they suffer from several problems.

1.   They are insufficiently precise. At this level of abstraction, they are as difficult to interpret and apply as the substantive law of some legal domain. Using these rules directly to regulate a legal proceeding will lead to frequent and unnecessary discourse-theoretical arguments about their intended meaning.

2.   They are too general. Alexy does not distinguish between different types of legal proceedings. Different rules of procedure are applicable to, for example, pleading, discovery, trial and appeal. There is more than one type of legal game.

3.   They fail to take resource limitations seriously. Although Alexy touches on the subject of resource limitations, their full significance is not reflected by the discourse norms he proposes. Rules such as [4, pp. 298-302]

   •   "Everyone may introduce any assertion into the discourse." and

   •   "It is possible for any speaker at any time to make a transition into a linguistic-analytical discourse."

   need to be qualified so as to assure that a decision is reached before the resources are exhausted.

4.   They fail to distinguish the roles of different players. The discourse rules applicable to a player should depend on his or her role in the proceeding, such as judge, attorney, plaintiff, defendant, or jury.

5.   Finally, and most importantly for our purposes, it is unclear how these discourse norms restrict judicial discretion. This is related to the previous point. As the rules apply to all speakers, regardless of their role, no attempt is made to balance the power of the judge relative to the legislature, the parties, legal philosophers or the press, for example.

   Despite these problems, Alexy's work is a major achievement, which points the way to overcoming the limitations of Hart's version of analytical jurisprudence. Judicial discretion should not be limited by the untenable line between hard and easy cases, but by fair rules of legal procedure. Although the meaning of procedural rules can be subject to doubt, in the same way and for the same reasons as substantive law, they are relatively few in number. Also, as the same procedural rules are applicable to every proceeding of a particular type, a sufficient degree of certainty is achieved through their repeated application. This is a matter of degree, not of kind. Substantive issues also recur, but not as frequently.

   Alexy is a German legal theorist and one might wonder to what extent his theory is acceptable to theorists in common law systems. One indication is John Rawls' treatment of the subject of procedural justice in his *A Theory of Justice* [99]. According to Michael Bayles, who also deals with this subject in his recent book, *Procedural Justice* [13,

p. 5], Rawls distinguishes between *pure*, *perfect* and *imperfect* procedural justice. In pure procedural justice, there are no independent criteria for determining whether the outcome of the procedure is just. The procedure itself defines the justice of the outcome. Bayles gives the example of a fair game of chance. Assuming, e.g., that a die is not malformed, a choice made in a game of chance by tossing it is certainly just. In the cases of perfect and imperfect justice, there is some independent test of justice or correctness, beyond the procedural rules. If the procedure is perfect, then the outcome obtained by the procedural is always the same as that determined by this independent test. If the procedure is imperfect, then the outcome may not be just according to this independent test. Bayles gives the example of cutting a pie into equal pieces. If the person cutting the pie chooses last, then everyone is likely to get an equal size piece. Bayles considers this procedure to be an example of perfect justice, but I think it is better classified as an example of imperfect justice: despite his best efforts the person cutting the pie may in fact fail to cut the pie perfectly.

What kind of justice is achievable by fair procedural rules for deciding legal cases? Although Alexy was not unfamiliar with Rawls' work on this subject [4, p. 99] he explicitly left the question of the relevance of Rawls' theory for a theory of legal reasoning open, noting that the focus of Rawls' book is the basic structure of the state, and not so much the decision of legal cases. Nonetheless, it may be interesting to try to evaluate Alexy's theory in terms of Rawls' framework.

At first glance, it appears that Alexy's is a pure theory of procedural justice, as he goes to great lengths to show that, in general, there are no independent objective criteria for evaluating the correctness of legal arguments. This analysis would be too simple. His theory is intended to cover the most general case. There may well be objective criteria for deciding some legal issues. The procedure used to decide such issues would be either perfect or imperfect, in Rawls' sense. More importantly, even when there are no independent objective criteria, Alexy takes care to explain, following Habermas, that conformance with the procedural norms only supports the *presumption* of justice. A fair procedure is designed to increase the likelihood that the decision will be just, but cannot guarantee this. Subsequent information, for example that a witness had lied during trial, can rebut this presumption. Thus, Alexy's theory discloses a weakness in Rawls' system of classification. Procedures can be imperfect even when there is no objective test of correctness. This insight is not so much a reason to reject Rawls' framework as an invitation to refine it. At this level of abstraction, the theories of Alexy and Rawls are mostly complementary.

3.4 Dimensions of Discourse Games

In the next chapter, several formal models of argumentation will be presented and evaluated. Ideally, it would be possible to derive from the discussion of legal philosophy in this chapter a set of requirements for a formal model of legal argumentation. As an important lesson of this chapter is that there are a variety of types of legal proceedings, each with its own discourse norms, this goal would be too abstract. Rather, a more promising approach might be to identify a particular type of legal proceeding relevant for resolving Article Nine priority conflicts, our chosen legal domain, and try here to abstractly specify its requirements. It would be premature to attempt this, however, as we are still completely in the dark about the formal tools available for modeling discourse games. The choice of a type of proceeding to model should depend on the possibilities opened by previous formal models of argumentation. It would be preferable to choose a proceeding to model which is within reach of the state of the art of formalization.

So, let us try instead to achieve the more modest goal of identifying the factors or dimensions of discourse games, some of which have been discussed in this chapter. These dimensions are intended to define the space of possible discourse games, and will be helpful for classifying and evaluating the formal models of argumentation discussed next.

Purpose.
What is the purpose of the game? Is the goal, for example, to identify the points of controversy, try facts, gather evidence, decide a claim, or review an argument on appeal?

Types of Data.
What types of data are used in speech acts? Is the data restricted to expressions of a formal language, or are natural language sentences, or perhaps even multimedia objects, such pictures, graphics, video or sound recordings, allowed? If this seems far-fetched, consider the types of exhibits which must be accounted for in a model of discovery or trial.

Dynamics.
Is the pool of data fixed at the beginning of the game, or can new data be introduced by players during the game? For example, can players introduce new terminology, rules, or evidence during the game?

Speech Acts.
What kinds of speech acts are modeled by moves of the game? Some possibilities are claims, proofs, questions, challenges, objections, and various kinds of arguments.

Commitments.
Do the previous moves of a player constrain his future moves? For example, are players committed to their claims? If so, are they also committed to consequences of these claims?

Resource Limitations.
Are moves constrained by resources? If so, what kinds? Some possibilities include time, the number of inference steps or length of proofs, the number of nodes expanded in some search space, or the number of cases or statutes cited. How are these resources divided among the players? Do these limitations assure termination of the game?

Players.
How many players are there? If there is more than one player, do they have different roles, such as plaintiff, defendant or judge? Do the rights and obligations of a player in the game depend on his or her role?

Subjects of Discussion.
What is subject to discussion during the game? Does the system support discussion about the truth of substantial claims, or is it restricted to only analytical truths (i.e., tautologies)? Other possible subjects include the validity of rules, priority relationships between rules, or the discourse norms of the game itself.

Chapter 4   Formal Models of Argumentation

As this is an artificial intelligence book, our goal is a *computational* model of some legal process. The discourse norms from Alexy's theory of legal argumentation are quite abstractly stated, and it is still less than clear how or whether they can be modeled in a computer program. One result of the previous chapter on legal philosophy is a set of dimensions for classifying discourse games. In this chapter, several existing formal models of argumentation will be described and then classified along these dimensions. The goal is not so much to assess their suitability for modeling legal argumentation as to gather ideas and techniques which can be adapted in a discourse game designed expressly for this purpose.

We will be looking at four formal systems in this chapter:

1.   Paul Lorenzen's *Dialogue Logic*, as described by Walter Felscher in [33];

2.   John Pollock's OSCAR system [91];

3.   Guillermo Simari and Ronald Loui's work on defeasible reasoning [116]; and

4.   Hector Geffner and Judea Pearl's logic of *conditional entailment* [41].

Lorenzen and Pollock are philosophers and logicians. The others are Artificial Intelligence scientists. With respect to *normative* models of argumentation, this is fairly representative selection. To my knowledge, there has been very little other work within AI on this subject. Some of this other work, as well as work on cognitive models of argumentation and hypertext issue-based information systems, will be discussed briefly in the conclusion of this chapter.

4.1   Lorenzen's Dialogue Logic

In the late 1950's, Paul Lorenzen proposed that arguments, which he calls dialogues, could provide a philosophical foundation for intuitionistic logic. That is, arguments are to play the role for intuitionistic logic that *models* play for classical logic, in Tarskian semantics. Although other foundations for intuitionistic logic have been developed, such as the "semantic interpretations" of Beth and Kripke [124, p. 229], dialogues and other "algorithmic" or "proof-theoretic" approaches reflect more closely the spirit of intuitionism as it was originally conceived by Brouwer at the beginning of the century. In Brouwer's view, mathematics is a form of mental activity; a mathematical object with particular properties exists for some person only if that person has been able to mentally construct such an object. Language and logic only comes into play when trying to convince others of the existence of such mathematical constructions. The goal of mathematical discourse is to assist other interested mathematicians in mentally reconstructing objects of the same type.

This epistemological approach to logic should be contrasted with the ontological approach taken in Tarskian model-theoretic semantics for classical logic. Here, the truth of a sentence is defined relative to an interpretation, that is, a mapping of symbols of the language to objects in some *external* domain or world. Sentences are *valid*, i.e., always true, only if they are true in every interpretation. That is, the validity of a proposition depends not on the existence of a mental construction, or proof, of the proposition, as in intuitionism, but solely on the properties of all possible interpretations of the proposition.

However, this is not the place to discuss the Formalists vs. Intuitionists debate in any detail. But I would like to point out that Intuitionism is not merely of historical interest. There is continuing interest in intuitionistic logic in both computer science and in AI and Law. In computer science, several theoreticians have argued that intuitionistic logic is the preferred basis for logic programming [74; 39; 80; 81]. Thorne McCarty has also proposed that intuitionistic logic programming is a good candidate for the core of a "language for legal discourse" [82]. Of more immediate relevance for my purposes here, an interesting analogy can be drawn between Brouwer's original arguments in favor of intuitionistic logic and Robert Alexy's discourse theory of justice. Just as, according to Brouwer, the "truth" of a mathematical proposition depends on a demonstration, or proof, that the proposition holds, in Alexy's view the justice of a legal decision depends of the process used to reach the decision. Both are procedural theories of validity. Indeed, as discussed in the previous chapter, Alexy was influenced by Lorenzen's school of practical deliberation, where an attempt was made to apply intuitionistic philosophy to ethical issues.

We need not be concerned too much here with whether or not Lorenzen and his successors were successful in their attempt to use dialogues as a foundation for intuitionistic logic. Walter Felscher, whose treatment of this subject in [33] was my primary source for this section, claims to have been the first to fully achieve this goal. But we are interested here in modeling legal argumentation, not finding an adequate foundation for intuitionistic logic. Whatever its merits, intuitionistic logic, like classical logic, has little to say about practical or "substantial" reasoning, to use Toulmin's term. Our goal here is a limited one: to use Lorenzen's model of dialogues as a starting point in our search for an adequate mathematical model of legal argumentation.

Dialogue logic is a two-person perfect-information game. The game begins when one player, the *proponent*, asserts a non-atomic first-order formula. The other player, the *opponent*, challenges or *attacks* the assertion by applying one of a set of *argument forms*. Which forms are applicable depends on the main connective of the proposition challenged, as will be explained in detail shortly. The proponent may then respond to the attack by *answering* it or, if the attack involved making a further assertion, by attacking this new assertion. The players take turns attacking and answering until no further move is permitted by the rules. The game is won by the player who made the last move.

A *move* is a triple $\langle e, n, k \rangle$, where e is an *expression*, defined next, n is a natural number or $\bot$, and k is one of A, D or $\bot$. The roles of n and k will be discussed shortly. An expression is either 1) a closed first-order formula, 2) one of the *special symbols* $\vee$, $\wedge_1$, $\wedge_2$, or $\exists$, which should not be confused with the connectives they resemble, or 3) a ground term of the language.

The moves permissible at a position in the game are determined by the argument forms and a few auxiliary rules. The argument forms are displayed in Table 4.1. There is one form for each connective and quantifier. Assertions and answers are formulas; attacks are expressions; w_i are well-formed formulas; and $[x/t]$ is a substitution of a variable x with a term t.

These forms are similar to inference rule schemata. For example, using the first form, two attacks are possible given the assertion $p \wedge q$, namely either one of the conjuncts, $\wedge_1(p)$ or $\wedge_2(q)$.

The role of a state of the playing board is played by *dialogues*, which are sequences of moves. That is, the state of the board after a move is the dialogue which results from appending the move to the dialogue of the previous state. Notice that dialogues are a somewhat unusual form of game state, as they are also a record of the entire history of the game so far.

Now we are in a position to explain the role of n and k in a move $\langle e, n, k \rangle$. The moves in a dialogue are numbered sequentially, beginning with 1. If a move is an attack or answer to another move, then n is the index of the move being responded to. k denotes the kind of move being made. Attacks are denoted by A, answers by D, for "defense". (As the opening move is neither an attack nor an answer, its n and k are marked by $\bot$.)

There are four auxiliary rules, which restrict the applicability of the argument forms:

1. The proponent may assert an atomic formula only after it has been previously asserted by the opponent.

2. If several attacks are still *open*, i.e., have yet to be answered, only the latest of them may be answered.

3. An attack may be answered at most once.

4. The *opponent* may attack an assertion at most once.

That's it. There are no further rules of the game. Although the explanation of the game has been rather terse, it is actually rather simple. Here is an example dialogue for the final state of a game in which the proponent won, successfully defending the claim that

$$(a \wedge b) \rightarrow (a \wedge b).$$

Odd moves were made by the proponent; Even moves by the opponent. (The moves have been labeled with P and O to make this clearer.) Assume that a and b are atomic formulas.

$\wedge$	assertion	$w_1 \wedge w_2$
	attack	$\wedge_i$
	answer	w_i
$\vee$	assertion	$w_1 \vee w_2$
	attack	$\vee$
	answer	w_i
$\rightarrow$	assertion	$w_1 \rightarrow w_2$
	attack	w_1
	answer	w_2
$\neg$	assertion	$\neg w$
	attack	w
	answer	*none*
$\forall$	assertion	$\forall x.w$
	attack	some term t
	answer	$w[x/t]$
$\exists$	assertion	$\exists x.w$
	attack	$\exists$
	answer	$w[x/t]$, for some term t

Table 4.1. Moves of Dialogue Logic

1. P: $\langle (a \wedge b) \rightarrow (a \wedge b), \bot, \bot \rangle$

2. O: $\langle a \wedge b, 1, A \rangle$

3. P: $\langle \wedge_1, 2, A \rangle$

4. O: $\langle a, 3, D \rangle$

5. P: $\langle \wedge_2, 2, A \rangle$

6. O: $\langle b, 5, D \rangle$

7. P: $\langle a \wedge b, 2, D \rangle$

8. O: $\langle \wedge_1, 7, A \rangle$

9. P: $\langle a, 8, D \rangle$

Notice that the proponent was permitted to attack, in moves 3 and 5, both conjuncts of the opponent's assertion in move 2, $(a \wedge b)$, but that the opponent was required to make a choice between the first or second conjunct when attacking the proponent's assertion in move 7. This is because of the fourth auxiliary rule, above, which permits the opponent to attack an assertion at most once. Also, the proponent was permitted to assert the atomic formula, a, in the last move, only because the opponent had already asserted it in move 4. As there are no open attacks by the proponent, the opponent is unable to make another move. (The proponent's attack in move 3 was answered in move 4; his only other attack, in move 5, was answered in move 6.) As the proponent made the last move, he wins the game.

Contrary perhaps to what might be expected, the fact that the proponent won this game does *not* imply that the opening formula $(a \wedge b) \rightarrow (a \wedge b)$ is intuitionistically valid, although it happens to be in this case. It is possible for the proponent to win the game, even when the formula is not valid. Here is an example:

1.   P: $\langle ((a \rightarrow b) \rightarrow a) \rightarrow a, \perp, \perp \rangle$

2.   O: $\langle (a \rightarrow b) \rightarrow a, 1, A \rangle$

3.   P: $\langle a \rightarrow b, 2, A \rangle$

4.   O: $\langle a, 3, D \rangle$

5.   P: $\langle a, 2, D \rangle$

The opponent lost this game because move 4 was strategically poor. He should have instead made the move $\langle a, 3, A \rangle$. Although in both cases, the opponent asserts the same formula, a, in the better move it is an attack, rather than an answer. Recall that rule 2 permits only the latest attack to be answered. According to the argument form for the $\rightarrow$ connective, the only answer to this better move, which would have been an attack on $a \rightarrow b$ in move 3, would have been b. However, due to rule 1, the proponent would not have been permitted to assert b, as the opponent had not asserted it previously. In the game, the proponent was able to answer the last open attack by the opponent, in move 2, by asserting a, as the opponent had asserted a in the previous move, in an *answer* to the proponent's attack in move 3.

Thus, it is clear that the Dialogue Logic game itself is not a calculus for intuitionistic logic. For this we need the notion of a *strategy*. For any opening move, a *game tree* can be generated by recursively applying all permissible moves to every node of the tree. A winning strategy for the proponent is a finite subtree of such a game tree with the following properties:

1.   Every branch of the tree ends in a leaf which is a dialogue won by the proponent.

2.   At every node for a move made by the opponent, there is just one successor node, for the next move by the proponent.

3.   At every node for a move made by the proponent, there is a successor node for every move permitted by the rules of the game for the opponent.

It is winning strategies for the proponent, not dialogues, which correspond to proofs, in the following sense: *There exists a winning strategy for the proponent of an assertion p if and only if p is provable in intuitionistic logic.* This is Felscher's principal theorem.

Thus, a *calculus* for intuitionistic logic based on dialogues might consist of a set of axioms and inference rules for winning strategies. To prove a formula using the calculus would involve searching the space of winning strategies for a strategy for the formula.

As it is strategies rather than dialogues which correspond to proofs, Dialogue Logic deviates considerably from Brouwer's original motivation for intuitionistic logic. Brouwer insisted that each inference step in the proof of some proposition be beyond doubt. In a Dialogue Logic game, however, the burden of making optimal moves is divided among the players, who may make mistakes. Moves do not correspond to sound inference steps. As we have seen, a player may lose even though he could have won. That is, at the end of the game, the proponent may have successfully defended a proposition for which no *proof* has been constructed.

There is an interesting parallel between this strategy interpretation of validity and Habermas' use of the ideal speech situation and Perelman's notion of the universal audience. In each case, validity or "truth" is assessed by trying to determine what the outcome of an ideal discourse about the issue would be. In the context of Dialogue Logic, this means supposing that each player makes the best moves possible.

The proof of the above theorem establishes the equivalence between winning strategies and intuitionistic logic proofs, but this alone does not provide a *foundation* for intuitionistic logic. One might suspect that the rules of this game were manipulated and tuned just for the purpose of establishing this equivalency. Interestingly enough, Lorenz has shown that a modification of the rules would result in a game for which the winning strategies would prove just the *classically* valid formulas [33, p. 352]. To be a foundation for intuitionistic logic, the rules of the game require independent philosophical justification.

Felscher claims to be able to provide just this kind of external justification. It would lead us too far astray to reproduce his complete argument here, but an example or two showing the kind of justification he offers will be useful. In the argument forms, there is no answer to an attack on $\neg p$. This is justified as follows. To avoid references to the semantical notions of truth or falsity, the concept of provability is enriched with the idea of absurdity or refutability. This can be done by introducing a propositional constant, $\bot$, denoting absurdity. Negated formulas, such as $\neg p$, are viewed as an abbreviation for the implication $p \rightarrow \bot$. The assertion of such an implication can be attacked as usual, by asserting p. The usual answer to this, according to the argument form for $\rightarrow$, would be to assert $\bot$. However, according to the principle of *ex absurdo quodlibet*, anyone who makes an absurd statement in an argument must be willing to accept absurd statements by his discourse partner, and thus must be willing to accept *any* assertion made by the partner, including the original assertion of the proponent. This would amount to conceding the game. To handle this, at least two discourse rules are possible. Either prohibit the assertion of $\bot$, or have the other player win the game immediately after $\bot$ is asserted. In Dialogue Logic, the first alternative was chosen, as it is reasonable to prohibit patent nonsense.

Another example is the justification for the rule prohibiting the proponent from asserting an atomic sentence until the opponent has already done so. To justify this, the *basic purpose* of this particular kind of discourse must be articulated. Felscher formulates the purpose as follows [33, p. 354]:

> Logically provable assertions shall be those which, for *purely formal* reasons, can be upheld by a strategy covering every dialogue chosen by [the opponent].

That is, the purpose of the discourse is artificially restricted to an analytical issue: whether or not the proposition asserted by the proponent can be "upheld" irrespective of truth or falsity of the atomic propositions occurring within it. Felscher then goes on to explain that all assertions made by the opponent are *hypothetical*, whereas those made by the proponent are all *contentions*. That is, when asserting an atomic formula p, the opponent is not contending that it is true, but only supposing it to be true for the sake of argument. If the proponent later confronts the opponent with his own hypothesis, by also asserting p, the opponent is in no position to object.

There are two important lessons implicit in the claim that discourse norms can serve as a foundation for some logic. If this claim is accepted, then after an *actual* debate about the validity of some proposition conducted in accordance with these norms, if the proponent wins the debate then the parties should be obliged to act as if the proposition is valid, *even though winning the debate does not prove the proposition*. Also, arguably dialogue logics can be developed for purposes other than establishing the formal validity of compound propositions, such as defending the kinds of substantial claims arising in legal discourse. The methodology suggested by Dialogue Logic is to first formulate the basic purpose of the class of dialogues to be regulated and develop discourse norms promoting this basic purpose. Then an attempt can be made to define a formal discourse game in which the moves permitted by the game are justified directly by these norms.

Enough has been said about Dialogue Logic to classify it along the dimensions mentioned at the end of the previous chapter. The purpose of the game is to check the validity of a first-order formula in intuitionistic logic. First-order formulas are the only kind of data. The pool of formulas is fixed by the proponent's opening move. There are two types of speech acts: attacks and defenses. Commitments are made by some moves. The game *does* impose resource limitations: at most one attack is allowed, and each attack may be answered at most once. (Thus, Dialogue Logic does divide the burden of proof among the players.) There are just two players, the proponent and opponent, and the moves permitted do depend on these roles: the proponent may assert a formula only after it has been asserted by the opponent, and the opponent may attack an assertion at most once. Finally, the subject matter of the dialogue is restricted to the analytical truth of sentences of first-order intuitionistic logic.

Dialogue Logic is not adequate, in general, for modeling legal reasoning, as it supports neither discussions about substantial claims, nor discussions about the validity or priority of rules.

For our purposes, the main points to retain about Dialogue Logic are:

1. Argumentation can be modeled as a formal game defined by argument forms and auxiliary rules.

2. Validity can be interpreted in terms of the existence of winning strategies.

3. In actual arguments conducted according to justified discourse rules, the parties should be bound to act *as if* the proposition is valid, when the proponent wins, even though validity has not been proven.

4. Dialogue Logic is a precedent for the claim that discourse norms can serve as a foundation for a logic.

4.2 Pollock's OSCAR Model of Defeasible Reasoning

In [91], the philosopher John Pollock modestly remarks that the first philosophical theories of defeasible reasoning were developed at "almost the same time" as the first AI work on nonmonotonic logics, by which he means between 10 and 20 years earlier than John Doyle's 1979 Artificial Intelligence article on his Truth Maintenance System! In that paper, Pollock presented a theory and computational model of defeasible reasoning, called OSCAR, which is the topic of this section. Although the theory suffers from several limitations, as we will see, it was one of the first attempts to base defeasible reasoning on arguments. Two recent systems influenced by Pollock's work, those of Simari and Loui, and of Geffner and Pearl, will be discussed in the following sections.

Once again, as was true for Dialogue Logic, the main goal of all three of these projects does not coincide directly with my goal of finding an adequate model of legal argumentation. These papers are not concerned with resolving disputes, but with prescribing the set of beliefs a single rational agent should hold, under certain simplifying assumptions. The dialogues or arguments in these systems occur between an agent and himself, introspectively. Many if not most of the discourse norms for regulating multi-agent arguments, such as those designed to fairly balance the burden of proof, resolve conflicts of interest, or to discourage dishonesty, would seem to have no place in dialogues with oneself.[1]

Nonetheless, it is not unreasonable to expect these theories and models of defeasible reasoning to prove useful to us. The single-agent case can be viewed as a simplification of arguments between several persons. Also, a complete normative theory of argumentation may well require a theory of rational belief; when allocating the burden of proof, the parties may be held to an objective, "reasonable person" standard. They may be expected to hold the beliefs prescribed by some theory of rationality. Finally, as was discussed at length in Chapter 3 on Legal Philosophy, substantive legal rules are usually organized as general

---

[1]Although a person can have competing interests and goals, it is unclear whether *discourse rules* are used to resolve them.

rules subject to exceptions of various kinds. Article Nine of the Uniform Commercial Code is full of examples of this, as was shown in Chapter 2. So, although this is not our central concern here, it will be interesting to see what these theories can tell us about reasoning with defeasible rules.

In Pollock's model, beliefs are first-order predicate logic formulas. The initial *epistemic basis* of an agent is an ordered triple $\langle F, D, R \rangle$, where F is a set of formulas for the *foundational states* of the agent, D is a set of *defeasible* inference rules and R is a set of *nondefeasible* inference rules. A foundational state is a proposition supported directly by perception, or a proposition recalled from memory. Pollock does not place any restrictions on the form of these propositions. The propositions in F are not necessarily believed; they are not "facts". Rather, belief in them is also defeasible, as perceptions can be mistaken and human memory is fallible. An object which appears red may turn out to have been illuminated by a red light. Regarding human memory, Pollock argues that it would take too much time to search memory for arguments supporting older beliefs. Later information could rebut the argument supporting an old belief; but if the arguments cannot be tractably retrieved, the person will not be able to determine whether or not this is the case. Pollock's proposal is to handle all past beliefs uniformly; they continue to be believed until defeated by new reasons, disregarding the original reasons.

The form of inference rules is not precisely defined in Pollock's model. He just gives several examples, described abstractly in natural language. First, he assumes there are sufficient nondefeasible rules for deriving any predicate calculus theorem. Second, there are defeasible rules for believing propositions in F, the set of foundational states. Finally, he mentions defeasible rules for probabilistic and inductive reasoning. An inference rule called *enumerative induction*, e.g., can defeasibly support belief in a universally quantified proposition. If all objects which have been observed to satisfy a predicate p have also been observed to satisfy a predicate r, then one may defeasibly infer $\forall x.p(x) \rightarrow r(x)$.

In the implementation of OSCAR, inference rules are modeled using $\langle X, p \rangle$ pairs, where p is a "proposition form" and X is a set of such forms [91, p. 512]. The details need not interest us here, but it is doubtful that these schemata are expressive enough to model some of the inference rules Pollock uses in his examples, such as enumerative induction. If the domain is infinite, a pattern language for X cannot express the constraint requiring a constant in X for every object observed.

In its simplest, linear form, an *argument* is a sequence of inference rules applied to an epistemic basis. More precisely, an argument is an ordered pair $\langle e, [l_1, ..., l_n] \rangle$, where e is an epistemic basis and each l is an *argument line*. An argument line is itself an ordered triple $\langle p, r, N \rangle$, where p is a proposition, r an inference rule and N a set of natural numbers referring to previous lines. We say that p is *supported* by the line. An argument supports some proposition p if and only if it contains a line supporting p.

Each proposition in a subset P of the foundational states F of some epistemic basis $\langle F, D, R \rangle$ is a *reason* to believe some proposition p just when there is an argument supporting p from $\langle P, D, R \rangle$. If a proposition q in P is an antecedent of an instance of a defeasible inference rule from D used in the argument, then q is a *prima facie* reason for believing p.

Another subset Q of F is a *defeater* of P as reasons for p if there is an argument from

$\langle Q, \mathbf{D}, \mathbf{R}\rangle$ supporting either $\neg p$ or $\neg(q_1 \wedge q_2, ..., q_n \rightarrow p)$, for each proposition q in P. If the argument using Q supports $\neg p$, then Q is called a *rebutting defeater* of P. Otherwise it is an *undercutting defeater*. A line j of an argument $\langle e, [l_1, ..., l_j, ..., l_n]\rangle$ *defeats* line i of an argument with the same epistemic basis $\langle e, [l_1, ..., l_i, ..., l_n]\rangle$ just when:

1. line i is $\langle p, r, N\rangle$, where r is an instance of a defeasible rule,

2. the prima facie reasons for p in e are $\{q_1, ..., q_n\}$, and

3. the proposition supported by line j is either $\neg p$ or $\neg(q_1 \wedge ... \wedge q_n \rightarrow p)$.

Pollock does not say how to determine the reasons for a line of an argument. Presumably these are minimal subsets of the foundational states allowing an argument with the line to be constructed.

With these definitions, Pollock goes on to discuss two different inference relations, for *warranted belief* and *justified belief*. The warranted beliefs are those an *ideal reasoner*, with no memory or computational limits, would hold, given some epistemic basis. The justified beliefs are those an agent is justified in holding, taking such pragmatic limitations into consideration. For example, according to Pollock an agent may be justified in holding inconsistent beliefs, if the reasoning required to discover this inconsistency is too complex, but such beliefs would not be warranted.

Warranted belief is defined in terms of *ultimately undefeated arguments*. These are defined iteratively. All arguments are level 0 arguments. A level $n + 1$ argument is one for which there is no level n argument with a line defeating one of its lines. An ultimately undefeated argument, then, is an argument for which there is some level m such that the argument is a level n argument for every $n > m$. To avoid certain paradoxes, this definition was modified slightly, by restricting level 0 arguments to those which are not *self-defeating*. See [91, pp. 494-496] for details.

Although Pollock does not discuss the properties of the warrant relation in computer science terms, he apparently feels it to be undecidable [91, p. 504]:

> ... But we cannot expect real epistemic agents to believe only warranted propositions. Warrant is a "global" concept defined in terms of the set of all possible arguments available to an epistemic agent at a single time. No one can actually survey that infinite totality and decide what to believe by applying the definition of "warrant" to it. That definition involves the comparison of infinitely many arguments ... This could not reflect the way we actually reason. Actual rules for reasoning must appeal exclusively to "local" considerations — readily accessible features of the epistemic situation.

Unfortunately, Pollock does not develop a precise mathematical definition of justified belief, but rather moves directly from a general philosophical discussion to the presentation of his OSCAR computer model, which is implemented as a production system. Here, I will just summarize his main points.

To make justified belief decidable and tractable, four modifications are made to the warranted belief relation:

1. An agent is no longer obligated to believe every proposition warranted by an epistemic state. Rather, the rules of the epistemic state are reinterpreted as *permissions*, allowing but not requiring the agent to believe their consequents when they are applicable. The agent is obligated to apply an inference rule only if he is also *interested* in the conclusion of the rule. Unfortunately, this concept of interest is not developed further. Moreover, this modification is not realized in the OSCAR computer model.

2. Three kinds of *rules of belief formation*, which should not be confused with the inference rules of an epistemic state, are introduced: 1) *adoption rules*, for introducing beliefs; 2) *defeat rules*, for challenging beliefs; and 3) *reinstatement rules*, for recovering beliefs after defeat. This is reminiscent of the assertions, attacks and answers in the argument forms of Dialogue Logic. The purpose of these rules is to reduce the potentially infinite comparison of arguments to just three phases, after which the agent is not obligated to continue reasoning.

3. The set of beliefs is partitioned into old beliefs and *newly adopted beliefs*. To avoid impractical memory searches, no reasons are recorded for old beliefs. Old beliefs may be rebutted by new contradictory beliefs, for any reason. This suggests the distinction between short-term and long-term memory. Beliefs are moved from the set of newly adopted beliefs as soon as no further beliefs are required to be adopted from the current epistemic state, by the rules of justified belief.

4. Reasons are recorded for newly acquired beliefs, but not all reasons. Rather, only the *immediate bases* for new beliefs are recorded. Although Pollock is not very clear about this, these seem to be the propositions of the foundational states which are used in the antecedent of just the *last defeasible step* of the argument supporting the belief. I do not quite understand Pollock's rationale for this. As both the arguments and the foundational states are finite, without further complexity analysis there is no reason to suppose that it would be impractical to compute the whole set of reasons for the new belief.

This completes the description of Pollock's system. It remains just to evaluate his contribution and decide how it may be useful to us in a model of legal argumentation. First, it is interesting to speculate whether Pollock was familiar with Toulmin's *Uses of Argument* [123], which he does not cite. They both are interested in the problems of practical, substantial reasoning, and both attempt to account for how humans combine deductive, defeasible, inductive and probabilistic reasoning. He also uses Toulmin's term "warrant", in a similar way. Moreover, as a normative theory of belief, Pollock's system is also subject to Alexy's criticism of Toulmin's work, that it is "empirical-definitional". Pollock acknowledges this, in fact, and argues that it is a mistake to think that normative epistemic rules are independent of psychology [91, p. 483]. On the contrary, he goes so far as to claim that actual human reasoning is governed by a system of rules of this type, and that human reasoning fails to conform to these rules on occasion only because "they are embedded in a larger system which can override them." However, Pollock does not himself provide substantial empirical support for his set of norms. His is a work of philosophy, and not natural science. But, in [91] at least, he also fails to provide sufficient philosophical justification for the epistemic norms proposed.

Unlike most of the AI literature on nonmonotonic reasoning, Pollock does not attempt to account for intuitively plausible examples of defeasible reasoning. Perhaps for this reason, his model also fails to account for the relative strengths of arguments. If two arguments defeat each other in Pollock's system, then an agent is not warranted in believing the proposition supported by either argument. This is an extreme form of "skeptical" defeasible reasoning. Other systems of defeasible reasoning resolve some of these conflicts, by ranking arguments by their specificity, for example. Indeed this is the central problem addressed in the field of nonmonotonic reasoning. Pollock does recognize the problem, but chose not deal with it in his OSCAR model [91, p. 508].

Pollock recognizes that a normative theory of reasoning must take computational limitations into consideration, including memory and time. It would be unjust to obligate persons to do the impossible. One consequence of this is that one may even be justified in holding inconsistent beliefs, when it is impractical to deduce this inconsistency. This is an issue which has received little attention in the field of nonmonotonic reasoning. Almost all of the proposed nonmonotonic inference relations in the literature are not even semidecidable. In Pollock's terms, they are theories of warranted belief, about what an ideal agent should believe, rather than of justified belief, about what persons should believe. This is one insight from Pollock's work that we will want to retain in a discourse model of legal argumentation.

To conclude this section, let's try to classify Pollock's system in terms of the dimensions of discourse games identified at the end of the previous chapter. Let us focus here on Pollock's OSCAR system, which implements his relation of justified belief. The purpose of the system is to compute the set of justified beliefs of an agent. The data consists of the formulas of the foundational state and inference rules. Although the formulas derived from this data are partitioned into old and new beliefs, and there may be some movement between these sets, it is unclear whether the foundational states and inference rules may change during the computation of the justified beliefs. There are three kinds of moves, for adopting, defeating and reinstating beliefs. The reasons recorded with new beliefs do serve to commit the agent to some extent; belief continues until defeated by other reasons. Resource limitations are a prime motivation for the design of the system: the agent may stop reasoning after searching for a single defeater and, if one is found, a single reinstating argument. Also, only the immediate basis for new beliefs are recorded, and the reasons for old beliefs are discarded. Interestingly, these resource limitations are not used to derive norms which restrict the moves permitted by the agent, but instead are used to relieve the agent of the obligation to continue reasoning. There is only one player; no roles are distinguished. The only subject of reasoning is whether to believe some formula. There is no reasoning about the validity of "inference rules" or their relative weight or priority.

4.3 Simari and Loui's System

In an AI Journal article [116], Guillermo Simari and Ronald Loui present a model of
defeasible reasoning based on Pollock's approach, but extended to rank competing
arguments by specificity. The particular measure of specificity used is due to David Poole
[92]. As we will see, however, they do not share Pollock's goal of finding a normative
theory of justified belief. Rather, like most work on nonmonotonic reasoning, their aim is
to find an elegant formal system capable of solving the usual benchmark problems in an
intuitively correct way. Although they do describe an implementation, no claims are made
about its computational properties, so it is unclear whether the system can be viewed as a
model of justified belief. At any rate, this is not a subject the authors address explicitly.

Like Pollock, it is not Simari and Loui's goal to develop a discourse model of
argumentation or conflict resolution. As their system is only indirectly relevant to our goals
here, a sketch of some of the principal definitions and theorems should suffice. Our focus
will be their interpretations of the notions of argument, counterargument and rebuttal, and
of course their solution to the problem of ranking competing arguments. The question also
arises whether the specificity of arguments alone is sufficient to resolve all of the types
of conflicts between legal rules that were discovered in our domain, Article Nine of the
UCC.

Just as Pollock begins with the idea of an epistemic basis, Simari and Loui begin with
the concept of a *defeasible logic structure*, which is a pair $\langle \mathbf{K}, \Delta \rangle$, where $\mathbf{K}$ is a set of closed,
well-formed first-order logic formulas, and Δ is a set of defeasible rules, to be defined
below. $\mathbf{K}$, which Simari and Loui call a *context*, is partitioned into two subsets: 1) the set
of ground formulas, called the *contingent formulas*, serve a function similar to Pollock's
"foundational states"; and 2) the nonground formulas, called the *necessary facts*, serve
the function of Pollock's nondefeasible rules. Unlike in Pollock's system, $\mathbf{K}$ is assumed
to be consistent. Recall that Pollock tried to account for the fact that perceptions can be
misleading. Thus it could happen that the foundational states are not consistent with the
nondefeasible rules. This is one of a number of places where Simari and Loui's work is
less ambitious than Pollock's.

A *defeasible rule* is a *nonclosed* material implication $\alpha \rightarrow \beta$, i.e., it may contain
free variables. In effect, a defeasible rule is a formula schema. A rule is *instantiated* by
uniformly replacing the free variables by constants from the language.[2]

Next, a *defeasible consequence relation* is defined, denoted $\vdash$, as follows. Suppose
there is an axiomatization of first-order classical logic such that the only inference rules
are *modus ponens* and *instantiation* of universally quantified formulas. Let G be a set
of formulas and p be a formula. $G \vdash p$ if and only if there exists a sequence of formulas
$[q_1, ..., q_n, p]$ such that each q_i is:

---

[2]Simari and Loui use another symbol, rather than $\rightarrow$, in defeasible rules, but explain that instances of these rules
are to be interpreted as material implications. Also, it is unclear whether Simari and Loui allow α and β to contain
other, bound variables, or whether instead an instance of a defeasible rule must be ground. In their examples,
they are all ground atomic formulas.

1.   an axiom, or

2.   a member of *G* or,

3.   derivable from the preceding formulas in the sequence using only the two inference rules of the calculus, modus ponens or instantiation.

Several remarks are called for here. First, despite its name and the use of the symbol ⊢ symbol, this derivability relation is monotonic.[3] The nonmonotonic derivability relation in Simari and Loui's system is the *justified in* relation, defined later. Second, it is unclear to me why sequences of formulas are used in this definition. Perhaps they are used because they resemble Pollock's "arguments", which are sequences of inference rule applications. However, unlike in Pollock's system, the sequences here serve no further purpose. As we will see, arguments are defined differently here. Finally, by limiting the inference rules to modus ponens and instantiation, Simari and Loui are trying to prohibit contrapositive inferences [116, p. 129]. But the axioms would also have to be restricted to achieve this affect. Here is an axiom, for example, which supports contrapositive reasoning with no other inference rule than modus ponens:

$$(p \rightarrow q) \rightarrow (\neg q \rightarrow \neg p)$$

Moreover, any axiomatization which does not allow contrapositive inferences would not be complete. What would be the semantics of the resulting logic?

In Pollock's system, arguments are sequences of inference rule applications, defeasible and nondefeasible. Here, an argument is a *set* of instances of defeasible rules only, and is defined as follows. Simari and Loui use $\Delta^{\downarrow}$ to denote the set of all instances of the defeasible rules in Δ. Let **K** be a context, as defined above, and *T* be some subset of $\Delta^{\downarrow}$. *T* is an *argument* for some proposition *h* if and only if it *implies h*, is *consistent*, and is *minimal* :

1. $\mathbf{K} \cup T \vdash h$,

2. $\mathbf{K} \cup T \not\vdash \perp$, where $\perp$ denotes inconsistency, and

3.   There is no subset *S* of *T* such that $\mathbf{K} \cup S \vdash h$.

Interestingly, although Simari and Loui don't mention this, arguments here are essentially the *abductive explanations* of *h*, where $\Delta^{\downarrow}$ is the set of hypotheses. Abduction will be discussed in greater detail in the next chapter.

As there may be competing defeasible rules, $\mathbf{K} \cup \Delta^{\downarrow}$ may be inconsistent. Thus, for any proposition *h*, there may be arguments in $\Delta^{\downarrow}$ for both *h* and $\neg h$. In Pollock's system,

---

[3]This may be confusing because some authors, such as Geffner [41], do use the ⊢ symbol for nonmonotonic derivability.

an agent would not be warranted in believing either proposition in this case. In Simari and Loui's system, an agent may believe h if there is an argument for h which is better than the arguments for $\neg h$. But when is one argument better than another? Simari and Loui adopt Poole's specificity criterion [92]; the more specific arguments are the better ones. Intuitively, one argument is more specific than another if it depends on more particular evidence or information. Philosophically, this can be justified by supposing that knowledge is organized as general rules and exceptions, where a general rule is applicable, by default, only so long as there is insufficient information to make an exception applicable. In the law, the principle giving precedence to more specific rules is uncontroversial. However, it is necessary to ask whether this principle *alone* is sufficient for ordering competing legal arguments. This question will be explored in detail in the next chapter.

Poole's specificity criterion is defined as follows. An *argument structure* is an ordered pair $\langle T, h \rangle$, where T is an argument for h, as defined above. Recall that a context $\mathbf{K}$ is partitioned into a set of necessary facts $\mathbf{K}_n$ and a set of contingent facts $\mathbf{K}_c$. Contingent facts are ground formulas; they correspond to evidence. One argument structure $\langle T_1, h_1 \rangle$ is *strictly more specific* than another $\langle T_2, h_2 \rangle$ just when more evidence is required to make T_1 an argument for h_1 than is required to make T_2 an argument for h_2, i.e., if and only if:

1. For every ground formula e, if $\mathbf{K}_n \cup \{e\} \cup T_1 \vdash h_1$ and $\mathbf{K}_n \cup \{e\} \nvdash h_1$ then $\mathbf{K}_n \cup \{e\} \cup T_2 \vdash h_2$, and

2. There exists a ground formula e such that

    a. $\mathbf{K}_n \cup \{e\} \cup T_2 \vdash h_2$, but

    b. $\mathbf{K}_n \cup \{e\} \cup T_1 \nvdash h_1$, and

    c. $\mathbf{K}_n \cup \{e\} \nvdash h_2$

The last condition assures that T_2 is not the "trivial", empty argument. Also, it is important to notice that e need not be a member of the particular contingent facts $\mathbf{K}_c$ of the context. Thus, when applying this definition to rank arguments, one is free to pick any ground proposition whatsoever to be e. This is intuitively reasonable; the relative specificity of "birds fly" and "penguins don't fly" should not depend on what we already know about some bird.

Here is an Article Nine World example of this kind specificity. According to A9W § 9-105 (h), a movable thing is a good, but money is not a good. This can be modeled with these two defeasible rules:

1. movable$(x) \rightarrow$ goods(x), and

2. money$(x) \rightarrow \neg$goods(x).

If the necessary facts $\mathbf{K}_n$ are

$$\{\forall x.\text{money}(x) \rightarrow \text{movable}(x)\},$$

then the argument

$$\{\text{money}(s) \rightarrow \neg\text{goods}(s)\}$$

is more specific than the argument

$$\{\text{movable}(s) \rightarrow \text{goods}(s)\}$$

because:

1. The only ground formula which satisfies the antecedent of the first argument is money(s), which also entails the antecedent of the second argument given the "necessary fact" that all money is movable; and

2. movable(s) is a ground formula which entails goods(s), using the second argument but not the first argument, given the necessary facts.

Let us now turn to Simari and Loui's definition of *justified belief*. Somewhat confusingly, this inference relation is not comparable to Pollock's notion of justified belief, but rather his idea of "warranted" belief: These are the propositions an ideal agent would believe given unlimited memory and time.

The definition of justified belief uses the concepts of *counterargument* and *defeating argument*. An argument structure $\langle T_1, h_1 \rangle$ is a counterargument to $\langle T_2, h_2 \rangle$ if and only if there exists an argument structure $\langle T, h \rangle$ such that:

1. $T \subseteq T_2$, and

2. $K \cup \{h_1, h\} \vdash \bot$

For example, $\langle \{a \rightarrow b\}, b \rangle$ is a counterargument to $\langle \{a \rightarrow \neg b, \neg b \rightarrow c\}, c \rangle$ in the context $\{a\}$, as $\langle \{a \rightarrow \neg b\}, \neg b \rangle$ is a subargument such that $\{a, b, \neg b\}$ is inconsistent.

Whenever these conditions are satisfied then both arguments cannot be consistently believed in the context, i.e., $K \cup T_1 \cup T_2 \vdash \bot$.[4] However, the inconsistency of two arguments is not sufficient to make them counterarguments. Rather, the definition requires one argument to contradict the *conclusion* of the other. For example, $T_1 = \langle \{a \rightarrow b, b \rightarrow c\}, c \rangle$ is *not* a counterargument to $T_2 = \langle \{a \rightarrow \neg b, \neg b \rightarrow c\}, c \rangle$ in the context $\{a\}$, although $\{a, a \rightarrow b, a \rightarrow \neg b, \ldots\}$ is clearly inconsistent, as T_1 does not contradict c.

Two counterarguments compete. In Simari and Loui's system, the more specific

---

[4]The proof is easy. According to the definition of argument, $T \cup K \vdash h$ and $T_1 \cup K \vdash h_1$. As T_2 is a superset of T, it is also the case that $T_2 \cup K \vdash h$, because of the monotonicity of $\vdash$. Thus, $K \cup \{h_1, h\} \vdash \bot$ implies $K \cup T_1 \cup T_2 \vdash \bot$.

argument rebuts the other one. Using Pollock's term for rebuttal, an argument $\langle T_1, h_1 \rangle$ is said to *defeat* another argument $\langle T_2, h_2 \rangle$ in a context **K**, if and only if:

1. $\langle T_1, h_1 \rangle$ counters $\langle T_2, h_2 \rangle$ at $\langle T, h \rangle$; and

2. $\langle T_1, h_1 \rangle$ is more specific than $\langle T, h \rangle$.

Unlike specificity, counterarguments — and therefore defeaters — do depend on the contingent facts of a particular context. The defeat relationship cannot be computed using just generic domain knowledge, i.e., the necessary facts, before gathering information about a particular case. However, once it is established that one argument defeats another, further information about the case cannot affect this conclusion. Looking at the definition of counterargument, it is easy to see that $K \cup \{h_1, h\} \vdash \perp$ remains satisfied in any context **K'**, where $K' \supset K$, due to the monotonicity of first-order derivability.

As in Pollock's system, a defeated argument can be *reinstated* by another still more specific argument which defeats the first defeater. Further case-specific facts may be required to make such a reinstating argument applicable.

An argument $\langle T, h \rangle$ *justifies* belief in h in a context **K**, if and only if, again as in Pollock's system, it is ultimately undefeated by any counterarguments that can be made using just the information available in **K**. Simari and Loui define this inductively in way quite similar to Pollock's definition of warranted belief above, using argument levels. The precise definition need not interest us here.

Given a defeasible logic structure $\langle K, \Delta \rangle$, belief in a proposition h is *justified* just when there exists an argument structure $\langle T, h \rangle$ justifying h in $\langle K, \Delta \rangle$. It is this "justified" relation which is the nonmonotonic inference relation of Simari and Loui's system. It is nonmonotonic, as additional evidence can activate arguments which would have been ultimately undefeated without this information.

The main theorem proved by Simari and Loui about their system asserts the existence of a unique set of justified beliefs, given a defeasible logic structure with only finitely many arguments [116, p. 142].

However, it is not so much this theorem as its proof which is interesting to us here. It uses a tree of arguments reminiscent of Dialogue Logic. Given an argument structure $\langle T, h \rangle$, a tree can be constructed in which the nodes are counterarguments and defeaters. Simari and Loui describe this tree as follows [116, p. 142]:

> This construction can be performed until we get a "tree" where the nodes of the tree are connected by the "counterargument" relation, the root to its children, or the "defeat" relation between the rest of the levels. This tree contains the whole dialectical structure for the argument being considered.

He goes on to explain that belief in h is justified if the length of *every* path in this tree, from the root to a leaf, is odd.[5]

It is easy to recast this in game theoretic terms. Suppose there are two players, a proponent and an opponent of $\langle T, h \rangle$ in a context **K**. After the opening move by the proponent, the opponent may assert any counterargument to $\langle T, h \rangle$. Thereafter, only defeating counterarguments are allowed. The players take turns asserting counterarguments until no further move is possible. (In this game, the contingent facts of **K** are fixed; the players may not bring forward new evidence.) The player who makes the last move wins. However, similar to Dialogue Logic, h is not proven to be a justified belief by the proponent winning the game. The opponent may have made a poor move. In Dialogue Logic, the assertion is proven only if the opponent made the best moves possible; i.e., only if a winning strategy for the proponent exists. This is the case in Simari and Loui's system too. A proposition is a justified belief when a strategy exists for defending the argument supporting the belief, no matter which counterarguments are made by the opponent.

Simari and Loui describe a computer program for checking whether a proposition is a justified belief. To decrease the complexity of this task, the defeasible rules and the necessary facts are restricted to Horn clauses and the contingent facts are restricted to ground, atomic sentences. The program first generates an argument supporting the proposition and then makes an exhaustive search of the game tree for this argument to try to defeat it. If the argument remains undefeated, then the proposition is a justifiable belief and the program terminates. Otherwise, the next supporting argument is generated and tested in the same fashion, until either an ultimately undefeatable argument is found or there are no more supporting arguments.

Simari and Loui do not make any claims about the computational properties of this task, but they are clearly concerned about efficiency. A section of their article is devoted to the problem of "discarding arguments", in order to reduce the size of the search space. Moreover, the purpose of Lemma 2.24 in the paper is to show how to reduce the complexity of determining whether one argument is more specific than another [116, p. 134]. Unfortunately, the proof of Lemma 2.24 was discovered by the authors to be erroneous. The proof could not be corrected. This motivated Loui to propose an alternative definition of specificity which does allow a comparable lemma to be proved [70].

The complexity of computing specificity, however, is not the only source of complexity in this task. As was mentioned previously, an argument in this system is equivalent to an abductive explanation of the proposition supported. It is well-known that the task of computing abductive explanations is intractably hard,[6] even when domain knowledge is restricted to propositional Horn clauses [112]. As this program must generate arguments before it can test whether they are defeating arguments, abduction is clearly a subtask which cannot be avoided. Thus, the problem of determining whether a proposition can be justifiably believed appears to remain intractable, even when the language for defeasible rules and domain knowledge is restricted to Horn clauses in this way, and regardless of the complexity of the specificity test. Thus, whatever the merits of Simari and Loui's system as a model of belief for an ideal agent, not subject to memory and time limitations, it cannot

---

[5]Simari and Loui decrease the branching factor of this tree by further restricting the moves allowed to the *most specific* counterarguments possible.

[6]Assuming $P \neq NP$.

be viewed as a model of justified belief in Pollock's sense.

Another problem with Simari and Loui's system concerns its semantics. They provide neither a model-theoretic semantics nor a foundation based on arguments, in the way Dialogue Logic is meant to serve as a foundation for intuitionistic logic. As we have seen, they do describe a dialectical game for computing justified belief, but to serve as a foundation for their system, the moves of the game would have to be *independently* justified. At the moment, their only justification is that they can be used to compute justified belief. Instead of providing a semantics, the authors show that the system gives the intuitively correct results when applied to a number of benchmark problems in the literature on nonmonotonic reasoning. Perhaps this can be viewed as a "case-based" approach to semantics.

However, whatever the significance of these limitations, Simari and Loui's system is of great interest to us, as it suggests how to model argumentation with defeasible rules as a two-person game, in the spirit of Dialogue Logic.

As we have done with the other systems examined thus far, let us classify Simari and Loui's system along the dimensions of discourse games. The purpose of the game is to test whether belief in formula is justified given a defeasible logic structure. The only data are first-order formulas and defeasible rules. The set of data is fixed by the defeasible logic structure before the game begins. No new data may be added during the game. The only moves are the assertion of arguments and counterarguments. Moves are not constrained by previous moves, but only by the structure of the dialectical tree. There are no resource limitations, other than the set of arguments which can be generated from the defeasible logic structure. There is only one player, and thus no differentiation of roles or burden of proof. The system does support substantial arguments, as defeasible beliefs are not necessarily true, but it does not support a discussion about the validity of the defeasible rules assumed in the defeasible logic structure. Priority relations between defeasible rules are also not debatable, but fixed by the specificity relation hard-wired into the game.

4.4   Conditional Entailment

Hector Geffner and Judea Pearl have developed an argument based system for defeasible reasoning [41] which, as we will see, is very much like the system of Simari and Loui just discussed. The main difference is that Geffner and Pearl provide a *model-theoretic semantics* for their system. The semantics facilitates a comparison with several other nonmonotonic logics. Geffner and Pearl divide these into two broad classes, the *extensional* systems, such as Reiter's Default Logic [100] and McCarthy's original form of Circumscription [75], and the newer *conditional* systems, such as those of Delgrande [28], Pearl [88] and Kraus, Lehmann and Magidor [62].[7] Each type of system has its advantages, but neither subsumes the other. An advantage of the extensional systems is

---

[7]Although the conditional systems are newer in Artificial Intelligence, they have their roots in Adam's early work on the logic of conditionals [1].

that additional *irrelevant* information cannot cause belief in some proposition to become unwarranted. The conditional systems, on the other hand, automatically order competing arguments according to their specificity. These relationships must be explicitly encoded in the extensional systems, which can be difficult to maintain and error prone. Geffner and Pearl's main achievement is the definition of a new nonmonotonic inference relation, called *conditional entailment*, which combines the advantages of both approaches.

Following Geffner and Pearl, we will discuss the model theory for conditional entailment before turning to their argumentation system, which they claim provides a complete and correct *proof theory*. Finally, there will be a brief discussion about Geffner and Pearl 's sketch of an implementation, which uses de Kleer's Assumption-Based Truth Maintenance System [27].

Let us begin with the model theory of classical first-order predicate logic, as the model theory of conditional entailment can be understood as a variation of it. Classical logic is intended to capture the idea of *necessary truth*: assuming some set of propositions is true, it defines what other propositions *must* also be true. This notion is made precise with the help of the concepts of language, interpretation and model. In the context of predicate logic, a *language* is the set of well-formed formulas, or sentences, which can be expressed given a particular set of constant, function and predicate symbols. An *interpretation* is a function mapping sentences to the set of truth values, {true, false}. In what follows, a set of sentences will often be called a *theory*. Finally, given such a theory T, a *model* of T is an interpretation I in which every sentence in T is true. That is, I is a model of T if and only if for every sentence p in T, it is the case that $I(p) =$ true.

The notion of logical necessity or consequence is captured in the classical entailment relation $\models$ by defining it in terms of truth in *all* models. That is, a formula p is entailed by T, denoted $T \models p$, if and only if, for all interpretations I, if I is a model of T then $I(p) =$ true. This implies that *every* formula is entailed by T if it has no models, i.e., if T is inconsistent.

The original motivation for the development of nonmonotonic logics in AI was the feeling that, for many tasks, such a planning actions with less than perfect information about the world, classical logic is too *weak*; it doesn't sanction enough beliefs. People need to plan their affairs based not only on firm knowledge about what is certainly or necessarily true, but also, for example, on informed guesses about what may be true. They use "rules of thumb" to "jump to conclusions" which are only plausible. If turning the key usually starts the car then, barring an indication that something is wrong, one is justified in believing the car will start when the key is turned. All nonmonotonic logics provide some means of expressing defeasible rules of this kind. They vary, however, in the set of plausible inferences sanctioned.

To make precise the sense in which classical logic is weaker than nonmonotonic logics, the notion of deductive *closure* is helpful. Given some entailment relation $\models$ and a theory T, the closure of T, denoted $C(\models, T)$, is the set of all sentences p such that $T \models p$. In other words, the closure is the set of all sentences entailed by the logic. One entailment relation $\models_1$ is *weaker* than another $\models_2$ just when, for every theory T, it is the case that $C(\models_1, T) \subset C(\models_2, T)$. Conversely, if $\models_1$ is weaker than $\models_2$, then $\models_2$ is *stronger* than $\models_1$.

It is not difficult to design an "entailment relation" stronger than classical entailment.

One could, for example, simply define *every* sentence of the language to be entailed by any theory Γ. However, it is seems clear that such an entailment relation would be much too strong; if the concept of plausibility is to be meaningful, there must also be some implausible sentences. The considerable number of nonmonotonic logics is largely due to conflicting intuitions about where to draw the line between plausibility and implausibility.

Shoham has developed a model theoretic framework for defining nonmonotonic logics which makes alternative intuitions about plausibility somewhat easier to compare [115]. The framework is based on a key observation. There is an inverse relationship between the number of models of a theory and the number of sentences in the closure of the theory: the fewer the models, the larger the closure. As propositions are added to a theory, fewer and fewer models will be able to simultaneously satisfy them all. Thus, to strengthen a logic it is sufficient to define entailment in terms of some "preferred" subset of the models, rather than all models. Shoham observes [115, p. 231]: "Nonmonotonic logics are the result of associating with a standard logic a preference relation on models."[8]

To be precise, a *preferential model structure* is an ordered pair $\langle \mathbf{I}, < \rangle$, where $\mathbf{I}$ is a set of interpretations and $<$ is strict partial order on these interpretations. Intuitively, $M < N$ means the interpretation M is *preferred* to the interpretation N.[9] An interpretation M in $\mathbf{I}$ is a *preferred model* of a sentence p if and only if M is a model of p and there does not exist an interpretation N in $\mathbf{I}$ such that $N < M$ and N is also a model of p. Finally, a sentence p is *preferentially entailed* by a theory T, denoted $T \models_< p$, if and only if p is true in *every* preferred model of T in $\mathbf{I}$.

To create a particular nonmonotonic logic using Shoham's framework, a strict partial order on models needs to be defined. In [115], he demonstrates how to recast a number of well-known nonmonotonic logics in this framework, including Circumscription [75], a version of Moore's Autoepistemic Logic [86] and an approximation of Reiter's Default Logic [100]. Strictly speaking, these logics are not *particular* nonmonotonic logics in his sense, as they do not define a partial order relation on models. Rather, they can be viewed as generic logics, or logic generators; they are functions which map a "knowledge base" into a preferential model structure. Usually, the partial order on models is derived from extralogical statements of the formalism. In Circumscription, for example, a set of predicates to be circumscribed must be selected. In Default Logic, the priority order is implicit in the default rules.

Finally, we are ready to sketch Geffner and Pearl's semantics for conditional entailment, which applies Shoham's framework. As is usual, the partial order on models is derived from the knowledge base, so we must first describe their method for representing defeasible rules. As in the systems of Pollock and Simari and Loui, discussed previously, knowledge is divided into evidence, strict rules and defeasible rules. A *default theory* is

---

[8]In what follows, we will assume the "standard logic" is classical first-order logic; but Shoham's framework is more general than this. For example, he defines a nonmonotonic logic using a partial order on the Kripke models of a modal logic.

[9]To avoid confusion later, I am using Geffner and Pearl's notation here. Shoham preferred the greater model.

a pair $\langle K, E \rangle$, where E is a set of ground sentences representing the evidence. K is itself a pair $\langle L, D \rangle$, where L is a set of closed sentences representing nondefeasible knowledge and D is the set of defeasible rules. Geffner and Pearl call defeasible rules *defaults*. As in Simari and Loui's system, defaults are schemata of the form $p \Rightarrow q$, where p and q are arbitrary formulas containing schema variables.[10] Instances of defaults are created by replacing schema variables by constants from the language. Unlike in Simari and Loui's system, default instances are not interpreted as ordinary sentences. Their use will be made apparent below.

As "a matter of convenience", Geffner and Pearl require that defaults be encoded in a particular format. For example, the rule that birds generally fly must be encoded using *two* expressions: a default $\text{bird}(x) \Rightarrow \text{bf}(x)$ and a sentence $\forall x.\text{bird}(x) \wedge \text{bf}(x) \rightarrow \text{flies}(x)$. Intuitively, these mean "If something is a bird then the bf default is applicable to it." and "If the bf default is applicable to some bird, then it flies." The bf predicate can be viewed as the *name* of the default.[11]

The *assumptions* of a default theory, denoted Δ, is the set of all instances of these default names. For example, if t is a constant then $\text{bf}(t) \in \Delta$. Each assumption is a ground atomic sentence. If the default theory is in the suggested format, the assumptions can be extracted from the conclusions of every default in D.

Given a default theory $\langle K, E \rangle$ in the prescribed format, the next task is to define a priority order on the models of sentences in the theory. But it also needs to be decided just what sentences of a default theory are to be regarded as the "theory" for this purpose. As a first attempt, let the theory be the set $L \cup E$ and let us define the partial order on models so as to *maximize* the number of assumptions they contain. Because of the format required for representing defaults, this would also have the effect of maximizing the number of defaults applied. If defaults are used to encode the way the world normally works, or should work, this preference relation could be understood as *minimizing* abnormality, as in Circumscription.

Like Circumscription, Default Logic and the other "traditional" nonmonotonic logics, this preference relation would result in what Geffner and Pearl call an *extensional* interpretation of defaults. It would capture some but not all intuitions about what the plausible inferences should be. Consider the standard "birds fly" example, where L is:

1. $\text{bird}(x) \wedge d_1(x) \rightarrow \text{flies}(x)$

2. $\text{penguin}(x) \wedge d_2(x) \rightarrow \neg \text{flies}(x)$

3. $\text{penguin}(x) \rightarrow \text{bird}(x)$

4. $\text{red bird}(x) \rightarrow \text{bird}(x)$

---

[10]Geffner and Pearl used the $\Rightarrow$ symbol for material implication and $\rightarrow$ for default rules. The opposite notation will be used in this chapter.

[11]This way of encoding defaults was used by Brewka in [23]. (See also [24].) It is also similar to McCarthy's use of "abnormality" predicates in circumscription [76].

The predicates d_1 and d_2 are the names for the first two formulas, which represent the defaults "birds fly" and "penguins don't fly". Let the evidence $\mathbf{E}$ = {bird(t)}. The assumptions then are {d_1(t), d_2(t)}. Variables are all universally quantified.

There are models of these sentences in which *both* assumptions are true; adding them both does not cause a contradiction. Thus, if the preferred models are those which maximizes the number of assumptions, as suggested, flies(t) would be preferentially entailed by this default theory, but not ¬flies(t). This is what one would expect.

Moreover, adding red bird(t) to the evidence would not change this result. This is what Geffner and Pearl mean when they write that the extensional interpretations of defaults "capture arguments of *irrelevance*." Being red has nothing to do with flying here, so the additional information that the bird is red should not cause the previous conclusion that he flies to no longer be entailed.

What happens if we now add penguin(t) to the evidence? Contrary to what one might expect, *neither* flies(t) *nor* ¬flies(t) is now preferentially entailed. The reason is that only one of the two assumptions can be consistently believed at once. There are two classes of preferred models, those containing d_1(t), in which case the bird flies, and those containing d_2(t), in which case he doesn't. This demonstrates a weakness of extensional nonmonotonic logics: they do not *automatically* use specificiy information contained in a default theory to further restrict the preferred models. Rather, to get the desired result here, one would have to add an additional sentence, such as

$$\text{penguin}(x) \rightarrow \neg d_1(x),$$

to the default theory.

According to Geffner and Pearl, this limitation can be overcome by adopting instead a "conditional interpretation" of defaults, as in the nonmonotonic logics of Delgrande [28] and Kraus, Lehmann and Magidor [62]. One way to ensure that a preferential model structure is of this type is to show that it satisfies certain "admissibility" conditions [63]. To be precise, a preferential model structure $\langle \mathbf{I}, < \rangle$ is *admissible* relative to a "background" $\mathbf{K} = \langle \mathbf{L}, \mathbf{D} \rangle$ if and only if:

1. It is *well-founded*. A preferential model structure is well-founded if, for every nonpreferred model M there exists a model N such that $N < M$; and

2. Every interpretation in $\mathbf{I}$ satisfies $\mathbf{L}$, and

3. For every instance $p \Rightarrow q$ of a default in $\mathbf{D}$,

   a. There exists a model of p in $\mathbf{I}$; and

   b. Every *preferred* model of p in $\mathbf{I}$ is also a model of q.

A default theory $\langle \mathbf{K}, \mathbf{E} \rangle$ *p-entails* a proposition if and only if it is true in every preferred model of $\mathbf{L} \cup \mathbf{E}$ of every admissible preferential model structure.[12]

This definition of p-entailment may appear somewhat confusing at first, or even ambiguous, as it is defined not in terms of *an* admissible model structure, but *every* one. In Shoham's original conception, a nonmonotonic logic is specified by choosing a particular partial order on models. In his reconstruction of several popular nonmonotonic logics, this choice is in part dependent on the default theory, but the logic and a theory together do determine a single partial order on models. In p-entailment, however, this is no longer true. Here, entailment is defined not in terms of a single partial order, but rather in terms of every admissible partial order. One consequence of this is that p-entailment is stronger than the logic which would result if a single admissible order on models were to be chosen.

It is easy to see that the preferential model structure proposed previously is not admissible. One of the default instances is $\text{penguin}(t) \Rightarrow d_2(t)$. However, there is a preferred model of $L \cup \{\text{penguin}(t)\}$ which is not a model of $d_2(t)$, namely the one in which $d_1(t)$ and $\text{flies}(t)$ are true. One has the choice of either adopting the assumption $d_1(t)$ and rejecting the default $\text{penguin}(t) \Rightarrow d_2(t)$ or adopting the assumption $d_2(t)$ and rejecting the default $\text{bird}(t) \Rightarrow d_1(t)$. If the first choice is made the second admissibility condition will be violated. As we will see next, Geffner and Pearl solve this problem by requiring the assumptions to be ordered such that the choice is always made which preserves admissibility. In this case, $d_2(t)$ is required to have higher priority than $d_1(t)$.

Although nonmonotonic logics satisfying these admissibility conditions use specificity to resolve conflicts between defaults, they do not necessarily handle irrelevant evidence in the expected way. Worse, some conditional logics do not sanction "default chaining"; one plausible sentence cannot then be used to derive others.[13] Geffner and Pearl's main contribution is the definition of a more restrictive admissibility criterion which avoids these problems. Logics which satisfy these conditions are a specialization of admissible preferential structures in which the partial order on models is determined by another partial order on assumptions.

First, a *prioritized preferential structure* is a preferential model structure $\langle I, < \rangle$ extended with a strict partial order on the assumptions of a default theory. The $<$ partial order on models is constrained to satisfy the following condition. Let M and N be two models. M is preferred to N, denoted $M < N$, if and only if for every assumption d_1 which is false in M but not N there is a higher priority assumption d_2 which is false in N but not M. An important property of this partial order is that the preferred models will have maximally many assumptions. This property preserves the extensional character of the resulting logic.

However, not all prioritized preferential structures are admissible, as no constraints have been placed on the partial order on assumptions. We saw in the previous example that this can be required. There it was necessary to give the assumption for "this penguin

---

[12]Geffner and Pearl use "preferential entailment" and "p-entailment" synonymously. However, I am using "preferential entailment" in this section in Shoham's sense, which is defined in terms of any preferential model structure, rather than just admissible ones.

[13]For example, suppose there is a defeasible rule stating that things with wings are normally birds. Such a conditional logic would allow us to conclude that a thing with wings is a bird, but not also that it flies.

doesn't fly" higher priority than the assumption for "this bird flies". Recall that the goal is to assure, for every default instance $p \Rightarrow d_1$, that the assumption d_1 is true in the preferred models of $L \cup \{p\}$. This condition is met if for every set of assumptions Δ, such that $L \cup \Delta \cup \{p, d_1\}$ is inconsistent, there is an assumption d_2 which is less preferred than d_1. Δ is said to be in *conflict* with the default instance $p \Rightarrow d_1$.

This observation leads to the following admissibility condition. A priority ordering on assumptions is *admissible* if and only if for every set of assumptions Δ in conflict with a default instance $p \Rightarrow d$ there is an assumption in Δ which is less preferred than d. A prioritized structure is admissible just when it is well-founded and its preference relation on assumptions is admissible.

Finally, we come to Geffner and Pearl's main definition. A default theory $\langle \mathbf{K}, \mathbf{E} \rangle$ *conditionally entails* a proposition p, denoted $\langle \mathbf{K}, \mathbf{E} \rangle \models_< p$, if and only if p is true in every preferred model of $L \cup E$ in every admissible prioritized structure. Notice that, just as was true for p-entailment, conditional entailment is defined in terms of *every* admissible structure.

A new entailment relation is only as interesting as its properties. Conditional entailment handles both irrelevant evidence and specificity in an intuitively correct manner. Conditional entailment is stronger than p-entailment, allowing for example default inferences to be chained. Moreover, if assumption predicates are only used to encode defaults, in the prescribed manner, conditional entailment is arguably not *too* strong; at least p and $\neg p$ will not be both entailed, unless they are also p-entailed. That is, under this condition a default theory is inconsistent in the logic of conditional entailment only if it would also be inconsistent using p-entailment. Finally, like other conditional logics, conditional entailment satisfies what Pearl in [41, p. 214] calls "the basic set of principles that any reasonable account of defaults must obey." These principles include, in addition to conditionality, *deductive closure*, meaning that the logic is at least as strong as classical predicate logic, and *cumulativity*, which roughly means that the addition of a defeasible conclusion to the evidence does not cause any sentence that had been entailed to no longer be entailed.[14]

As conditional entailment includes all of classical logic, it also permits contraposition. In the bird example, if the only evidence is bird(t), then not only is flies(t) entailed, but so too is ¬penguin(t). There is a "clash of intuitions" in the defeasible reasoning community about whether or not such inferences are plausible. Recall, for example, that Simari and Loui want to prohibit this. However, in this example at least, it does not seem counterintuitive to suppose that a known bird is not a penguin, not knowing anything else. This has also been an issue in the AI and Law community. Allen [9] and Prakken [96] have both used unintended contrapositive inferences to argue that material implication should not be used to model legal rules. Allen has proposed that Anderson's weaker relevance logic [10] be used instead. Prakken suggests legal rules may be represented as inference

---

[14]Notice that many well-known nonmonotonic logics, such as Default Logic, are therefore not reasonable accounts of defaults in Pearl's view. Reiter's original version of Default Logic was not cumulative. Brewka has developed a cumulative version [25], but neither version satisfy Pearl's conditionality requirement.

rules as in Reiter's Default Logic.

Let us take a look at how conditional entailment handles a propositional version of Prakken's self-defense example, which led him to reject contraposition:

1. killing $\wedge d_1 \rightarrow$ murder

2. killing $\wedge$ defense $\wedge d_2 \rightarrow \neg$murder

3. attack $\wedge d_3 \rightarrow$ defense

These are the sentences in **L**. They are intended to mean "Killing is murder.", "Killing in self-defense is not murder." and "If you have been attacked, then you are reacting in self-defense." The defaults in **D** are

1. killing $\Rightarrow d_1$

2. killing $\wedge$ defense $\Rightarrow d_2$

3. attack $\Rightarrow d_3$

The assumptions are $\{d_1, d_2, d_3\}$. Let us suppose the evidence **E** is $\{$killing, attack$\}$. Given this evidence, the maximally consistent sets of assumptions are $\{d_1, d_2\}$, $\{d_1, d_3\}$ and $\{d_2, d_3\}$, as there are no models in which both murder and $\neg$murder are true. However, any ordering on models is admissible so long as the models containing the assumptions in $\{d_2, d_3\}$ are preferred to those containing $\{d_1, d_3\}$.[15] Admissibility does not require a preference between $\{d_2, d_3\}$ and $\{d_1, d_2\}$. *Thus, given this evidence, neither* $\neg$murder *and* defense, *nor their negations, are conditionally entailed.* The reason is that conditional entailment does not require a choice between these two classes of models. This is exactly the problem Prakken would like to avoid. He claims $\neg$murder and defense should be entailed here. But in the preferred class of models containing the assumptions $\{d_1, d_3\}$, the first rule can be used to derive murder from which, together with the second rule, used contrapositively, $\neg$defense can be derived.

To obtain the result Prakken argues is intuitively correct, it would be sufficient to prefer d_3 to d_1. But what is the basis for the intuition that the rules named by these assumptions should have this relative priority? Why should the rule about an attack being sufficient justification for self defense be preferred to the rule about killing being murder? One is not more specific than the other; so this is not a counterexample to the claim that conditional entailment handles specificity properly. Indeed, it does not appear that these two rules have anything to do with one another. Thus, in retrospect it should come as no surprise that we are free to choose either one to avoid a contradiction. The desired result could be obtained

---

[15]To determine an admissible ordering, first find the conflict sets for each default. In this example, there is a just one, $\{d_1\}$, which conflicts with the second default. Thus any ordering preferring d_2 to d_1 is admissible.

here by making the rule about attacks strict instead of merely defeasible. But this would not be a general solution. Presumably it is only a default rule in criminal law; not all attacks justify killing in self defense. Although it is not entirely clear what the correct result should be in this example, conditional entailment's skepticism here does not appear unintuitive.

How does conditional entailment compare to Simari and Loui's system? A more thorough comparison will have to wait until Geffner and Pearl's argument-based proof theory has been described, but a few initial observations can be made. Both systems handle specificity, but it is still completely unclear to what extent their interpretations of specificity coincide. Unfortunately, Geffner and Pearl do not compare them. Although Simari and Loui do not explicitly discuss irrelevance, it appears that their system also handles it properly. They show how their system handles the Royal Elephants benchmark, where Clyde being an African Elephant, as well as Royal, does not inhibit the conclusion that he is not gray. Simari and Loui do not measure their system against Pearl's "basic set of principles". It is clear, however, that at least one of the principles is not satisfied, namely deductive closure. Recall that Simari and Loui weakened their logic so as to prohibit contraposition. Their system is, by design, not stronger than classical logic.

Pearl's set of principles need further justification. Their value should depend, I think, on the purpose of the logic. They may make sense if the goal is to model the warranted beliefs of an ideal agent, in Pollock's sense. But they are much too restrictive if the goal is to model justified belief. A normative theory of justified belief cannot fairly expect agents to be "logically omniscient". Common sense reasoning is subject not only to limited and imperfect information about the world, but also limited computational resources. Persons "jump to conclusions", not only due to lack of information, but also due to lack of time.

Geffner and Pearl have developed a complete and correct proof theory to accompany their model theory for conditional entailment. It is of special interest to us, as it too adopts the metaphor of arguments. Derivability is defined in terms of "stable" arguments, which are similar to Pollock's ultimately undefeated arguments.

Given a default theory $\mathbf{T} = \langle \mathbf{K}, \mathbf{E} \rangle$, an *argument* for a proposition p is a consistent set Δ of assumptions from which p may be derived. That is, Δ is an argument if and only if:

1. $L \cup E \cup \Delta \nvdash \bot$, and

2. $L \cup E \cup \Delta \vdash p$

Here, $\vdash$ denotes classical derivability and $\bot$ falsity, or inconsistency, as usual. This definition of argument is almost the same as Simari and Loui's. There the argument was a set of instances of defaults. Here the argument is a set of assumptions, which are names for instances of defaults. Simari and Loui further required that an argument be minimal. Here, minimality is a property of some arguments, but not a part of their definition.

If $L \cup E \cup \Delta \vdash \bot$, then the set of assumptions Δ is called a *conflict set*. A preferential model structure is well-founded if there are only finitely many *minimal* conflict sets.[16]

Two arguments A and B *conflict* if and only if their union is a conflict set:

---

[16]In ATMS terminology, minimal conflict sets are called "nogoods" [27].

$L \cup E \cup A \cup B \vdash \perp$. In Geffner and Pearl's terminology, conflicting arguments and *counterarguments* are synonymous. This differs from Simari and Loui's notion of counterargument somewhat, where inconsistency is necessary but not sufficient. Notice that if $A \cup \{d\}$ is a minimal conflict set, then A is a counterargument to any argument for d. Geffner and Pearl show that a counterargument exists for an assumption if and only if there is a minimal conflict set containing the assumption.

Using arguments and conflict sets, Geffner and Pearl state four different syntactic conditions sufficient for proving conditional entailment.[17] These are all correct, but vary in their degree of completeness. For example, the first such lemma states that an *assumption* d is conditionally entailed if it has no counterarguments, i.e., using the above result, if there does not exist a minimal conflict set C such that $d \in C$. This criterion is incomplete, as it does not use specificity to choose between counterarguments, when they exist. The next test does handle some specificity arguments: An assumption d_1 is conditionally entailed if for every minimal counterargument Δ, there exists an assumption $d_2 \in \Delta$ such that d_1 is preferred to d_2 in every admissible priority order on assumptions. Notice that both of these tests are applicable only to assumptions, not arbitrary propositions. The syntactic test for establishing whether or not an assumption has higher priority than another in every admissible ordering is described later.

The next, more powerful entailment test uses the notion of defeat. An argument A *defeats* another argument B if and only if they are counterarguments and for every assumption d_1 in A there is a less preferred assumption d_2 in B.[18] An argument is *stable* if it defeats all of its counterarguments in every admissible priority order on assumptions. Now we come to the first entailment test applicable to any proposition: *a proposition is conditionally entailed if there exists a stable argument for it.* Stable arguments are reminiscent of Pollock's notion of "ultimately undefeated arguments", which was also adopted in Simari and Loui's definition of justification. As was discussed previously, one reason Simari and Loui's logic is weaker than conditional entailment is that it forbids contraposition. Thus we already know that the two systems are not equivalent. Nonetheless it is interesting to speculate whether stable arguments would be equivalent to justified belief, if the restriction against contraposition were lifted. But this question is not important enough for our purposes to pursue further here.

This test, however, is still not complete, which indicates that conditional entailment may be stronger than Simari and Loui's system for reasons other than their omission of contraposition. Geffner and Pearl claim [41, p. 228] the concept of stable arguments is "very powerful and accounts for most of the natural inferences authorized by conditional entailment". However, stability fails to account for certain kinds of "disjunctive arguments". To gain completeness, the notion of a stable argument is extended to stable *covers*, where a cover is a set of alternative arguments, each of which supports the same proposition. Ignoring the details here, Geffner and Pearl arrive at this main theorem: a

---

[17]They are "syntactic" because calculi exist for first-order logic.

[18]Rebuttal is a related notion in Geffner and Pearl's system [41, p. 231]: B is a rebuttal of A if they are counterarguments but A does not contain a defeater of B.

proposition is entailed *if and only if* it is supported by a stable cover. Interestingly, their implementation does not handle covers. Rather it checks only whether a proposition is supported by a stable argument. To this extent the implementation is admittedly incomplete.

All of these entailment tests, except the first, require checking whether an assumption is preferred to any other one in a set of assumptions. Precisely, given an assumption d_1 and a set of assumptions D, the question is whether there exists an assumption $d_2 \in D$ such that d_1 is preferred to d_2 in all admissible orderings. Fortunately there is a syntactic method for determining this. Recall that there is a default instance $p \Rightarrow d_1$. The assumption d_1 is preferred to some assumption in D in all admissible preference orders on assumptions if and only if $D \cup \{p\} \vDash \neg d_1$.

Geffner and Pearl describe an implementation of conditional entailment, which makes heavy use of de Kleer's Assumption-Based Truth Maintenance System (ATMS) [27]. One of the principal functions of an ATMS is to compute the minimally inconsistent sets of assumptions, called "nogoods" in ATMS terminology. As we have seen, these minimal conflict sets are used in each of the tests for conditional entailment. Using the first test, for example, an assumption is conditionally entailed if (but not only if) it is not a member of any nogood.

The program is intended to compute whether or not a stable argument for some proposition exists. The ATMS computes the minimal arguments supporting some proposition. None of these minimal arguments is necessarily stable, however. Geffner and Pearl's program iterates over these minimal arguments, searching for one that either is stable because no arguments rebut it, or can be made stable by consistently extending it with the propositions of arguments defeating each rebuttal.[19] As defeaters can themselves be rebutted, this leads to a recursive algorithm, the base case of which is an argument having no rebuttal.

The similarity between this program and the one used by Pollock and by Simari and Loui cannot be overlooked. But there are some obvious differences. Simari and Loui prohibit contrapositive inferences; so their logic is weaker in this respect. Simari and Loui use Poole's specificity criterion, whereas Geffner and Pearl use the kind of specificity realized in conditional logics. (The exact relationship between these two forms of specificity is unclear.) Finally, Geffner and Pearl, but not Simari and Loui, use an ATMS to cache minimal arguments and conflict sets, but this is just a means of improving efficiency.

At least one benchmark problem in the nonmonotonic literature, the Yale Shooting Problem, is solved by Simari and Loui's system but not by Geffner and Pearl's. This may also be a result of Simari and Loui's rejection of contraposition. Interestingly, weakening the underlying monotonic logic can cause some inferences to become plausible. We saw this in the murder example. Had contraposition been suppressed, as Prakken suggests, there would have been no counterargument to the self-defense argument, allowing

---

[19]Actually, the pseudocode on page 231 of [41] incorrectly considers only a single rebuttal for each supporting argument, rather than all rebuttals. Presumably, this was an oversight.

¬murder to be entailed. This may seem to be a disadvantage of conditional entailment, but Geffner and Pearl, following Shoham, argues that the Yale Shooting Problem requires temporal reasoning, which one should not expect to be subsumed by specificity.

Geffner and Pearl point out that the program is not complete for conditional entailment, as it does not handle the kind of disjunctive arguments for which covers were introduced into the proof theory.[20] Also, although Geffner and Pearl suggest the program could be made efficient enough for practical purposes with some "additional refinements", the problem it solves is intractable. That is, no theoretically efficient algorithm exists. This was also true for Simari and Loui's system and for the same reason: abduction of the kind used in these systems is intractable, even when the domain is represented using only propositional Horn clauses. The problem of finding minimal arguments and minimal conflict sets, performed by the ATMS here, is an abduction task. Whether or not the program is efficient enough for some practical purposes is an empirical question, but Geffner and Pearl do not provide any data about practical experience with the program.

To conclude this section on conditional entailment, let me reiterate the main points. Geffner and Pearl's main contribution is their model theory. As we have seen, Simari and Loui's system is also able to handle both specificity and irrelevance in an intuitive manner, so this is not a unique advantage of Geffner and Pearl's system. The value of the model theory for conditional entailment, in my opinion, is that it provides another perspective on the argument based proof theory. In some cases, the model theory makes it easier to anticipate the inferences sanctioned by the system. It also makes it easier to compare this logic with others having a model theory. But the model theory does not provide a "semantics" or foundation for conditional entailment in any meaningful sense. Rather, the model theory of a defeasible logic itself needs to be justified by philosophical arguments and examples which, together, persuasively support the claim that it has captured the intuitive meaning of plausibility. But arguments of this type can just as well be used to support the proof theory directly. A model theory is neither a necessary nor sufficient foundation for a logic. This is not to say that conditional entailment lacks sufficient philosophical justification, but only that this justification comes from the arguments and examples which support the claim that it handles specificity and irrelevance in an intuitively reasonable manner.

For our purposes, a major weakness of Geffner and Pearl's model is that no attempt has been made to justify the permitted argument moves. (This was also a limitation of the other models of argumentation discussed in this chapter, except Dialogue Logic.) Rather, the discourse rules have been designed simply with the goal of assuring that all and only the conditionally entailed sentences are derived when an *exhaustive* search of the game tree is performed. Real arguments cannot usually be resolved this way. A fair resolution

---

[20]They also say that the program requires a commitment to a single admissible priority ordering on assumptions [41, p. 230]. This would further impair completeness, but not affect correctness, as a superset of the preferred models which respect all admissible orderings respect any one of these admissible orderings. That is, every formula which is satisfied by all of the models which respect this single ordering are also satisfied by that subset of these models which respect every admissible ordering. However, Geffner and Pearl do not make it clear why the program is thought to require this commitment to a single ordering.

of the issues cannot require all possible rebuttals to be defeated. Rather, as in Dialogue
Logic, the burden of bringing forth arguments and defending claims should be divided
among the parties. To assure termination within a reasonable time, each party is allocated
only a limited number of opportunities to present arguments. The allocation of this burden
of proof itself needs philosophical justification. This is one problem addressed in the next
chapter, describing my model of argumentation.

How does conditional entailment, viewed as a game, fit into my classification
scheme for discourse games? Conditional entailment is a mathematical relation, with no
input-output direction, so let us focus on Geffner and Pearl's implementation of a theorem
prover. Similar to Simari and Loui's system, the purpose of the game is to test whether a
formula is conditionally entailed by a default theory. The data consists of default rules and
formulas of first-order logic. The data doesn't change after the game begins; nothing may
be added or removed from the default theory during play. The only kinds of moves are
the assertion of supporting arguments, rebuttals and defeating counterarguments. Moves
are constrained by the relationships of support, rebuttal and defeat, but not by the moves
actually made along some path of the dialectical tree. There are no resource limitations,
other than the space defined by the dialectical graph of arguments. There is only a single
player, and no role differentiation. Substantial arguments about the truth of propositions,
given the information in the default theory, are supported. The default rules, strict sentences
and evidence in the default theory are not debatable. It is not possible to argue about
priority relationships between defaults. As can be seen, in terms of these dimensions at
least, there are no significant differences between conditional entailment and Simari and
Loui's system.

4.5   Related Work

The few systems described in this chapter hardly make a dent in the space of normative
discourse games, given the dimensions of my classification scheme. Of course, none of
these systems were designed expressly from this point of view. Despite the broader goals
of the Erlangen School, Dialogue Logic is mainly intended to be a calculus for proving
theorems of first-order intuitionistic logic. It is most interesting for us as a starting point
for designing two-player argumentation games, and as a precedent for the idea of using
procedural norms as a foundation for a formal system of logic, rather than model theory.
Pollock's OSCAR system is a normative model of rational belief, for a single agent
introspecting about its knowledge. It is the only one of the systems examined which
takes resource limitations seriously. The systems of Simari and Loui and of Geffner
and Pearl are state-of-the-art nonmonotonic logics. They provide the central techniques
necessary for handling defeasible legal rules, as found in Article Nine, in an argumentation
framework.

However, these systems leave us with several problems which will presumably have to
be solved in most *legal discourse games*. None of these systems allow such things as facts,
rules or evidence to be introduced during the game, nor do they support a discussion about
the validity or priority of rules. Specificity is but one factor to be considered when ordering

legal rules. Finally, the roles of the parties will play a major role in legal discourse games. Dialogue Logic is the only system to have multiple players, and to differentiate the moves permitted on the basis of their roles. It will provided some guidance, but represents only a small first step in this direction.

It has of course not been possible to discuss all prior work on argumentation systems. For the sake of completeness, I would like to at least briefly mention several others.

In addition to Lorenzen's system, there have been several other dialogue logics, by Lorenz [68], Rescher [102], and Mackenzie [71]. Like Lorenzen's Logic, Lorenz's and Mackenzie's systems do not support substantial arguments. Lorenz was the first to suggest resource bounds, by restricting the permitted number of responses. Mackenzie's system was the first to constrain moves by previous statements, using a "commitment store". His system was also novel in allowing players to retract claims. Rescher's system was an early attempt to handle defeasible arguments and the first to rank them by specificity.

Although not formal systems like the ones presented in this chapter, nonetheless relevant are hypertext systems, such as [73] and [109], which have used Toulmin diagrams for organizing and browsing arguments. Logical dependencies are not used in these systems to constrain or facilitate the development of arguments. They also do not distinguish the roles or interests of the parties; thus the idea of regulating argument moves using discourse norms does not appear.

Layman Allen has designed many logical games for several players, such as Wff 'n Proof [7] and the Plain Language Game [8]. These are early examples of resources allocation games which divide up the burden of proof among the players. Moves of the Plain Language Game included making claims about what statements could be proved within certain resource limits, asking questions of a neutral judge, and challenging claims of the opponent.

In AI, Trevor Bench-Capon and his colleagues have developed two discourse games, applied to the problem of improving the explanations of expert systems. One is based on Mackenzie's system [17], the other on Toulmin's theory [18]. Ronald Loui and William Chen have designed an argument game [69] based on a variant of the logic by Simari and Loui described in this chapter.

There are surely some interesting relationships to explore between case-based models of legal reasoning and argument, such as [22; 12; 117], and models of legal decision-making procedures, like the Pleadings Game. A thorough comparison will have to await another occasion, but a few initial comments can be made here. The kinds of argument moves modeled in the Pleadings Game are generic; they do not depend on the kind of backing used to support rules. The case-based models, on the other hand, develop a richer model of the kinds of argument moves which can be made using cases, such as generalizing or restricting the scope of a precedent. Conversely, the case-based models have focussed their attention on the kinds of moves which can be made with cases, without embedding these moves in a general, procedural model of argumentation. Finally, case-based approaches have typically modeled the behavior of generating good arguments from cases, whereas the object modeled by the Pleadings Game are procedural norms of legal argument. That is, while the case-based models might be useful for assisting lawyers find good arguments, models like the Pleadings Game are more likely to be useful in mediating an argument to help assure that procedural norms are respected. To sum up, it appears that models like the Pleadings Game largely compliment these case-based models of legal reasoning.

The research which has culminated in this work began in 1981, when I attempted to write a legal expert system in EMYCIN for Article Nine of the Uniform Commercial Code, the same legal domain used here. Using EMYCIN's rule language, I was unable to find a satisfactory way to represent the many kinds of defeasible rules which appear in the article. The two versions of OBLOG were my initial attempts to develop a system for defeasible legal reasoning [42; 43; 44]. In [45], the first normative arguments for using nonmonotonic logic for legal reasoning are presented. In 1989, I began to develop models based on Fiedler's theory construction view of legal reasoning. These efforts include an abductive theory of issue spotting [46; 47] and a theory construction approach to assembling legal documents [48]. Karsten Schweichhart's Argument Construction Set [110] was also developed in our group during this period.

Chapter 5   The Pleadings Game

There are many kinds of legal proceedings, each with its own set of norms. Alexy's thesis is that the norms of legal argumentation are a specialization of the moral norms of general, practical discourse. This is agreeable if "specialization" is understood to mean that these general norms are defeasible rules which may be overridden by the particular norms for some type of legal proceeding. Similarly, the rules for legal discourse Alexy proposes may also have to be refined and adapted to further the particular goals of some type of proceeding. ·

This chapter presents the main contribution of the book: *The Pleadings Game*. It is a formal, normative model of a particular type of legal proceeding. Pleading is the first of a series of proceedings which can occur along the way toward the decision of a civil case. Very roughly, but sufficient for our purposes, this series of proceedings can be depicted as in Figure 5.1. The purpose of pleading is to identify the legal and factual issues of the case. What is the conflict about? The purpose of *discovery* is to gather evidence which may be relevant for deciding the factual issues, such as documents and the written statements of witnesses. The purpose of *trial* is to decide the legal and factual issues. Of course, the evidence gathered during discovery is presented at the trial. Finally, the purpose of *appeal* is review the decision and procedure of the trail court. There may be several levels of appeal, ending in a review by the Supreme Court.

In the chapter on legal philosophy, the main question addressed was how judicial discretion can be rationally restricted, to preserve the balance of power between the legislative and judicial branches of government. A model of pleading alone would not demonstrate how judicial discretion may be restricted by fair procedural rules, as the judge does not participate in pleading. However, as shown above, pleading is but a part of a series of proceedings, including the trial and appellate proceedings where judges do make decisions. A very basic formal *Trial Game* will also be defined in this chapter, to demonstrate how a judge's discretion may be sensibly restricted by the issues, and the dependencies between issues, identified during pleading.

In terms of my system of classification for discourse games, the Pleadings Game can be described as follows:

- The purpose of the game is to identify the legal and factual issues of the case.

- The "data" of the game are defeasible rules and sentences of first-order logic.

- Using the terminology of conditional entailment, the "default theory" is not fixed at the beginning of the game, but may be extended by asserting defeasible rules, nondefeasible rules and "evidence" during the game.

Figure 5.1. Series of Civil Proceedings

- There are four kinds of speech acts, for conceding, denying and defending propositions, and for asserting defeasible rules.

- Players are committed to the known consequences of their claims. The concept of an *issue* is used to focus the discussion, by prohibiting further arguments about statements which have become irrelevant.

- A resource limitation is imposed: each player may make at most one argument or counterargument.

- There are two players, the plaintiff and defendant. The rights and obligations of a player do depend to a limited extent on his or her role, as the plaintiff has the burden of proving the main claim.

- Finally, permissable subjects of argument include not only substantial claims, but also the validity and priority of defeasible rules. The discourse rules of the game, however, are not subject to dispute.

Even at this abstract level, certain novel features of the game may be apparent. To my knowledge it is the first formal game in which: 1) defeasible reasoning is modeled as a dialogue between two speakers; 2) inference is used to commit players to the known consequences of their claims; 3) the goal of the game is to identify issues, rather than decide them; 4) discourse is focussed using the concept of an issue, and 5) the speakers may argue about the validity and priority of defeasible rules.

The rest of this chapter is organized as follows. We begin by describing pleading in more detail and presenting an Article Nine World example. Next, a formal language for defeasible rules is defined, and shown to be sufficient and convenient for representing the kinds of relationships between legal rules identified in Chapter 2. The semantics of this language is given by a mapping into conditional entailment default theories. Then the Pleadings Game is defined, followed by a formalization of the example. Next a simple Trial Game is defined. The theory of issues used in these games depends on the structure of the dialectical graph for the main claim. These dialectical graphs are discussed next. The final section presents the theory of issues itself.

5.1   Civil Pleading

The purpose of pleading is to identify the *issues* to be decided by the court. My model of pleading is more akin to common law practice than to the "modern" law of civil procedure in the United States. At common law, the goal of pleading was to reduce the issues to be tried to a minimum. There appears to be no limit to the number of pleadings which could be filed by the parties [20]:

Pleading

... The process performed by the parties to a suit or action, in alternately presenting written statements of their contention, each responsive to what precedes, and each serving to narrow the field of controversy, until there evolves a single point, affirmed on one side and denied on the other, called the "issue," upon which they then go to trial.

The individual allegations of the respective parties to an action at common law, proceeding from them alternately, in the order and under the distinctive names following: The plaintiff's *declaration*, the defendant's *plea*, the plaintiff's *replication*, the defendant's *rejoinder*, the plaintiff's *surrejoinder*, the defendant's *rebutter*, the plaintiff's *surrebutter*, after which they have no distinctive names.

In modern legal systems, typically the rules of civil procedure do not require the parties to explicitly make legal arguments during pleading; rather, they merely assert or deny "essential" facts which are believed to entitle them to legal relief, such as monetary compensation for damages, or are believed to constitute a defense. The number of pleadings which may be filed is reduced, in the usual case, to three:

1. The plaintiff begins by filing a *complaint*, in which the facts are asserted which he believes entitles him to legal relief. The complaint also includes a demand for some specific relief.

2. The defendant may then file an *answer*, in which each of the assertions in the complaint is admitted or denied, or a *motion to dismiss for failure to state a claim*, also known as a *demurrer*, in which it is asserted that the law does not entitle the plaintiff to the relief demanded, even if the facts asserted are true. If the defendant files an answer, he may also assert facts which he believes constitute an *affirmative defense*. In our terminology, these are facts which make an exception to some rule applicable.

3. Finally, if the defendant's answer includes an affirmative defense, the plaintiff may file a *reply*, to answer any claims made by the defendant in an affirmative defense, or a demurrer, to assert that the facts claimed in the answer do not constitute a defense.

Notice that this procedure does not account for the possibility that the plaintiff may assert additional facts in his reply which are believed to constitute, in effect, a defense to the defense. There are often exceptions to exceptions in the law, but modern civil procedure terminates pleading, somewhat arbitrarily, after the plaintiff's reply. Unlike common law pleading, the purpose here is not so much to refine and limit the issues to be tried, but only to establish whether or not there is a genuine legal conflict.

The Pleadings Game model deviates from the modern law of civil procedure as our goal is a normative model of pleading, founded on first principles, inspired by Robert Alexy's discourse theory of legal argumentation.

Having decided that the basic purpose of pleading should be to identify the factual and legal issues of a case, we can begin to consider which discourse norms would promote this purpose. As discussed in the introduction to this chapter, the norms proposed by Alexy were not designed with the goals of a particular legal proceeding in mind. So we may not adopt them uncritically. Moreover, recall that Alexy admits that one purpose of having explicitly formulated a set of discourse norms for legal argumentation was to "reveal their shortcomings the more plainly" [4, p. 17]. In trying to formalize some of these norms, some of these shortcomings became apparent. Rather than trying to formalize all of the norms Alexy proposes, I have selected a few to start with, which appear both relevant to pleading and amenable to formalization:

(1.1) No speaker may contradict him or herself.

(1.3) Every speaker who applies a predicate F to an object a must be prepared to apply F to every other object which is like a in all relevant respects.

(2) Every speaker must give reasons for what he or she asserts when asked to do so, unless he or she can cite reasons which justify a refusal to provide a justification.

(2.2)(a) Everyone may problematize any assertion.

(3.3) Whoever has put forward an argument is only obliged to produce further arguments in the event of counter-arguments.

Again, these few principles by no means exhaust those proposed by Alexy. There would seem to be no way to formalize the constraint, e.g., that "Every speaker may only assert what he or she actually believes."

It might be helpful to restate these norms in a form which more closely resembles the result of my attempt to formalize them:

1. No party may contradict himself.

2. A party who concedes that a rule is valid must be prepared to apply the rule to every set of objects which satisfy its antecedent.

3. An argument supporting an issue may be asserted only when the issue has been denied by the opponent.

4. A party may deny any claim made by the opponent, if it is not a necessary consequence of his own claims.

5. A party may rebut a supporting argument for an issue he has denied.

6. A party may defeat the rebuttal of a supporting argument for one of his own claims, if the claim is an issue.

The first principal just comfirms Alexy's rule 1.1.

The second principal is an operational restatement of Alexy's rule 1.3. Two objects (more precisely, two sets of objects) are considered to be alike "in all relevant respects", relative to some rule, when they both satisfy the antecedent of the rule. Notice, however, that an exception may be applicable to one of the objects, but not the other. Thus, after all rules have been considered, it may well be that the predicate of the conclusion of the general rule is "applied" to only one of objects, even though the antecedent of the rule is satisfied by both.

Neither Alexy nor I require an uncontested claim to be supported by an argument. However, Alexy's principal 2 obliges the proponent of the challenged claim to support it with an argument, whereas my third principal permits, but does not require, a supporting argument to be made. Moreover, Alexy leaves open whether or not an argument may be made when the claim has not been challenged. In my system, an argument is permitted only when the claim has been denied and is still an issue.

The fourth principal is my version of Alexy's principal 2.2(a). Alexy permits "everyone to problematize any assertion." My principal is more restrictive. Only the parties may deny claims, not just anyone. And the claim may be denied only if it is not a necessary consequence of his own claims. It might be thought that Alexy's principal 1.1 implies this second condition. Although principal 1.1 prohibits a speaker from asserting statements which contradict his previous claims, it is unclear whether this principal prohibits the speaker from denying the necessary consequences of his claims.

My fifth and sixth principals correspond to Alexy's principal 3.3. As in the principal for supporting arguments, counterarguments are permitted in my system, rather than obligatory, as in Alexy's. (Strictly speaking, Alexy only seems to require defeating counterarguments to be asserted, but leaves open whether rebuttals are also obligatory.) As for supporting arguments, rebuttals and defeating counterarguments are allowed only so long as the claim they are about are still an issue.

To complete this introductory section, and to facilitate an intuitive understanding of the Pleadings Game model, consider the following hypothetical exchange of allegations, concerning an Article Nine priority conflict between two secured transactions.

The plaintiff, Smith, and the defendant, Jones, have both loaned money to Miller for the purchase of an oil tanker, which is the collateral for both loans. Miller has defaulted on both loans, and the practical question is which of the two lenders will first be paid from the proceeds of the sale of the ship. These facts are uncontested. One subsidiary issue is whether Smith *perfected* his security interest in the ship or not. This is where we enter the pleadings.

Plaintiff. My security interested in Miller's ship was perfected.

Defendant. I do not agree.

Plaintiff. A security interest in goods may be perfected by taking possession of the collateral (UCC § 9-305). I have possession of Miller's ship.

Defendant. What makes you think ships are goods for the purposes of Article 9? Also, prove you have possession.

Plaintiff. Except for money and instruments, movable things are goods, according to UCC § 9-105-h.

Defendant. Although a ship is surely movable, I do not agree that this is sufficient for being a good according to the UCC. Furthermore, according to the Ship Mortgage Act, a security interest in a ship may only be perfected by filing a financing statement.

Plaintiff. I have filed a financing statement. But I do not agree that this is required by the Ship Mortgage Act. Moreover, even if you are right, the UCC would take precedence, as it is newer than the Ship Mortgage Act.

Defendant. But the Ship Mortgage Act is Federal Law, which takes precedence over state law such as the UCC, even if the state law was enacted later.

At the end of this exchange several issues have been identified. The parties disagree about whether or not Smith has possession of the ship, and whether he has filed a financing statement. These are factual issues. They also disagree about whether ships are goods in the sense of Article Nine, and whether the Ship Mortgage Act requires filing to perfect a security interest in a ship. These are legal issues. There is also the issue about whether the Ship Mortgage Act has priority over the UCC. The plaintiff argued that it does not, using the principle of *Lex Posterior*, which gives the newer rule priority. The defendant responded with the principle of *Lex Superior*, which gives the rule supported by the higher authority priority. Finally, there may be an issue about which of these two principles has priority.

It is tempting to stratify these issues into three levels. The legal and factual issues would be at the object level. The principles for resolving conflicts at the object level, such as *Lex Superior*, would be at the meta level. And the rules for ordering these principles would be at the meta-meta level. A simpler approach is taken in the Pleadings Game: all rules are first-order objects. Conflicts are resolved by partially ordering rule instances. Levels can be simulated, if desired, by giving all rules at some level priority over all lower level rules. An advantage of this approach is that one is not limited to an a priori number of levels. The next section describes the rule language of the Pleadings Game, which realizes this approach.

5.2   A Language for Explicit Exceptions

One of the features of Geffner and Pearl's theory of conditional entailment is that it uses specificity information to order conflicting defeasible rules. Some see this as an advantage. It is argued that the task of maintaining a set of defeasible rules using systems which require the user to rank conflicting rules explicitly, such as Reiter's Default Logic, is unduly burdensome and error prone. Others, such as McCarty [84], have argued just the opposite, claiming that it can be easy to write and maintain sets of defeasible rules using explicit exceptions. Ideally, the system would provide the means for representing defeasible legal rules in a way which reflects the way statutes are usually written. As we have seen in Chapter 2, on Article Nine of the Uniform Commercial Code, this requires support for *both* implicit and explicit exceptions. However, one empirical observation can be made at this point: a brief scan of Article Nine shows that explicit exceptions are prevalent. Here are a few examples of explicit exceptions of the kind we would like to be able to handle, from our Article Nine World:

§ 9-102. (1) Except as provided in Section 9-104 on excluded transactions, this Article applies ...

§ 9-105. (h) "Goods" include all things movable ... but does not include money or instruments.

§ 9-302. (1) A financing statement must be filed to perfect all security instruments except the following: (a) a security interest in collateral in possession of the secured party under Section 9-305.

Notice that there are two types of explicit exceptions in these few examples: 1) those which state that one section does not apply when another section does apply, such as the first and third examples; and 2) those which create an exception by explicitly stating the conditions under which the section does not apply, as in the second example, where money and instruments are excepted from the definition of goods.

Conditional entailment uses specificity to implicitly order defaults. As Geffner and Pearl's system is attractive for several reasons, such as its support for partially ordered defaults, its model-theoretic semantics, and its interesting argument-oriented proof theory, the question arises whether it is possible to somehow encode explicit exceptions using specificity. The answer is yes. This section describes one method. Moreover, the method has the advantage, as will be demonstrated, that rules can be structured in a way that is quite similar to the way statutes are written.

The rest of this section assumes familiarity with Geffner and Pearl's theory of conditional entailment, to the extent described in Chapter 4.

Let us begin by defining a first-order language. First, there is a set of *symbols*, S, and a triple $\langle R, F, C \rangle$, where R, F and C are members of 2^S, the power set of S. R, F and C are sets of *predicate*, *function* and *constant* symbols, respectively. Each symbol in R and F is associated with an integer giving its *arity*. A *constant* may be viewed as a function symbol whose arity is 0, but the use of a separate set C for constants allows the same symbol to be used as both a constant and a function with some other arity. There is also a set of special symbols for the usual quantifiers, the connectives and a set of variables. The language **L** is the set of terms and formulas determined by $\langle R, F, C \rangle$. To facilitate the layout of rather complex formulas in examples from Article Nine, a Lisp-like notation will be used.

Definition 1 (Terms)

The set of *terms* of **L** is inductively defined, as follows:

1. A variable is a term.

2. If `c` is a constant symbol in *C*, then `c` is a term.

3. If `f` is a function symbol in *F*, with arity *n*, and `t1 ... tn` are terms, then `(f t1 ... tn)` is a term.

4. Nothing else is a term.

A *closed term* has no variables.

Definition 2 (Atomic Formulas)

An expression `(r t1 ... tn)` is an *atomic formula* if `r` is a predicate symbol in *R* and `t1 ... tn` are terms. The symbol `false` is an atomic formula.

Definition 3 (Formulas)

The set of formulas of **L** is inductively defined as follows:

1. An atomic formula is a formula.

2. If `p` is a formula, then `(not p)` is a formula.

3. If `p` and `q` are formulas, then `(if p q)` is a formula.

4. If `p1 ... pn` are formulas, then `(and p1 ... pn)` and `(or p1 ... pn)` are formulas.

5. If `p` is a formula and `x1 ... xn` are variables, then `(all (x1 ... xn) p)` and `(exists (x1 ... xn) p)` are formulas.

6. Nothing else is a formula.

The basic set of connectives included here does not exhaust the possibilities, but any first-order predicate logic sentence can be expressed using these.

What is the semantics of **L**? Geffner and Pearl's system of conditional entailment is defined relative to some monotonic consequence relation. In their paper, this relation was assumed to be the ordinary entailment relation of classical logic, but any consequence relation may be used. To model legal argumentation, it will be necessary to use two different consequence relations, denoted $\models$ and known, where known is a weaker, decidable subset of $\models$. The known relation will be defined precisely below. For the purposes of the formalization of legal argument, it is unimportant which monotonic consequence relation is chosen for $\models$. Let us assume in the rest of this chapter that it is classical entailment. (In the computational model described in the next chapter, we will use a somewhat weaker logic, to avoid some of the computational complexity of classical logic.)

Recall that a *default theory* for conditional entailment is a pair $\langle K, E \rangle$, where K, the *background context*, is itself a pair $\langle L, D \rangle$. E and L are sets of closed formulas from **L**, representing the case-specific *evidence* and the nondefeasible generic knowledge of the domain, respectively. D is a set of *defaults* from Δ, the domain of defaults. A default is a $\langle p, q \rangle$ pair, denoted $p \Rightarrow q$, where p and q are formulas which may contain free variables. Let us call p and q the *antecedent* and *consequent* of the default, respectively. A default instance is created by systematically replacing free variables by closed terms of **L**. Let **D** be the set of all instances of D. The *assumptions* of a default theory, denoted **A**, are the set of consequents of all default instances in **D**. These assumptions may be viewed as names of instances of defaults.

Conditional entailment uses specificity to implicitly order conflicting default rules. To cancel the applicability of a default instance named d, when some condition q is satisfied, it is sufficient to add (if q (not d)) to L. The problem of explicitly ranking default instances is more subtle. To give an assumption d1 priority over another assumption d2, it is not sufficient to assert (if d1 (not d2)), as this is equivalent to (if d2 (not d1)). The key to understanding how to explicitly order default instances is contained in the syntactic test for determining whether one assumption d is preferred to another in some set of assumptions A in all admissable priority orderings [41, p. 220]. If the default instance for d is p $\Rightarrow$ d, then it is preferred to some assumption in A in all admissable orderings if and only if $A \cup \{p\} \models$ (not d). Thus, to encode an explicit preference for d1 over another assumption d2, it is sufficient to add the formula (if (and p d2) (not d1)) to the set of nondefeasible sentences L, where p is the antecedent of the default instance for d1.

Rather than encoding defeasible rules, whether or not they have explicit exceptions, directly in this format, we develop a more convenient notation for such rules, whose semantics is given by a mapping into defaults and sentences of K:

Definition 4 (Rules)
A *rule* is a quintuple $\langle d, [x_1, ..., x_n], a, c, e \rangle$, where d is a constant symbol naming the rule, $[x_1, ..., x_n]$ is a vector of n distinct variables for the *parameters* of the rule, and a, c, and e are formulas, which may include free variables, for the *antecedent*, *consequent*, and *exception* of the rule, respectively. Every free variable in a, c, and e is a member of $[x_1, ..., x_n]$. For convenience, a rule will be denoted by

```
(rule d (x1 ... xn) if a then c unless e),
```

or, if e is false, simply as

```
(rule d (x1 ... xn) if a then c).
```

For example, Section 9-105 of A9W, about which things are goods, might be represented in this format as:

```
(rule s9-105 (x)
        if (movable x)
        then (goods x)
        unless (or (money x) (instrument x)))
```

Here, s9-105 is the name of the rule, x is its only parameter, (goods x) is its consequent, (movable x) is its antecedent and

```
(or (money x) (instrument x))
```

is its exception.

The semantics of rules is given by the following mapping into defaults and formulas of a default theory for conditional entailment.

Definition 5 (Interpretation of Rules)

Let the language L include four distinguished unary predicates (applies, antecedent, ap, and backing) and two function symbols (inst and parms). Then the *interpretation* of a rule

```
(rule d (x1 ... xn) if a then c unless e)
```

is a background context $\langle L, D \rangle$, where L is the set of formulas:

```
{ (all (x1 ... xn)
      (if (and a (backing delta))
          (antecedent (inst delta
                            (parms x1 ...  xn))))),

  (all (x1 ... xn)
      (if (and a
              (backing delta)
              (ap (inst delta (parms x1 .. xn))))
          (applies (inst delta (parms x1 ... xn))))),

  (all (x1 ... xn)
      (if (applies (inst delta (parms x1 ... xn)))
          c)),

  (all (x1 ... xn)
      (if (and e
              (ap (inst delta (parms x1 ... xn))))
          false)) }
```

and D is a singleton set containing the default

```
(antecedent (inst delta (parms x1 ... xn))) =>
(ap (inst delta (parms x1 ... xn)))
```

Given a rule r, whose interpretation is $\langle L, D \rangle$, let $\mathrm{strict}(r) = L$ and $\mathrm{defaults}(r) = D$.

As a notational convenience, let $\mathrm{I}(R)$ denote the interpretation of a set of rules R. If R is $\{r_1, ..., r_n\}$, then

$$\mathrm{I}(\{r_1, ..., r_n\}) = \langle \bigcup_i^n \mathrm{strict}(r_i), \bigcup_i^n \mathrm{defaults}(r_i) \rangle$$

Thus, the interpretation of the example above, for § 9-105, is the background context consisting of the strict sentences

```
(all (x)
    (if (and (movable x)
             (backing s9-105))
        (antecedent (inst s9-105 (parms x))))))

(all (x)
    (if (and (movable x)
             (backing s9-105)
             (ap (inst s9-105 (parms x))))
        (applies (inst s9-105 (parms x))))))

(all (x)
    (if (applies (inst s9-105 (parms x)))
        (goods x)))

(all (x)
    (if (and (or (money x) (instrument x))
             (ap (inst s9-105 (parms x))))
        false))
```

and the default

```
(antecedent (ap (inst s9-105 (parms x)))) =>
(ap (inst s9-105 (parms x)))
```

If the exception had been false, rather than

```
(or (money x) (instrument x)),
```

the last sentence of the background context in this example would have been

```
(all (x)
    (if false
        (not (ap (inst s9-105 (parms x)))))),
```

which is a tautology. Thus, this last sentence can be safely omitted from the translation when a rule has no exception.

Notice that I have deviated somewhat from Geffner and Pearl's suggested encoding of defeasible rules. Their encoding of a defeasible rule, such as movable things are (normally) goods, is the sentence

```
(all (x)
    (if (and (movable x)
             (s9-105 x))
        (goods x)))
```

and a default (movable x) $\Rightarrow$ (s9-105 x), where a ground instance of atomic formula (s9-105 x) is the name of an instance of the rule. The set of such names make up the set of *assumptions* maximized by conditional entailment.

In my encoding, on the other hand, following a suggestion by Ulrich Junker [56], rule instances are named by ground *terms*, rather than ground atomic formulas, and the set of assumptions consists of ground instances of applicability sentences such as

```
(ap (inst s9-105 (parms x))).
```

The advantages of this approach will be discussed next, after this definition:

Definition 6 (Rule Instance)
 A *rule instance* is obtained from a rule

```
(rule d (x1 ... xn) if a then c unless e)
```

by systematically substituting every parameter in x1 ... xn by a ground term from **L**. The term

```
(inst d (parms t1 ... tn)),
```

where t1 ... tn are ground terms, is the *name of the rule instance* obtained by substituting t1 ... tn for the parameters x1 ... xn in the rule named d. The formula

```
(ap (inst d (parms t1 ... tn)))
```

is the *applicability assumption* for this rule instance.

This change in the naming convention for rule instances has no effect on Geffner and Pearl's theoretical results concerning conditional entailment. But it is of practical importance for us here, as it allows us to reason about rule instances without leaving first-order logic. Rules, and rule instances, are *reified* in this system. It is possible to write rules making statements about rules. Moreover, properties of rules can be expressed. For example, when legal statutes are represented as rules in this form, we can state such properties as the date of their enactment, their authority or source, and the article of the code in which they appear. As it turns out, this ability makes it possible to handle all of the kinds of exceptions and principles for resolving conflicts between rules we have identified in Article Nine.

For a first example of the utility of reification, notice that a *backing condition* is included in the translation of rules into background formulas. In the example for § 9-105, the relevant formula was

```
(all (x)
     (if (and (movable x)
              (ap (inst s9-105 (parms x)))
              (backing s9-105))
```

```
(applies (inst s9-105 (parms x))))).
```

Reification allows Toulmin's distinction between warrants and backing to be handled. The role of warrants is played by rules. One type of challenge to a conclusion of a rule is to attack the rule by requesting its backing. In the legal context, this is usually reduced to the issue of the authority for the rule. Using Susskind's terminology, the rule is a law "statement" which may be backed by an authoritative law "formulation" [119, pp. 36-37]. Pragmatically, there is a discourse rule allowing the parties to agree that a rule is backed, just as any other claim may be conceded, without making an issue out of this. However, the opponent may instead challenge the rule, in which case the proponent will have to present an argument for the backing claim, just as is the case for every other disputed claim, in order to use the rule to derive its consequent. In our example, the (backing s9-105) claim may be conceded, but if it is denied, the proponent will have to support the backing claim with an argument in order to use s9-105 to support (goods t), for any constant t. The discourse rules are described in detail below.

It is the rule, s9-105 here, which must be backed, not just a rule instance, such as (inst s9-105 (parms t)). If the backing condition for a rule is falsified, e.g., if (not (backing s9-105)) is conditionally entailed by the default theory, then the rule is effectively cancelled.

For another example of the utility of reification, let us represent § 9-302, in which § 9-305 is referred to explicitly in the exception. Recall that § 9-302 states, in part:

> (1) A financing statement must be filed to perfect all security instruments except the following: (a) a security interest in collateral in possession of the secured party under Section 9-305.

Here, one needs to also be familiar with § 9-305 to interpret § 9-302; the "security interest in collateral in possession of the secured party" phrase is not an additional condition on the applicability of § 9-302, but rather a redundant restatement of part of the antecedent of § 9-305, presumably intended to help the reader identify or remember § 9-305.

Now, § 9-302 can be represented by the following rule:

```
(rule s9-302 (p s g)
    if (and (perfected s)
            (not (filed s)))
    then false
    unless (applies (inst s9-305 (parms p s g))))
```

Five means of resolving conflicts between legal rules used in Article Nine were identified in Chapter 2: 1) authority 2) time 3) express exceptions 4) specificity, and 5) scoping and applicability rules. I have already shown how express exceptions can be handled in our rule language. Specificity is handled by conditional entailment. This leaves authority, time and scoping provisions to be discussed. The reification of rules makes it possible to represent these other conflict resolution principles as well.

This next example will show one way of using both authority and time to order conflicting rules. According to the principal known as *Lex Superior*, rules with higher authority have precedence over rules with lower authority. For example, federal law has priority over state law. On the other hand, the principal of *Lex Posterior* states later rules have priority over conflicting earlier rules. Moreover, both of these principles are themselves defeasible. When they conflict, *Lex Superior* prevails over *Lex Posterior*. For example, a federal law has priority over a conflicting later state law.

We begin with a few formulas about rules. One rule instance conflicts with another if they are not both applicable.

```
(all (r1 r2)
     (if (not (and (ap r1) (ap r2)))
         (conflicting r1 r2)))
```

Using our convention for representing assumptions, the formula for encoding an explicit preference for the default instance d1 over the default instance d2 would be

```
(if (and (antecedent d1)
         (ap d2))
    (not (ap d1))).
```

To allow explicit preferences to be asserted in a more convenient manner, let us add the following formula to **L**, introducing a `preferred` predicate.

```
(all (x y)
     (if (preferred x y)
         (if (and (antecedent x)
                  (ap y))
             (not (ap x)))))
```

which is equivalent to

```
(all (x y)
     (if (and (preferred x y)
              (antecedent x)
              (ap y)
              (ap x))
         false))
```

To see how this can be used, let us now state the rule for ordering rule instances by authority. Let us assume there are predicates for ranking authority and ordering dates. (higher a1 a2) is intended to mean that a1 is a higher authority than a2. (before d1 d2) is intended to mean that the date d1 is before d2.

```
(rule lex-superior (r1 p1 r2 p2)
```

```
if  (exists (a1 d1 a2 d2)
       (and (conflicting (inst r1 p1) (inst r2 p2))
            (authority  r1 a1 d1)
            (authority  r2 a2 d2)
            (higher a1 a2)))
   then (preferred (inst r1 p1) (inst r2 p2)))
```

The (conflicting (inst r1 p1) (inst r2 p2)) condition in this example
is not unimportant. Without it, the previous formula for preferred above would imply
a conflict between the two rule instances, even if they were not otherwise in conflict. It
would have made it impossible to apply state and federal law together in one argument.

As explained previously, in the interpretation of rules of this formalism, one condition
of the antecedent of a default instance (inst r parms), is the proposition (backing
r), meaning that the rule is well supported or founded. This next formula simply states
that legal authority is one form of backing. (authority r a d) is intended to mean
that the rule r was enacted by the authority a on the date d.

```
(all (r a d)
    (if (authority r a d)
        (backing r)))
```

The following representation of the rule for ordering conflicting rules by time is similar
to the rule for ordering them by authority, but includes an exception for rules backed by
higher authority.

```
(rule lex-posterior (r1 p1 r2 p2)
      if (exists (a1 d1 a2 d2)
            (and (conflicting (inst r1 p1) (inst r2 p2))
                 (authority r1 a1 d1)
                 (authority r2 a2 d2)
                 (before d2 d1)))
      then (preferred (inst r1 p1) (inst r2 p2))
      unless (applies (inst lex-superior
                             (parms r2 p2 r1 p1))))
```

Alternatively, we could omit the exception from lex-posterior and add another rule
ordering instances of lex-posterior and lex-superior in cases of conflict:

```
(rule lex-posterior (r1 p1 r2 p2)
      if (exists (a1 d1 a2 d2)
            (and (conflicting r1 r2)
                 (authority r1 a1 d1)
                 (authority r2 a2 d2)
                 (before d2 d1)))
      then (preferred (inst r1 p1) (inst r2 p2))
```

```
(rule superior-over-posterior (p1 p2)
    if   (conflicting (inst lex-superior p1)
                      (inst lex-posterior p2))
    then (preferred (inst lex-superior p1)
                    (inst lex-posterior p2)))
```

Notice that this later rule orders the lex-superior and lex-posterior rules, and thus only indirectly the "object-level" rules in conflict.

These two versions of lex-posterior are not equivalent. In the first version, the backing for lex-posterior is also backing for the prinicipal that authority has priority over time. That is, anyone who asserts this version of the rule may not dispute that it is subordinate to the lex-superior rule. In the second version, the principal of authority over time is factored out, and represented independently in a rule of its own. Thus, in this version, a party could accept lex-posterior while disputing superior-over-posterior. Moreover, the exception in the first version is not defeasible. The second version leaves open the possibility of there being exceptions to the principle that authority takes precedence over time.

Finally, here is an example showing how to use this scheme to represent a scoping provision. § 9-102 (2) of the A9W simplification of UCC Article Nine states "This article does not apply to statutory liens except as provided in Section 9-301." This may be represented using a rule such as:

```
(rule s9-102-2 (e)
    if (exists (r p c d)
              (and (substantive r)
                   (event (inst r p) e)
                   (security-interest e)
                   (collateral e c)
                   (statutory-lien e)
                   (authority r A9W d)
                   (ap (inst r p))))
    then false
    unless (applies (inst s9-301 (parms e))))
```

The predicates substantive, event, security-interest, collateral, and statutory-lien here are domain specific. (substantive r) is intended to mean that a rule r is one of substantive law, rather than, e.g., a scoping provision. (event r e) is intended to mean that r is a rule instance involving an event e. (security-interest e) means that the event creates a security interest. (collateral e c) means c is the collateral of the security interest, and (statutory-lien e) is intended to mean that e is a statutory lien. A9W is a constant naming Article Nine World.

Notice that § 9-102 is self-referential — it purports to regulate the scope of the article in which it itself appears — but this section is certainly not intended to mean that it, § 9-102, is not applicable to statutory liens. Presumably it means that only those sections

of Article Nine affecting interests in the collateral are not applicable to such liens. The
(substantive r) condition of the representation of § 9-102 makes this condition
explicit.

5.3   The Pleadings Game

Now we are ready to formally define the Pleadings Game itself. It is structured as a formal,
two-person game, comparable to Dialogue Logic. We will be defining the "playing board",
the moves permitted by the rules of the game, and a termination criterion for determining
when the game is over. It will also be defined what it means to "win" this game. When
there are issues remaining at the end of the pleadings, then neither party wins and the case
proceeds to trial.

To begin, the game is played against a particular *background*. (Recall that I is the
interpretation function of Definition 5, above.)

Definition 7 (Background)
    A *background* is a triple $\langle \phi, S, R \rangle$, where ϕ is a formula, S is a set of formulas and R
    is a set of rules. ϕ is the *main claim*, the claim the plaintiff ultimately would like to
    prove. S and R are formulas and rules, respectively, about which the parties agree.
    Both sets may be empty. Together, S and R determine the *initial background context*
    K_0 for conditional entailment. $K_0 = \langle L \cup S, D \rangle$, where $\langle L, D \rangle = I(R)$.

The main claim is also the *ultimate issue* of the case, so long as it is an issue.

The only players of the game, during pleading, are the *plaintiff* and the *defendant*. The
judge, or court, enters the game only during the trial. The moves available during pleading
are assertions of various kinds of statements:

Definition 8 (Statements)
    There are four kinds of *statements*, defined inductively as follows:

1.   If p is a formula, then (claim p) is a statement.

2.   If A is a set of formulas and p is a formula, then (argument A p) is a
      statement.

3.   If A and C are sets of formulas and p is a formula, then (rebuttal A p C)
      is a statement.

4.   If s is a statement, then (denial s) is also a statement.

5.   Nothing else is a statement.

These statements are not moves of the game. Rather, the moves are assertions about statements.

Definition 9 (Assertions)
There are also four kinds of *assertions*, defined as follows:

1. If s is a statement, then (concede s) is an assertion.

2. If s is a statement, then (deny s) is an assertion.

3. If s is a statement and A is a set of formulas, then (defend s A) is an assertion.

4. If r is a rule, then (declare r) is an assertion.

5. Nothing else is an assertion.

Statements and assertions completely define the type of moves possible, but we have yet to give the rules of the game prescribing when an assertion of a particular type may be made, and with what effect on the playing board. The playing board here will be called the *record*, which is a legal term for the pleadings and other documents filed at the court by the parties. Each rule has a precondition. If this precondition is satisfied by the record, then the player *may* choose to apply the rule. Application of a rule modifies the record, according to the *effects* defined for the rule. The rules below define when an assertion is *permitted*, not *obligated*. However this does not imply that no assertions are obligatory. As will be described in more detail below, when discussing control and termination, a party is required to answer every *relevant* statement, not yet answered, on each turn. Pleading terminates when no relevant statements remain to be answered.

Before describing these production rules, the structure and certain properties of the record, used in the preconditions of the rules, need to be defined.

Definition 10 (Statements of a Party)
The *statements* of a party are a triple $\langle O, D, C \rangle$, where O, D and C are each sets of statements. O is the set of *open* statements, which have not yet been responded to by the opponent. D is the set of statements which the opponent has *denied*. Finally, C is the set of statements which the opponent has *conceded*.

Definition 11 (The Record)
The *record* is also a triple, $\langle b, \pi, \delta \rangle$, where b is the background $\langle \phi, S, R \rangle$ of the game, and π and δ are the statements of the plaintiff and defendant, respectively.

Definition 12 (Arguments)

An *argument* is a set of formulas. An *argument for some proposition* is a pair $\langle A, p \rangle$, where A is a set of formulas and p is a formula. Given a default theory $\langle K, E \rangle$, where $K = \langle L, D \rangle$, an argument A is a *supporting argument* for p if and only if $L \cup E \cup A \models p$. The *claims* of an argument are all of its formulas which are not assumptions.

Definition 13 (Counterarguments)

An argument R is a *counterargument* to another argument A in a default theory $\langle K, E \rangle$ if and only if $R \cup A \cup L \cup E \models$ false. R is a *defeating counterargument* of A if and only if they are counterarguments and every assumption in R is preferred to some assumption in A. R is *protected from A* if and only if R contains a subargument which defeats A. Finally, a counterargument R of A is a *rebuttal* if and only if A is not protected from R.

The definition of *supporting* argument here is similar to Geffner and Pearl's definition of argument [41, p. 225], except that an argument may consist of arbitrary formulas, not just assumptions, and $L \cup E \cup A$ is not required here to be consistent. The definitions of counterarguments, defeating counterarguments and rebuttals are the same as Geffner and Pearl's. They are repeated here for the sake of completeness.[1]

Here are some auxiliary functions and values used in the rules for assertions. Each of these is defined relative to the current state of the record. A phrase such as "the open statements of the plaintiff", e.g., means his open statements in the current record.

opponent : statements $\rightarrow$ statements

Maps the statements of one party into the statements of the opposing party. Recalling that π and δ are the statements of the plaintiff and defendant, respectively, opponent$(\pi) = \delta$ and opponent$(\delta) = \pi$.

rules : 2^{rule}

The union of the rules of the initial background and all rules subsequently declared by either party. The rules declared by a party are $\{r \mid (\text{declare } r) \in C\}$, where C is the set of conceded statements of the party. Let Π be the rules stated by the plaintiff and Δ be the rules stated by the defendant. Then, rules $= R \cup \Pi \cup \Delta$.

$K : 2^L \times 2^\Delta$

The current *background context*. $K = \langle L \cup S, D \rangle$, where $\langle L, D \rangle = $ I(rules).

---

[1] These definitions differ slightly from the ones I used in [47]. There an argument is what I have chosen to call a valid argument here. A rebuttal there is what Geffner and Pearl call counterarguments, as defined above. A counterargument there was a special kind of rebuttal.

$L : 2^L$

   The nondefeasible part of the current background context, $\langle L, D \rangle = K$.

facts : 2^L

   These are the conceded claims of both parties. They are what Geffner and Pearl, in their system for conditional entailment, call "evidence". The conceded claims of a party are $\{f \mid (\text{claim } f) \in C\}$, where C is the set of conceded statements of the party. Let Π be the conceded claims of the plaintiff, and Δ be the conceded claims of the defendant. Then facts $= \Pi \cup \Delta$.

$\Theta : 2^L$

   The current *context*, the union of the nondefeasible sentences of the background context and the facts. $\Theta = L \cup$ facts.

claims : statements $\rightarrow 2^L$

   The claims of a party. If the statements made by the party are $\langle O, D, C \rangle$, then claims$\langle O, D, C \rangle = \{f \mid (\text{claim } f) \in (O \cup D \cup C)\}$.

arguments : 2^A

   The arguments which have been made by the parties. If the statements made by a party are $\langle O, D, C \rangle$, his arguments are the union of

$$\{\langle A, c \rangle \mid (\text{argument } A \ c) \in (O \cup D \cup C)\}$$

and

$$\{\langle A \cup R, \text{false} \rangle \mid (\text{rebuttal } A \ c \ R) \in (O \cup D \cup C)\}.$$

   Let Π be the arguments made by the plaintiff and Δ be the arguments made by the defendant. Then arguments $= \Pi \cup \Delta$.

   Two predicates, issue and known play an important role in this model. known is explained next, but a proper explanation of the issue predicate requires more space than I want take here. For now, the following should suffice. issue(q, p) is true if and only if the formula q is *relevant* to the goal of proving the formula p. (See Section 5.7, below, for further details.)

   The known relation, which is a subset of $2^L \times L$, is relatively easy to define. The intended meaning of known(A, p), is that p is known to be entailed by A and some set of premises Θ. Intuitively, one would expect a knowledge relation to be decidable, and tractably so. One's own knowledge can be efficiently retrieved. If a difficult problem must first be solved, then intuitively one can be said to know the answer only after the problem has been solved. Thus, the knowledge relation should be some tractably decidable subset of the entailment relation.

Definition 14 (Known Relation)
   Recall that a supporting argument for a proposition is a pair $\langle G, p \rangle$ where $G \cup \Theta \models p$ in the context Θ. Given this context and a set of supporting arguments A, a formula p is *known* to be entailed by an argument G, denoted $\mathrm{known}_{\langle A, \Theta \rangle}(G, p)$, if and only if:

1. p is a member of $G \cup \Theta$,

2. $\mathrm{known}_{\langle A, \Theta \rangle}(G, \mathtt{false})$, or

3.   there exists an argument $\langle H, p \rangle \in A$, such that, for every formula $q \in H$, $\mathrm{known}_{\langle A, \Theta \rangle}(G, q)$.

When the context and set of arguments is clear, we will simply write $\mathrm{known}(G, p)$, without the subscript.

   As arguments are isomorphic to propositional Horn clauses, not only is the problem of deciding whether $\mathrm{known}(G, p)$ holds decidable, its worst-case time complexity is *linear* [29].
   A well-defined knowledge relation surely requires more than tractability. For an extreme example, the empty set is clearly also a tractably decidable subset of any entailment relation, but it would not seem plausible to suggest that nothing is known. Arguably, the knowledge relation should be a *consequence relation*, satisfying the usual Tarskian properties:

Inclusion.
   $G \subset \mathrm{closure}(G)$, where the closure of G is the set of all formulas p, such that $\mathrm{known}_{\langle A, \Theta \rangle}(G, p)$.

Idempotence.
   $\mathrm{closure}(G) = \mathrm{closure}(\mathrm{closure}(G))$.

Monotonicity.
   If $G \subset H$ then $\mathrm{closure}(G) \subset \mathrm{closure}(H)$.

The known relation is a consequence relation in Tarski's sense.
   We are ready to define the rules controlling assertions. There are three types of assertions (concessions, denials and defenses); the rules for each type will be presented together. Altogether there are ten rules; they will be numbered for future reference. A precondition of all rules is that the statement being responded to be in the set of open statements of the opponent. If the party making the move is x, this set is denoted by O in $\langle O, D, C \rangle = \mathrm{opponent}(x)$. An effect of most moves is to delete the statement from O and add it to either the denied statements, D, or the conceded statements, C. If a response by the opponent to this new assertion is possible, then another effect is to add the assertion to the set of open statements of the party making the move.

No response is required or permitted to the mere declaration of rules, i.e., to an assertion of the form (declare r), where r is a rule. What may be controversial is the claim that such a rule is *backed*, for example by legal authority. Recall that nothing can be derived from a rule which is not backed. These backing claims, which have the form

```
(claim (backing r)),
```

may be conceded or denied in the same way as other claims.

The syntax used here for production rules is informal.[2] Each rule consists of a *statement pattern*, which is matched against the statement for which this move is a response, a set of *preconditions* which must be satisfied if the move is to be applicable, and a sequence of *effects*, which are executed in the order they appear when the move is applied. In every rule, p denotes statements of the party making the move, which is intended to be mnemonic for *proponent*, and o, denotes the statements of the *opponent* of p, i.e., $o = \text{opponent}(p)$. Also, as a notional convenience, the open, denied and conceded statements of the parties are denoted using subscripts. For example, if $\langle O, D, C \rangle = p$ then $O_p = O$. In effects, $\leftarrow$ denotes assignment.

There are three rules for concessions. Claims, arguments and rebuttals may be conceded; denials may not be conceded. Conceding the denial of one's own assertion would violate the principle against self-contradiction. For the same reason, a claim may be conceded only if it is not known to be inconsistent with the other claims of the party making the concession. There are no further preconditions on concessions; no artificial barriers are placed on the willingness of the parties to agree. By conceding an argument or rebuttal, the party gives up the opportunity to make a counterargument.

1. **move** (concede (claim c))

   preconditions

   - (claim c) $\in O_o$

   - $\neg\text{known}(\text{claims}(p) \cup \{c\}, \text{false})$

   effects

   1. $O_o \leftarrow O_o \setminus \{(\text{claim c})\}$

   2. $C_o \leftarrow C_o \cup \{(\text{claim c})\}$

---

[2]Although it would also have been possible to formalize these rules as operators in a planning language, such as STRIPS [38; 65], these productions rules are simpler and sufficient for our purposes here.

2. **move** (concede (argument A c))

   preconditions

   - (argument A c) $\in O_o$

   effects

   1. $O_o \leftarrow O_o \setminus \{(\text{argument A c})\}$

   2. $C_o \leftarrow C_o \cup \{(\text{argument A c})\}$

3. **move** (concede (rebuttal A c R))

   preconditions

   - (rebuttal A c R) $\in O_o$

   effects

   1. $O_o \leftarrow O_o \setminus \{(\text{rebuttal A c R})\}$

   2. $C_o \leftarrow C_o \cup \{(\text{rebuttal A c R})\}$

There are only two rules for denials. Only claims and denials may be denied. Arguments and rebuttals may not be denied as we will require the proponent to prove an argument or rebuttal when it is asserted. (See below.) A party may deny a claim only if it is not known to be entailed by his own claims. This is another use of the principle against self-contradiction. By denying a denial the party leaves any issues raised by the claim for trial and forfeits the opportunity to make an argument supporting his claim.

Denying a statement is not the same as claiming the negation of the statement, because of the division of the burden of proof. The pragmatic effect of a denial is to request the other party to bear his burden of proof. Conversely, a concession relieves the opponent from the burden of proving one of his claims.

4. **move** (deny (claim c))

    preconditions

      • (claim c) $\in O_o$

      • $\neg$known(claims(p), c)

    effects

    1. $O_o \leftarrow O_o \setminus \{(\text{claim c})\}$

    2. $D_o \leftarrow D_o \cup \{(\text{claim c})\}$

    3. $O_p \leftarrow O_p \cup \{(\text{denial (claim c))}\}$

5. **move** (deny (denial s))

    preconditions

      (denial s) $\in O_o$

    effects

    1. $O_o \leftarrow O_o \setminus \{(\text{denial s})\}$

Declaring a rule simply adds it to the rules of the background of the record. The only precondition is that there not already be another rule of the same name. (In the membership test below, two rules are considered equal if they have the same name.)

6. **move** (declare r)

    preconditions

      • r $\notin$ rules

    effects

    1. rules $\leftarrow$ rules $\cup \{r\}$

Finally, there are several defenses. Rather than merely denying or conceding a statement asserted by the opponent, a defense makes an argument against the statement. If the opponent has denied some claim, the defense is an argument supporting the claim. If the opponent has made an argument, the defense is a rebutting counterargument. If the opponent has asserted a rebuttal, the defense is either a counterargument defeating the rebuttal, or a rebuttal of the rebuttal.

A defense usually asserts new claims. For example, when defending a claim with a supporting argument (argument A c), one not only asserts that c is a necessary consequence of A, but claims that each of the formulas in A is true. However, each claim is asserted at most once. If it is known that some previous claim entails some formula in A, then this previous, stronger claim is the only one which is open to debate. No claim is asserted for the weaker statement. This rule encourages making claims which are only as strong as required to prove an argument. Stronger claims than necessary should be held back until they are required. For example, rather than claiming that the collateral is consumer goods, in a context where a good of any kind would suffice, one should claim only that the collateral is a good. If one fails to show that collateral is a consumer good, there may not be another opportunity to show that it is a good for some other reason.

One effect of a defense is to concede all of the open claims of the opponent known to be entailed by the argument of the defense. This is just a matter of convenience, as one precondition of denials is that the claim to be denied not be known to be entailed by the claims of the party making the denial. Thus, the only move permitted is to concede the claim, which is thus done automatically by defenses.

Applicability assumptions in arguments are also not asserted as claims. A rule is challenged by denying its backing, not by contesting the applicability assumption of one of its instances. Conversely, a rule is supported by an argument for its backing, not by arguments for an applicability assumption. These assumptions are included in arguments for technical reasons related to the way conditional entailment realizes defeasible reasoning. They are maximized by conditional entailment. See Section 4.4, on Geffner and Pearl's system, for details.

A rebuttal may, but need not, assert further claims. When no claims are made, the rebuttal asserts the argument being rebutted is inconsistent. For example, one rebuttal of an argument (argument A c) would be a proof that A is inconsistent. Similarly, a rebuttal (rebuttal A c R) may itself be rebutted by a proof that R is inconsistent. Here we see one reason why rebuttals have their own syntactic form, rather than being represented as (argument (union A R) false). Although to make a rebuttal one must prove that $A \cup R$ is inconsistent, the opponent should be given the opportunity to counter by proving that R alone is inconsistent. This opportunity is preserved by representing rebuttals so as to distinguish A and R.

Rebuttals and defeating counterarguments accept the argument against which they are a defense "for the sake of argument." Intuitively, when making one of these defenses, one says "Even if all the facts you claim are true, which I deny, you are still wrong, because of these other facts." For example, suppose one party has argued that Article Nine does not apply to the transaction because the security interest was created by a statutory lien,

§ 9-102 (2). This argument gives rise to three statements, each of which may be answered. The first is the claim that the interest was created by a statutory lien. The second is the argument that if an interest was created by a statutory lien then it is excluded from Article Nine. The third is that Article Nine provides authority for the proposition that statutory liens are excluded. (This is the question of backing.) The opponent can respond to each of these statements. He can deny that there is a statutory lien, deny that Article Nine excludes statutory liens and at the same time argue, in a rebuttal, that even if statutory liens are excluded, this security interest is covered by Article Nine, appealing to e.g., § 9-310. The only limitation here is that a party may not both deny that there is a statutory lien and claim that it is a special type of statutory lien.

The burden of proof is divided between the parties in this system. The party making an argument (argument A c) must prove $\Theta \cup A \models c$. However, he need not also show that $\Theta \cup A$ is consistent. The opponent of the argument has the burden of proving its inconsistency, by asserting a rebuttal. Similarly, the party asserting a rebuttal (rebuttal A c R) must prove $\Theta \cup A \cup R \models false$, but his opponent may prove that R alone is the source of the inconsistency: $\Theta \cup R \models false$. Recall that a rebuttal is a counterargument which is not defeated by some subset of the argument it is intended to rebut. Rather than requiring the proponent of the rebuttal to prove that all parts of this test are met, here too the burden of proof is divided between the parties. The proponent of the rebuttal must only show that it is a counterargument which is not *known* to be defeated by some subset of the other argument. The opponent has the burden of proving, using the stronger entailment relation, $\models$, that the supposed rebuttal is in fact defeated by some subset of the other argument. When asserting a defeating counterargument, however, the party making the assertion has the full burden of proving that it is a defeating counterargument.

The burden of proving that the preconditions of a discourse rule are satisfied is to be borne by the party making the move, not by the person (or machine) mediating the game, to assure that the rules are followed. When a precondition of a discourse rule requires proof of consistency, for example, *the party making the move is required to present the proof in such a form that it may be efficiently checked.* That is, the problem of checking the proof is required to be decidable and tractable. The rules of the Pleadings Game do not specifiy how this condition is to be met. There are at least two possibilities: 1) The proof can be packaged as a sequence of applications of inference rules in some calculus, i.e., as a path through the search space. To check the proof, one need only confirm that each inference rule application is correct. 2) The proof can be represented by a set of settings for some reference theorem prover, such as a particular heuristic evaluation function, selection of a search strategy, and such resource bounds as a depth or time limit. To check the proof then, the mediator need only run the theorem prover using these settings. The proponent is considered to have met his burden of proof only if the reference theorem prover succeeds in finding a proof using these settings.

A defense to a claim (claim c), argument (argument A c) or rebuttal (rebuttal A c R) may be made only if the formula c is an *issue*. This restriction prevents the assertion of irrelevant claims and arguments, which would unduly prolong pleading. Irrelevant claims and arguments *may* be denied or conceded, to remove them from the set of open statements requiring a response. However, one must be careful when choosing between conceding or denying statements, even when they are irrelevant. If the claim is conceded, only those claims are permitted later which are not known to be inconsistent with it and the other claims made or conceded by the party. If the claim is denied, the party may not later make claims known to be entailed by it.

The purpose of the prohibition against making arguments using claims which one has denied is to discourage obstinacy. A claim should be denied only in good faith. However, good faith is not something which can be formally determined. Thus this rule brings with it the risk that a party will be prohibited from using a claim denied in good faith, even when he has become convinced by arguments made to support the claim. To plug a potential loophole in this rule, an open claim must be conceded before it may be used in an argument. Otherwise, it would have been possible to avoid this rule by first making the argument and then denying the claim used in the argument.

For similar reasons, a rule may be applied in an argument only if the party has not denied that the rule has backing.

In this system, exactly one answer to any statement is permitted. Technically, this is realized by permitting responses only to statements in the set of open statements of the opponent. As one effect of every move is to delete this statement from the open set, at most one answer is possible. This restriction also applies to defenses. For example, just one argument may be made supporting a claim denied by the opponent. Each party has the burden of making the best argument available. The purpose of this rule is to prevent a party from making spurious arguments, intended only to delay resolution of the conflict. Conceivably, this rule could be relaxed somewhat, by allowing some small number of defenses, rather than just one.

There is no formal requirement that arguments be minimal. That is, to make an argument (argument A c), the proponent need not first prove that there is no subset B of A such that $\Theta \cup B \models c$. There are two reasons for this. First, as the proponent has the burden of proving all the formulas in A, it is in his own self-interest to keep A as small as possible. A formal check is not necessary here to promote the goal of avoiding unnecessary claims. Second, when a rebuttal is defeated by asserting a counterargument, it is known not to be minimal in this sense, as it is a superset of the argument rebutted. The purpose of the additional formulas in the counterargument is not to prove the claim, but to defeat the rebuttal.

7. **move** (defend (denial (claim c)) A)

preconditions

- (denial (claim c)) $\in O_o$

- issue(c, ϕ)

- $\neg(\exists q \in A.$(claim q) $\in (O_o \cup D_o))$

- $\neg$known(claims(p) $\cup$ A, false)

- $\Theta \cup A \models c$

effects

1. $O_o \leftarrow O_o \setminus \{$(denial (claim c))$\}$

2. for each (claim q) $\in O_o$ if known(claims(p) $\cup$ A, q) then

    1. $O_o \leftarrow O_o \setminus \{$(claim q)$\}$

    2. $C_o \leftarrow C_o \cup \{$(claim q)$\}$

3. for each q $\in$ A, if

    1. $\neg$known(claims(p), q), and

    2. q is not an applicability assumption

    then $O_p \leftarrow O_p \cup \{$(claim q)$\}$

4. $O_p \leftarrow O_p \cup \{$(argument A c)$\}$

8. **move** (defend (argument A c) R)

   preconditions

   - (argument A c) $\in O_o$

   - issue(c, ϕ)

   - $\neg(\exists q \in R$. (claim q) $\in (O_o \cup D_o))$

   - $\neg$known(claims(p) $\cup$ R, false)

   - $\Theta \cup A \cup R \models$ false

   - A does not contain a subset which is known to be a defeating counterargument to R.

   effects

   1. $O_o \leftarrow O_o \setminus \{(\text{argument A c})\}$

   2. for each (claim q) $\in O_o$ if known(claims(p) $\cup$ R, q) then

      1. $O_o \leftarrow O_o \setminus \{(\text{claim q})\}$

      2. $C_o \leftarrow C_o \cup \{(\text{claim q})\}$

   3. for each q $\in$ R, if

      1. $\neg$known(claims(p), q), and

      2. q is not an applicability assumption

      then $O_p \leftarrow O_p \cup \{(\text{claim q})\}$

   4. $O_p \leftarrow O_p \cup \{(\text{rebuttal A c R})\}$

9. move (defend (rebuttal A c R) {})

preconditions

- (rebuttal A c R) $\in O_o$

- issue(c, ϕ)

- $\Theta \cup R \models$ false

effects

1. $O_o \leftarrow O_o \setminus \{(\text{rebuttal A c R})\}$

2. $C_p \leftarrow C_p \cup \{(\text{argument R false})\}$

10. **move** (defend (rebuttal A c R) D)

   preconditions

   - (rebuttal A c R) $\in O_o$

   - issue(c, ϕ)

   - $\neg(\exists q \in D.$ (claim q) $\in (O_o \cup R_o))$

   - $\neg$known(claims(p) $\cup$ D, false)

   - D is a defeating counterargument of R.

   effects

   1. $O_o \leftarrow O_o \setminus \{(\text{rebuttal A c R})\}$

   2. for each (claim q) $\in O_o$ if known(claims(p) $\cup$ D, q) then

      1. $O_o \leftarrow O_o \setminus \{(\text{claim q})\}$

      2. $C_o \leftarrow C_o \cup \{(\text{claim q})\}$

   3. for each q $\in$ D, if

      1. $\neg$known(claims(p), q), and

      2. q is not an applicability assumption

      then $O_p \leftarrow O_p \cup \{(\text{claim q})\}$

   4. $O_p \leftarrow O_p \cup \{(\text{argument}(A \cup D)c)\}$

This completes the definition of the set of discourse rules. We now turn to the subject of control and termination. How does pleading begin? What are a player's obligations at each turn? When is pleading over? Can one of the parties "win" at this stage, without the case proceeding to trial? These are the main questions to be answered next.

As is usual in games, the players take turns making moves until some termination criterion is satisfied. The defendant takes the first turn. (Recall that the plaintiff's claim is considered to be part of the initial background context.) On each turn, a player *must* continue to make moves until no *relevant* statement remains to be answered. However, an irrelevant statement *may* also be answered, so long as some move is applicable to it. The

pleading phase of the game is over when no relevant statements remain to be answered at
the beginning of a party's turn to move. Thus, to state these rules precisely, we first need
to define relevance.

Definition 15 (Relevance of Statements)

A statement is *relevant* if and only if the formula it is about is an issue. There are
four cases, one for each kind of statement. A statement of the form (claim c),
(argument A c) or (rebuttal A c D) is relevant if and only if c is an
issue. Finally, (denial s) is relevant if and only if s is relevant.

Now let us formulate the rules for pleading, in pseudocode, as a recursive procedure:

```
procedure plead (p: statements);
  var s: statements;
  var m: assertion;
begin
  if opponent(p) has relevant open statements then
    begin
      while open relevant statements remain do
        begin
          s := one of the statements;
          m := some move applicable to s;
          execute m;
        end;
      plead(oppenent(p));
    end;
end;
```

There are two choice points in this procedure, the choice of a statement to answer and
the choice of a move applicable to that statement. Although there are only finitely many
open statements to answer, for any such statement there are infinitely many applicable
moves. (For example, any new rule may be declared and the domain of rules is infinite.)
Heuristic methods will thus be required to play the game, whether it is to be played by a
person or an AI system.

The pleadings game is set up by the plaintiff first making a claim and the parties
agreeing, by some unspecified procedure, to sets of background sentences and rules. One
possibility is that they will agree to include a whole "knowledge base" about some area of
law. In the worst case these sets will be empty, and the game begins with a "clean slate".
Here is the initial state of the *background context*. Notice that the only open statement of
the plaintiff initially is the main claim.

```
const background = (c,S,R);
var plaintiff: statements := ({{(claim c)},{},{}});
var defendant: statements := ({},{},{});
```

The game is then started by the defendant taking the first turn:

```
plead(defendant);
```

At the end of pleading, the plaintiff is the "winner" if and only if there are no issues and the main claim, c, is conditionally entailed by the default theory ⟨K, facts⟩, where K is the final background context. For this purpose, the monotonic consequence relation for testing conditional entailment is the weaker, decidable known relation, not ⊨. The defendant "wins" if the main claim is not conditionally entailed, also using the known relation, and there are no issues to be decided. If neither party has won at this stage, the pleadings game ends in a "draw" and the case proceeds to trial.

In terms of the law of civil procedure, a party would be entitled to a *summary judgment* if he wins the pleadings game. A summary judgment is to be granted in favor of a party when [20, p. 1287] "there is no genuine issue of material fact and he is entitled to prevail as a matter of law."

5.4 A Detailed Example

This section demonstrates how the Pleadings Game is played, using the hypothetical case of Smith vs. Jones presented near the beginning of this chapter. The code shown in this section is from an actual transcript of a game played using the implementation described in the next chapter. Some of the commands available for interacting with the system will also be explained here, when they are first used.

Recall that Miller is the debtor on two loans secured by his ship, one from the plaintiff, Smith, and the other from the defendant, Jones. Miller has defaulted on both loans, and the practical question is which of the two security interests has priority. However, for the purposes of this example we will focus on a subsidiary question, whether or not Smith had perfected his security interest, as he claims. Let us suppose that pleading begins by Smith filing a complaint in which he claims that his security interest, s1, is perfected.

```
p: (argument bg
       (set (all (x y)
                 (if (and (preferred x y)
                          (antecedent x)
                          (ap y)
                          (ap x))
                     false))))
p: (complaint (perfected s1) bg)
```

The argument command defines an argument. Here bg is the background set of formulas assumed to be accepted by both players before the game begins. It contains just the formula discussed in section 5.2, for conveniently expressing a preference between two rules.

The `complaint` command sets up the game by adding the main claim, that `s1` is perfected, to the set of open statements of the plaintiff, and declares `bg` to be part of the background. It is the defendant's turn:

```
d: (statements)
(claim (perfected s1))

d: (issues)
((perfected s1))

d: (deny (claim (perfected s1)))
```

The defendant begins by first asking for information. The `statements` command lists the relevant open statements of the opponent. Here the only such statment is the main claim. The `issues` command lists the current set of issues, which also is just the claim the `s1` is perfected. The next move denies that the security interest is perfected, applying rule 4 of the Pleadings Game. A claim c may be denied only if it is not known to be entailed by the claims of the proponent. One effect of this move is to add

```
(denial (claim c))
```

to the open statements of the proponent, to give the opponent an opportunity to make a supporting argument. There are no further relevant, open statements to answer, so it's the plaintiff's turn.

```
p: (statements)
(denial (claim (perfected s1)))

p: (rule ucc-9-305 (p s g)
      if (and (secured-party s p)
              (collateral s g)
              (goods g)
              (possession g p))
      then  (perfected s))
```

The only statement to answer is the defendant's denial of the main claim. The plaintiff then declares a rule, `ucc-9-305`, which he believes is an adequate representation of UCC § 9-305, which says that a security interest in goods may be perfected by taking possession. The (`rule <symbol> ...`) form associates the symbol with the rule and then declares it, applying rule 6 of the Pleadings Game. The rule is intended to state that goods may be perfected by taking possession. Rules are translated into a set of formulas and a default and added to the background context. The name of the rule may not have been used previously, for some other rule. There are no other preconditions, and no response is required or permitted to the mere declaration of rules.

```
p: (argument a1 (apply ucc-9-305 (smith s1 ship1)))
```

Next, the plaintiff defines an argument, a1, using a function, apply, which constructs an argument by applying a rule to a tuple of terms. This is just a convenient utility.

```
p: (defend (denial (claim (perfected s1))) a1)
```

The plaintiff responds to the defendant's denial of his claim by asserting a supporting argument, applying rule 7 of the Pleadings Game. The system checks that the argument is indeed a supporting argument, using a theorem prover. When asserting a supporting argument the claim must be at issue. No formula in the argument may have been claimed by the opponent, but denied or not yet answered by the proponent. The argument may not be known to be inconsistent with the previous claims of the proponent. Finally, the proponent has the burden of proving that the argument is a supporting argument for the claim. One effect of this move is to concede all open claims of the opponent which are known to be entailed by this argument and the other claims of the proponent. Also, all claims (i.e., non-assumptions) of this argument which are not known to be entailed by the proponent's previous claims are asserted as new claims, to be answered individually by the opponent, as is the statement for the argument itself. It is the defendant's turn.

```
d: (statements)
(claim (backing ucc-9-305))
(claim (secured-party s1 smith))
(claim (collateral s1 ship1))
(claim (goods ship1))
(claim (possession ship1 smith))
(argument
     ((possession ship1 smith)
      (goods ship1)
      (collateral s1 ship1)
      (secured-party s1 smith)
      (backing ucc-9-305)
      (ap (inst ucc-9-305 (parms smith s1 ship1))))
     (perfected s1))
```

The defendant first asks which statements of the plaintiff are open and relevant. Notice that the claims of the plaintiff's supporting argument, a1, where added to his set of open statements, as was the argument itself.

```
d: (deny (claim (goods ship1)))
d: (concede (claim (collateral s1 ship1)))
d: (deny (claim (possession ship1 smith)))
d: (concede (claim (secured-party s1 smith)))
```

Here, the defendant simply denies and concedes some of these new claims, using rules 1 and 4 of the game. A claim may be conceded only if it is not known to be inconsistent with the claims of the proponent, because of the discourse norm against self-contradiction. Denials may not be conceded. A party is not permitted to retract claims.

```
d: (rule sma-1 (s g)
      if (and (collateral s g)
              (ship g)
              (not (filed s))
              (perfected s))
      then false)
```

A rule representing the (hypothetical) § 1 of the Ship Mortgage Act is declared. It states that it is inconsistent to suppose that a security interest in a ship is perfected if a financing statement has not been filed.

```
d: (argument r1
      (set (ship ship1)
           (collateral s1 ship1)
           (backing sma-1)
           (ap (inst sma-1 (parms s1 ship1)))
           (not (filed s1))))
```

The defendant defines an argument, r1, explicitly. The convenient apply function could not be used here, as the defendant does not want to concede that s1 is perfected, which is the plaintiff's main claim. (A difference function would have been of assistance here, but hasn't been implemented.)

```
d: (defend (argument a1 (perfected s1)) r1)
```

The defendant rebuts a1 with r1, applying rule 8 of the Pleadings Game. The system checks that r1 is a counterargument to a1 which is not known to be protected from it. To assert (defend (argument A c) R) the formula c must be an issue, no formulas in R may be unconceded claims of the opponent, and R must not be known to be inconsistent with the previous claims of the proponent. The proponent has the burden of proving that R is a counterargument which is not known to be defeated by A. If R is empty, A itself is shown to be inconsistent. Rebuttals and defeating counterarguments accept the claims of the argument they counter for the sake of argument, without conceding them. The effects of a rebuttal are similar to those of supporting arguments: All open claims known to be entailed by the rebuttal are conceded, all claims in the rebuttal which are not known to be entailed by the previous claims of the proponent are asserted as new claims, and finally, the statement (rebuttal A c R) is asserted. There are no further relevant statements to be answered, so it is the plaintiff's turn again.

```
p: (statements)
(denial (claim (goods ship1)))
(denial (claim (possession ship1 smith)))
(claim (if (filed s1) false))
(claim (backing sma-1))
(claim (ship ship1))
(rebuttal
     ((possession ship1 smith)
      (goods ship1)
      (collateral s1 ship1)
      (secured-party s1 smith)
      (backing ucc-9-305)
      (ap (inst ucc-9-305 (parms smith s1 ship1))))
      (perfected s1)
     ((ship ship1)
      (collateral s1 ship1)
      (backing sma-1)
      (ap (inst  sma-1 (parms s1 ship1)))
      (not (filed s1))))

p: (issues)
((ship ship1)
 (possession ship1 smith)
 (goods ship1)
 (perfected s1)
 (backing sma-1)
 (not (filed s1)))
```

Again, the system is first queried about the relevant open statements of the opponent, here the defendant, and the current set of issues.

```
p: (deny (denial (claim (possession ship1 smith))))
p: (deny (claim (not (filed s1))))
p: (deny (claim (backing sma-1)))
p: (concede (claim (ship ship1)))
p: (rule ucc-9-105-h (x)
       if (movable x)
       then (goods x)
       unless (money x))
p: (argument a2 (apply ucc-9-105-h (ship1)))
p: (defend (denial (claim (goods ship1))) a2)
```

In his last turn, the defendant denied that ships are goods and that the plaintiff has possession. Here, the plaintiff first denies the denial of his possession claim, using rule 5 of the game. Denying a denial, without asserting further arguments, just has the effect of leaving the statement open for trial. Next, he supports his claim that ships are goods by arguing that movable things are goods, according to UCC § 9-105(h).

```
p: (rule lex-posterior (r1 p1 a1 d1 r2 p2 a2 d2)
        if (and (conflicting (inst r1 p1) (inst r2 p2))
                (authority r1 a1 d1)
                (authority r2 a2 d2)
                (before d2 d1))
           then (preferred (inst r1 p1) (inst r2 p2))
           unless (applies (inst lex-superior
                                (parms r2 p2 a2 d2
                                       r1 p1 a1 d1)))))
p: (argument d1
        (apply lex-posterior
          (ucc-9-305 (parms smith s1 ship1) ca 1972
          sma-1 (parms s1 ship1) us 1960)))
p: (defend (rebuttal a1 (perfected s1) r1) d1)
```

Here, the plaintiff defeats the rebuttal to his argument that a security interest in a ship can be perfected by possession, by arguing that the UCC takes precedence over the Ship Mortgage Act, because it is newer.[3] He admits that *Lex Superior* has priority over *Lex Posterior*, by including it as an exception. The assertion of defeating counterarguments is regulated by rule 10 of the game.

A (defend (rebuttal A c R) D) move asserts a defeating counterargument D to the rebuttal R of A. The precondition and effects of this move are analogous to those for rebuttals, except that the proponent must show that D defeats R. If D is equivalent to A, then R is not a rebuttal of A, but this had not been known. The burden of proving defeat rests on the party in whose interest it is to show defeat. As D must defeat R, and not merely be protected from it, D may not include any assumptions which are not preferred to some assumption in R. An effect of this move is to assert the stronger argument (argument (union A D) c), giving the opponent another opportunity to construct another rebuttal.

There are no further relevant open statements, so it is the defendant's turn.

```
d: (issues)
((before 1960 1972)
 (authority ucc-9-305 ca 1972)
 (authority sma-1 us 1960)
 (conflicting
```

---

[3]The long parameter lists of the lex-posterior and lex-superior rules could have been avoided by using an existential quantifier in their antecedents. A variable need be a rule parameter only if it occurs in the conclusion or exception of the rule.

```
    (inst ucc-9-305 (parms smith s1 ship1))
    (inst sma-1 (parms s1 ship1)))
(movable ship1)
(possession ship1 smith)
(goods ship1)
(perfected s1)
(backing ucc-9-105-h)
(backing lex-posterior)
(backing sma-1)
(not (filed s1)))


d: (statements)
(denial (claim (not (filed s1))))
(denial (claim (backing sma-1)))
(claim (backing ucc-9-105-h))
(claim (movable ship1))
(argument
    ((movable ship1)
     (backing ucc-9-105-h)
     (ap (inst ucc-9-105-h (parms ship1))))
(goods ship1))
(claim (backing lex-posterior))
(claim
    (conflicting
        (inst ucc-9-305 (parms smith s1 ship1))
        (inst sma-1 (parms s1 ship1))))
(claim (authority ucc-9-305 ca 1972))
(claim (authority sma-1 us 1960))
(claim (before 1960 1972))
(argument
    ((before 1960 1972)
     (authority sma-1 us 1960)
     (authority ucc-9-305 ca 1972)
     (conflicting
        (inst ucc-9-305 (parms smith s1 ship1))
        (inst sma-1 (parms s1 ship1)))
     (possession ship1 smith)
     (goods ship1)
     (collateral s1 ship1)
     (secured-party s1 smith)
     (backing lex-posterior)
     (backing ucc-9-305)
     (ap (inst lex-posterior
                (parms ucc-9-305 (parms smith s1 ship1) ca
```

```
1972
                        sma-1 (parms s1 ship1) us 1960)))
     (ap (instance ucc-9-305 (parms smith s1 ship1))))
  (perfected s1))
```

As usual, the defendant first lists the current issues and relevant open statements.

```
d: (deny (denial (claim (not (filed s1)))))
d: (deny (denial (claim (backing sma-1))))
d: (deny (claim (backing ucc-9-105-h)))
d: (concede (claim (movable ship1)))
d: (concede (claim (backing lex-posterior)))
d: (concede
       (claim (conflicting
                  (inst ucc-9-305 (parms smith s1 ship1))
                  (inst sma-1 (parms s1 ship1)))))
d: (concede (claim (authority ucc-9-305 ca 1972)))
d: (concede (claim (authority sma-1 us 1960)))
d: (concede (claim (before 1960 1972)))
```

Next, several new claims by the plaintiff are denied or conceded. The backing claims for the representations of UCC § 9-105(h) and *Lex Posterior* are conceded, so these potential legal issues have been avoided. Notice that claims *about* UCC § 9-305 and the Ship Mortgage Act have been made and conceded, such that § 9-305 is California law enacted in 1972, without leaving the object-level.

```
d: (concede (argument a2 (goods ship1)))
```

Here, the defendant concedes the argument that ships are goods, because they are movable, although he had initially denied the claim that ship1 is a good. The concession of arguments is controlled by rule 2 of the game. An argument may be conceded at any time. The argument conceded is already known to be correct, as this is a precondition of making the argument in the first place. Conceding an argument gives up the opportunity to make a counterargument.

Conceding this argument does not violate the norm against self-contradiction, because the defendant never claimed that ships are not goods. He only demanded that the plaintiff bear his burden of proving that ship1 is goods. Denying a claim p is not the same as claiming (not p).

```
d: (rule lex-superior (r1 p1 a1 d1 r2 p2 a2 d2)
       if (and (conflicting (inst r1 p1) (inst r2 p2))
               (authority r1 a1 d1)
               (authority r2 a2 d2)
               (higher a1 a2))
```

```
     then (preferred (inst r1 p1) (inst r2 p2)))

d: (argument r3
      (apply lex-superior
            (sma-1 (parms s1 ship1) us 1960
             ucc-9-305 (parms smith s1 ship1) ca 1972))))

d: (defend (argument (union a1 d1) (perfected s1)) r3)
```

Here the defendant accepts the plaintiff's invitation to rebut *Lex Posterior* using the
Lex Superior exception.
   It's the plaintiff's turn again.

```
p: (statements)
(denial (claim (backing ucc-9-105-h)))
(claim (backing lex-superior))
(claim
    (conflicting
         (inst sma-1 (parms s1 ship1))
         (inst ucc-9-305 (parms smith s1 ship1))))
(claim (higher us ca))
(rebuttal
    ((before 1960 1972)
     (authority sma-1 us 1960)
     (authority ucc-9-305 ca 1972)
     (conflicting
          (inst ucc-9-305 (parms smith s1 ship1))
          (inst sma-1 (parms s1 ship1)))
     (possession ship1 smith)
     (goods ship1)
     (collateral s1 ship1)
     (secured-party s1 smith)
     (backing lex-posterior)
     (backing ucc-9-305)
     (ap (inst lex-posterior
               (parms ucc-9-305 (parms smith s1 ship1)
                      ca 1972 sma-1 (parms s1 ship1)
                      us 1960)))
     (ap (inst ucc-9-305 (parms smith s1 ship1))))
     (perfected s1)
    ((higher us ca)
     (authority ucc-9-305 ca 1972)
     (authority sma-1 us 1960)
     (conflicting
```

```
        (inst sma-1 (parms s1 ship1))
        (inst ucc-9-305 (parms smith s1 ship1)))
    (backing lex-superior)
    (applicable
        (instance lex-superior
            (parms sma-1 (parms s1 ship1) us 1960
                   ucc-9-305 (parms smith s1 ship1)
                   ca 1972)))))
```

```
p: (issues)
((higher us ca)
 (conflicting
     (inst sma-1 (parms s1 ship1))
     (inst ucc-9-305 (parms smith s1 ship1)))
 (possession ship1 smith)
 (goods ship1)
 (perfected s1)
 (backing ucc-9-105-h)
 (backing lex-superior)
 (backing sma-1)
 (not (filed s1)))
```

First the plaintiff lists the current issues and open, relevant statements.

```
p: (deny (denial (claim (backing ucc-9-105-h))))
p: (concede (claim (backing lex-superior)))
p: (concede
     (claim (conflicting
         (inst sma-1 (parms s1 ship1))
         (inst ucc-9-305 (parms smith s1 ship1)))))
p: (concede (claim (higher us ca)))
p: (concede (rebuttal (union a1 d1)(perfected s1) r3))
```

Then the plaintiff just denies or concedes the remaining open relevant statements, including the rebuttal $r3$. According to rule 3 of the game, any rebuttal may be conceded, but at the cost of losing the opportunity to assert a defeating counterargument.

After this last move, there are no relevant statements left to answer, for either party, so the game is over. There are issues remaining, so the Pleadings Game ends in a draw:

```
> (issues)
((possession ship1 smith)
 (perfected s1)
 (goods ship1)
```

```
(backing ucc-9-105-h)
(backing sma-1)
(not (filed s1)))
```

The show command lists all formulas of an argument. The symbol facts is bound
to the set of formulas which are currently accepted by both parties. At the end of this
particular game, the facts are:

```
> (show facts)
((secured-party s1 smith)
 (ship ship1)
 (collateral s1 ship1)
 (movable ship1)
 (before 1960 1972)
 (higher us ca)
 (authority ucc-9-305 ca 1972)
 (authority sma-1 us 1960)
 (conflicting
     (inst sma-1 (parms s1 ship1))
     (inst ucc-9-305(parms smith s1 ship1)))
 (conflicting
     (inst ucc-9-305(parms smith s1 ship1))
     (inst sma-1 (parms s1 ship1)))
 (backing lex-superior)
 (backing ucc-9-305)
 (backing lex-posterior))
```

5.5   The Trial Game

In this model of legal argumentation, if the pleadings game was played to a draw, the case
proceeds immediately to trial. The model does not account for the motions and "devices",
such as those designed to discover evidence, which may take place after pleading and
before trial.

Another simplification is that the only player at trial is the court. In practice, the
parties, through their attorneys, present evidence at the trial, for which there are elaborate
procedural rules. Also, the fact-finding and law-finding roles of the court are merged here,
although they may be divided between a judge and jury in practice.

The court has a relatively "passive" role in this model. The legal and factual issues
are completely determined by the parties, during pleading. The court's role is restricted
to choosing which of the claims to accept. It is not free to make arguments on its own
initiative.

Although there is only one player, the court, the trial is also modeled as a game, although it is much simpler than the one for pleading. Here the game board is called the proceedings, which includes the record of the pleadings.

Definition 16 (Proceedings)
> The *proceedings* is a triple $\langle r, A, R \rangle$, where r is the record of the pleadings, and A and R are sets of formulas for claims *accepted* and *rejected* by the court, respectively.

There are only two moves; the court may decide to accept or reject some claim.

Definition 17 (Decisions)
> There are two kinds of *decisions*, defined inductively as follows:

- If c is a formula, then (accept c) is a decision.

- If c is a formula, then (reject c) is a decision.

- There are no other decisions.

The accepted formulas become part of the facts. Technically, the definition of facts used during pleading is modified to include the accepted claims as well as those conceded by the parties. The issues are to be determined using this new definition.

Definition 18 (Facts at Trial)
> The facts are the conceded claims of both parties and the claims accepted by the court. If the record is $\langle b, \pi, \delta \rangle$, then
>
> $$\text{facts} = \{ f \mid (\text{claim } f) \in (C_{\pi} \cup C_{\delta}) \vee f \in A \}.$$

The court is not free to choose just any disputed claim to decide. Rather, the preconditions of the moves are designed so as to focus the court's attention on those issues with the most potential for reducing the number of issues which must ultimately be addressed to decide the case and to assure that no relevant arguments made by the parties are ignored. The concept of an *active issue* is introduced for this purpose. It plays a role analogous to that of relevant statements during pleading. Active issues are defined in section 5.7.

Here are the production rules prescribing when a decision is applicable, and the effect of making the decision.

move (accept c)

    preconditions

       •   c is an active issue.

    effects

      1. $A \leftarrow A \cup \{c\}$

move (reject c)

    preconditions

       •   c is an active issue.

    effects

      1. $R \leftarrow R \cup \{c\}$

The trial is over when no further move is possible, i.e., when no active issues remain. The prescribed procedure for conducting the trial, again in pseudocode, is:

```
const r: record = (b, pi, delta), where b is (c, L, D);
var A: set of L = {};
var R: set of L = {};

while there are applicable decisions do
  begin
    select an applicable decision;
    make the decision;
  end;
```

At the end of the trial, the court shall enter judgment for the plaintiff if and only if the main claim, c, is conditionally entailed by the default theory $\langle \mathbf{K}, \texttt{facts} \rangle$, where **K** is the final background context of the record. Otherwise the court shall enter judgment for the defendant. As in determining whether a party is entitled to a summary judgment after pleading, conditional entailment here is to be determined using the decidable known consequence relation, not the stronger $\models$ relation.

How much discretion does the court have in this model? On the one hand, the court is free to decide issues in any way it chooses. Here the model surely gives the court too much discretion. A more realistic model should at least address the law of evidence. For example, one constraint might be that at least some evidence supporting the claim must be presented at the trial before the court may accept the claim. On the other hand, the parties have complete control over the delineation of the factual and legal issues in this model. The court is not permitted to make arguments on its own initiative. Moreover, the court must address all of the arguments made by the parties, so long as they are relevant.

In the chapter on legal philosophy, I argued that legal judgments need not be formulated as deductive proofs. The main point was that deductive proof alone is neither sufficient nor necessary for limiting judicial discretion and subjecting judgments to review. It is not sufficient, as the court should be obligated to address the arguments made by the parties, and should not be permitted to merely assume that which is to be proven. It is not necessary, as elliptical arguments, in which uncontested premises remain unstated, should be permitted. The model presented in this chapter remains faithful to these points.

5.6 Dialectical Graphs

The issues surrounding a claim depend on the dialectical structure of arguments pro and contra the claim. This section precisely defines this dialectical structure. Recall that an argument is a set of formulas. Let A denote the domain of arguments. The following functions will be defined here:

supports : $L \rightarrow 2^A$
   The set of minimal supporting arguments for some formula.

rebuttals : $A \rightarrow 2^A$
   The set of minimal rebuttals of an argument.

defeaters : $A \rightarrow 2^A$
   The set of minimal defeating counterarguments of an argument.

Given a formula p, these three functions can be used to generate the complete *dialectical graph* of arguments and rebuttals for p. Each node of the graph is a set of formulas. The root of the graph is the singleton set $\{p\}$. The rest of the graph of arguments can be partitioned into *layers*. The arguments of the first layer are the minimal supporting arguments of p. The next layer consists of the rebuttals of these supporting arguments. The third layer consists of the defeating counterarguments of these rebuttals, and so on.

Figure 5.2 shows one path through the dialectical graph for the example at the beginning of this chapter, about whether or not a security interest in a ship had been perfected.

Let us begin by defining the supports function. This will be shown to be a well-founded, but tractable, form of abduction.

The supports : $L \rightarrow 2^A$ function maps a formula to the *minimal*, consistent

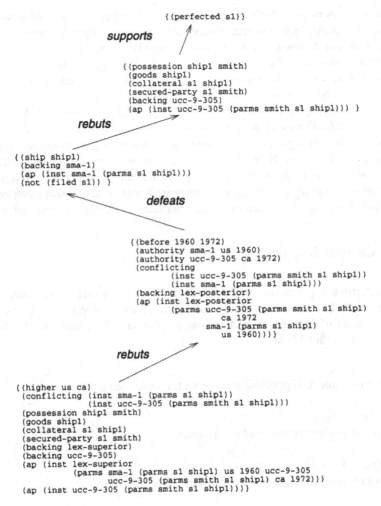

```
                                    {(perfected s1)}

            supports                      ↗
                                         /

                        {(possession ship1 smith)
                         (goods ship1)
                         (collateral s1 ship1)
                         (secured-party s1 smith)
                         (backing ucc-9-305)
                         (ap (inst ucc-9-305 (parms smith s1 ship1))) }

              rebuts                 ↗

     {(ship ship1)
      (backing sma-1)
      (ap (inst sma-1 (parms s1 ship1)))
      (not (filed s1)) }
                                    defeats
            ↖
                                       ↙

                        {(before 1960 1972)
                         (authority sma-1 us 1960)
                         (authority ucc-9-305 ca 1972)
                         (conflicting
                                (inst ucc-9-305 (parms smith s1 ship1))
                                (inst sma-1 (parms s1 ship1)))
                         (backing lex-posterior)
                         (ap (inst lex-posterior
                                (parms ucc-9-305 (parms smith s1 ship1)
                                            ca 1972
                                            sma-1 (parms s1 ship1)
                                            us 1960))))}

                rebuts              ↗

     {(higher us ca)
      (conflicting (inst sma-1 (parms s1 ship1))
                   (inst ucc-9-305 (parms smith s1 ship1)))
      (possession ship1 smith)
      (goods ship1)
      (collateral s1 ship1)
      (secured-party s1 smith)
      (backing lex-superior)
      (backing ucc-9-305)
      (ap (inst lex-superior
              (parms sma-1 (parms s1 ship1) us 1960 ucc-9-305
                     ucc-9-305 (parms smith s1 ship1) ca 1972)))
      (ap (inst ucc-9-305 (parms smith s1 ship1))))}
```

Figure 5.2. One Path in a Dialectical Graph

arguments known for the formula. As a first attempt, we might consider defining
supports as follows. Given a set of arguments A and a context Θ, $S \in$ supports(p)
if and only if:

1.   known(S, p), and

2.   ¬known($S,$ false), and

3.   ¬($\exists T . T \subset S \land$ known(S, p))

The problem of computing the supports of a formula using this definition can easily be shown to be isomorphic to the problem of finding the abductive "explanations" of a proposition from a set of propositional Horn clauses. More precisely, let $\langle A, \text{supports} \rangle$ be a structure, where A is a set of arguments. The supports function of this structure can be simulated by the explanations function of a $\langle C, \text{explanations} \rangle$ structure, where C is a set of propositional Horn clauses.

A literal is either a propositional letter p, called a positive literal, or its negation $\neg p$, a negative literal. Propositional Horn clauses are often defined as sets of literals with at most one positive literal. A clause $\{p, \neg q_1, ..., \neg q_n\}$, for $n \geq 0$, is interpreted to be equivalent to a formula in disjunctive normal form $p \vee \neg q_1 \vee ... \vee \neg q_n$. Such a formula is of course equivalent to the material implication $q_1 \wedge ... \wedge q_n \rightarrow p$. A definite Horn clause has exactly one positive literal. In the following, we will restrict our attention to definite clauses, which can be more conveniently represented as pairs $\langle \{q_1, ..., q_n\}, p \rangle$, where n may be 0.

With these preliminaries, the explanations function can be defined as follows .

Definition 19 (Propositional Horn Clause Abduction)
Given a set of propositional, definite Horn clauses, C, the *abductive explanations* of a propositional letter p, denoted explanations(p), are all sets of propositional letters E such that:

1. $E \cup C \models p$, and

2. $E \cup C$ is satisfiable, and

3. There does not exist a subset D of E such that $D \cup C \models p$.

This definition is similar to the definition of "minimal supports" given by Reiter and de Kleer in [101, p. 184], except that their definition is for arbitrary clauses, not just definite Horn clauses.

Now, it is easy to create a $\langle C, \text{explanations} \rangle$ structure to simulate the supports function of $\langle A, \text{supports} \rangle$. First a bijective function f mapping the arguments of A to propositional Horn clauses is constructed. This only requires naming each formula in A by a propositional letter. Let f^{-1} be the inverse function of f. Then S is a minimal supporting argument of a formula p, for which there is an argument in A, if and only if there is a set of propositional letters $\{q_1, ..., q_n\}$ such that:

$$S = \bigcup_1^n f^{-1} p_i$$

where

$$\{q_1, ..., q_n\} \in \text{explanations}(f(p))$$

Other than showing that the problem of determining the minimal supporting arguments of a formula can be viewed as an abduction problem, this result is interesting for another reason. As discussed by Selman and Levesque [112] this problem of generating the abductive explanations of a propositional letter from a set of propositional Horn clauses is NP-complete. (In the worst case, there can be exponentially many such explanations.) Thus, the problem of finding the minimal supporting arguments of a formula, using the above definition, is also NP-complete. Selman and Levesque have shown that the problem of finding a *single*, nontrivial explanation from a set of propositional Horn clauses can be solved in time $O(kn)$, where k is the number of propositional letters and n is the number of occurences of literals in the set of Horn clauses. But this result is of no assistance to us here, as we are interested in testing whether a formula is an issue, which requires, in the worst case, all minimal supporting arguments to be examined.

This result is unsettling. One could just accept that there is no efficient algorithm for computing minimal supporting arguments, and thus issues, and leave it at that. However, this contradicts my intuitions about the concept of an issue. In a dispute about some subject, the parties know what issues have been raised. Recalling the issues is not a hard problem. Constructing arguments and rebuttals can be hard, or even undecidable, but keeping track of the arguments which have been made, and the dependencies between arguments and issues, should be an easy task. To use the metaphor of civil procedure, this should be a job for the *clerk* of the court. The arguments made in the pleadings of the parties are filed with the clerk, who should then be able to report about the record of the pleadings, including listing the issues. This should be a simple, bookkeeping task. The burden of solving any undecidable or hard problems should be distributed fairly among the players, rather than delegated to the clerk. Thus, rather than accept the intractability of the problem of generating supporting arguments, I view this as an indication of a potential flaw in the model of argumentation.

The source of this unwanted computational complexity must be the third prong of the provisional definition of supports above, regarding minimality. The first two conditions just check whether a tuple is a member of the known relation, which is a tractable problem of linear complexity, as mentioned previously. To gain tractability, let us weaken this minimality requirement. Instead of requiring that there not be a subset D of E such that the formula of interest, p, is known to be entailed by D, let us instead require merely that no smaller argument for p than E has been made by one of the parties. This shifts the burden of finding minimal arguments from the clerk to the parties, giving us the following definition.

Definition 20 (Supports)
    Given a set of arguments A and a context Θ, an argument $S \in$ supports(p) if and only if:

1.   known(S, ϕ),

2.   ¬known(S, false), and

3. $\neg(\exists T . T \subset S \wedge \langle T, p \rangle \in A)$

What has been lost by adopting this tractable version of the idea of minimal supporting arguments? It brings with it the risk that the parties will waste resources arguing about claims which could have been shown to be irrelevant to the main claim. However, as each party bears the burden of proving his claims, there is a natural incentive to avoid irrelevant claims. Thus, from a pragmatic point of view, there is no need for the clerk to try to solve the same hard problem that presumably one of the parties has already tried to solve.

Using this tractable definition of minimal supporting arguments, has its relationship to abduction also been lost? Perhaps minimal supporting arguments could be considered an incomplete form of abduction, in Selman's sense [113]. However, this characterization is not quite satisfactory, as the adjective "complete" here seems out of place. The minimal supporting arguments of a formula are not a subset of some "complete" set of abductive explanations. (Indeed they are a *superset* of the minimal supporting arguments generated using the definition isomorphic to propositional Horn clause abduction.) Instead, I will argue that the supports function is simply a tractable instance of a more abstract concept of abduction.

To clarify this idea, a suitably abstract definition of abduction is needed. There is no one authoritative definition of abduction. According to the *Encyclopedia of Philosophy* [31, vol. 5, p. 57], abduction is:

(1) A syllogism whose major premise is known to be true but whose minor premise is merely probable. (2) C. S. Pierce's name for the type of reasoning that yields from a given set of facts an explanatory hypothesis for them.

The second definition is still widely used [26; 60; 94]. Here, abduction is the process of inferring potential causes or explanations of observed effects from general knowledge about how the world functions. That is, according to this view, abduction is another name for diagnosis. It is a kind of task, or a class of problems, rather than a particular kind of *formal* reasoning. From this point of view, it is not incoherent to speak of solving abduction problems deductively [32].

Others, however, contrast deduction, abduction and induction, using purely formal criteria. Hector Levesque, e.g., has adopted this view [64, p. 1061] :

Using the terminology of C. S. Pierce, given sentences α, β and $(\alpha \rightarrow \beta)$, there are three operations one can consider: from α and $(\alpha \rightarrow \beta)$, one might *deduce* β; from α and β, one might *induce* $(\alpha \rightarrow \beta)$; and from β and $(\alpha \rightarrow \beta)$, one might *abduce* α.

Abduction can be thought of as a form of hypothetical reasoning. To ask what can be abduced from β is to ask for an α which, in conjunction with background knowledge, is sufficient to account for β. When α and β are about the physical world, this normally involves finding a cause α for an observed effect β. ... But not all abduction is concerned with cause and effect. If we happen to know that Marc is 3 or 4 years old, the fact that he is not yet 4 does not *explain* his being 3, although it does imply it, given what is known. ...

Levesque goes on to propose a very general description of abduction, in terms of the "simplest explanations" of a proposition in an "epistemic" state. Every particular form of abduction has a "belief operator" and a partial order on explanations, where the smallest explanations in the order or considered to be the "simplest". For example, Levesque proposes the number of distinct literals in an explanation as a measure of simplicity.

I would like to propose a similar signature for abduction here. Let **A** denote the domain of arguments, 2^L. An abduction structure is a quadruple $\langle L, \vDash, <, e \rangle$, where:

1. L is some logical language (i.e., a possibly infinite set of formulas);

2. $\vDash$ is a consequence relation on $\mathbf{A} \times L$;

3. $< : L \rightarrow 2^{\mathbf{A} \times \mathbf{A}}$ maps a formula to a strict partial order on arguments (denoted $<_p$, for a formula p) and

4. $e : \mathbf{A} \times L \rightarrow 2^{\mathbf{A}}$ is a function satisfying the following properties. $E \in e(A, p)$ only if:

    a. $E \cup A \vDash p$,

    b. $E \cup A \nvDash \texttt{false}$, and

    c. There does not exist an argument D such that

        i. $D \cup A \vDash p$,

        ii. $D \cup A \nvDash \texttt{false}$, and

        iii. $D <_p E$.

The principal innovation here is to make the ordering on "explanations" dependent on the formula to be explained.

This signature is general enough to capture several common forms of abduction. Propositional Horn clause abduction, for example, is an abduction structure $\langle L, \models, <, e \rangle$, where L is restricted to propositional Horn clauses, and $D <_p E$ if and only if $D \subset E$. e here is a partial function: $e(C, p)$ is defined only if C is a set of definite Horn clauses and p is a propositional literal. Recall that a signature like this states only the defining properties of a class of structures. Particular instances may satisfy additional constraints.

The ordering relation on explanations used for propositional Horn clause abduction is partially *semantic*, as it prefers the smallest sets of formulas which *entail* the formula to be explained. Entailment is a semantic concept. However, in many applications of abduction, the preference relation on explanations is defined by purely syntactic criteria. Levesque goes so far as to argue that syntactic criteria are *necessary* to capture some notion of simplicity [64, p. 1063].

David Poole's Theorist system also uses a syntactic method to order explanations; the preferred explanations consist only of formulas drawn from a set of *hypotheses* [94; 92]. A Theorist structure is a quadruple $\langle L, F, H, f \rangle$, where L is a logical language, F is a set of closed formulas from L, called the "facts", and H is a set of hypotheses. A *scenario* is a subset D of H such that $D \cup F$ is (classically) consistent. The *explanations* of a formula p in Poole's system, $f(p)$, are every scenario D such that $D \cup F$ (classically) entails p. Thus, a Theorist structure $\langle L, F, H, f \rangle$ is an abduction structure $\langle L, \models, <, e \rangle$, where $\models$ is classical entailment, $D <_p E$ is always false, and $e(F, p) = f(p)$. Notice that explanations are not ordered in Theorist. Also, as in the previous example, e here is a partial function; it is defined only for F.

As a final example, here is the abduction structure for my theory of minimal supporting arguments. Given a set of arguments A and a context Θ, the abduction structure is

$$\langle L, \text{known}_{\langle A, \Theta \rangle}, <, \text{supports} \rangle,$$

where L is the set of first-order formulas occurring in A and $D <_p E$ if and only if $D \subset E$ and $\langle D, p \rangle \in A$.

The `rebuttals` and `defeaters` functions remain to be defined. These are the smallest known arguments which are presumed to rebut an argument, or known to defeat an argument, respectively.

These definitions use Geffner and Pearl's syntactic test for whether an assumption is necessarily preferred to some assumption in a set of assumptions, except that here we use the decidable `known` relation in the test, instead of $\models$.

Once it is known that one argument defeats another, no additional amount of inference will require this conclusion to be retracted, as the `known` relation is monotonic. Recall, however, that one argument is a rebuttal of another only if this other argument does not contain a defeating counterargument of the first argument. Thus, it is only *presumed* that one argument rebuts another when using the weak `known` relation to check whether or not the other argument is protected. If after additional reasoning it becomes known that it is protected, then this presumption should be retracted.

Definition 21 (Rebuttals and Defeaters)

Let A and B be arguments. A and B are *known counterarguments* if and only if known($A \cup B$, false). A is a *known defeating counterargument* of B if and only if they are known counterarguments and for every assumption $d \in A$ it is the case that known($\{q, d\} \cup D$), false), where q is the antecedent of the default instance for the assumption d and D is the set of assumptions in B. A is *known to be protected* from B if and only if A contains a subargument which is known to defeat B. A is a *presumed rebuttal* of B if and only if they are known counterarguments and B is not known to be protected from A.

$A \in$ rebuttals(B) if and only if:

1. A is presumed to be a rebuttal of B, and

2. There does not exist a subset of A which is presumed to be a rebuttal of B.

$A \in$ defeaters(B) if and only if:

1. A is known to be a defeater of B, and

2. There does not exist a subset of A which is known to be a defeater of B.

5.7   The Concept of an Issue

The concept of an *issue* has been used in a number of places: in the preconditions of defenses, the definition of relevant statements and in the *active issues* of the Trial Game. In this section the concept of issue will be formally defined. The theory of issues presented here is a refinement of previous work of mine [46; 47]. There are however some important differences, due first of all to the adoption of Geffner and Pearl's system of conditional entailment as the basis for defeasible reasoning.[4] Using conditional entailment, the concept of issue can no longer be restricted to formulas in minimal arguments supporting some formula. Propositions in rebuttals and defeating counterarguments must also be considered. Recall for example that defeating counterarguments are supersets of minimal supporting arguments.

Minimality still has a role to play however. Now we are interested in minimal counterarguments, as well as minimal supporting arguments. For example, if A is an argument and D is a rebuttal of A, then intuitively a proposition p should be an issue *because of D* only if $D \setminus \{p\}$ is not a rebuttal of A.

---

[4]Relying on David Poole's work in [93], I had thought defeasible legal reasoning could be modeled using abduction. However, it is now clear that the kind of defeasible reasoning possible with abduction is too limited for modeling the variety of exceptions found in Article Nine.

There is another complication to be considered. Suppose that $\{a, b\}$ is the only argument supporting c. Both a and b have been denied. In a defense to the denial of a, a supporting argument $\{d, e\}$ has been made. Both of these claims have also been denied. No counterarguments have been made. What are the issues concerning c? Using the theory of issues in [47], the answer would be just $\{a, b\}$, as these are the only members of minimal supporting arguments of c. In the context of our discourse model of argumentation, this seems intuitively wrong. The formulas of the argument supporting a surely should also be issues, to allow the proponent an opportunity to defend them. These considerations lead to a new definition of issue.

The issues of a claim depend on arguments in the dialectical graph for the claim. The exact structure of the dialectical graph is unimportant. The function *join* constructs the union of all the arguments in the dialectical graph for a claim by iterating over the successive layers of the graph, starting with the minimal supporting arguments of the claim.

Definition 22 (Join)
  The function

$$successors : 2^{\mathbf{A}} \to [2^{\mathbf{A}}]$$

generates the *successor layers* of a set of supporting arguments. Let S be a set of supporting arguments $\{A_1, ..., A_n\}$. If S is empty then $successors(S)$ is the empty sequence. Otherwise, let R be the union of the rebuttals of each argument in S

$$R = \bigcup_{1}^{n} \texttt{rebuttals}(A_i)$$

and D be the union of the defeaters of each rebuttal

$$D = \bigcup_{1}^{n} \texttt{defeaters}(R_i).$$

Then,

$$\texttt{successors}(S) = R, D, \texttt{successors}(D).$$

Let append denote sequence catenation. Now

$$\texttt{join}(p) = \bigcup_{1}^{n} D_i,$$

where

$$[D_1, ..., D_n] = \texttt{append}(\texttt{supports}(p), \texttt{successors}(\texttt{supports}(p)))$$

A formula q is an issue with respect to some claim p if and only if q is a claim which is not known to be derivable from Θ, the context of conceded formulas, and is a member of the dialectical graph for p or, recursively, an issue with respect to some formula in the graph.

Definition 23 (Issues)

A formula q is an *issue* relative to a *goal* formula p, denoted $\mathrm{issue}(q, p)$, if and only if

1. q is a claim,

2. $\neg\mathrm{known}_{\langle A,\Theta\rangle}(\varnothing, q)$, and

3. a. $q = p$,

    b. $q \in \mathrm{join}(p)$, or

    c. $\exists r \in \mathrm{join}(p).\mathrm{issue}(q, r)$.

"One small blemish" [47, p. 106] of my former theory is corrected here. There, rebuttals did not raise issues. Only the propositions of arguments not known to be inconsistent were issues, and rebuttals are, by definition, inconsistent. The new definition checks whether a formula is a member or any rebuttals, as well as supporting arguments.

In Figure 5.3, the issues regarding (perfected s1) have been highlighted. The figure shows the relevant portion of the dialectical graph for (perfected s1), as well as the graph for one of its issues, (goods ship1). Notice that the question of whether or not § 9-105(h) is authority for the proposition that movable things are goods is an issue relative to (perfected s1) because it is an issue in the dialectical graph for (goods ship1). All of the other formulas in these graphs are not issues, either because they are known to be a consequence of the context (i.e., the conceded formulas), or because they are applicability assumptions.

In the model of the trial, the court may decide an issue only if it is *active*. This restriction is designed to further two goals:

1. To minimize costs and avoid the decision of unnecessary legal issues, those issues should be decided first which have the most potential of making other issues moot. This can be achieved by requiring the issues of supporting arguments to be decided before those of rebuttals. If an issue of the supporting argument is decided against its proponent, the rebuttal becomes moot. Thus, the issues of higher levels in the dialectical graph should be considered before those of lower levels.

2. The court should be obligated to address relevant arguments brought forward by the parties. Thus, if an argument A for an issue p has been made, the issues of A should be decided before p may be decided directly. However, once the issues of A are decided, p may cease to be an issue and no longer require a decision.

To understand how both of these goals can be achieved, we need to first define the *leaves* of an argument. Given a formula and the supports function, an *and/or graph* of formulas can be generated. (If the formula has no supporting arguments, then the only node

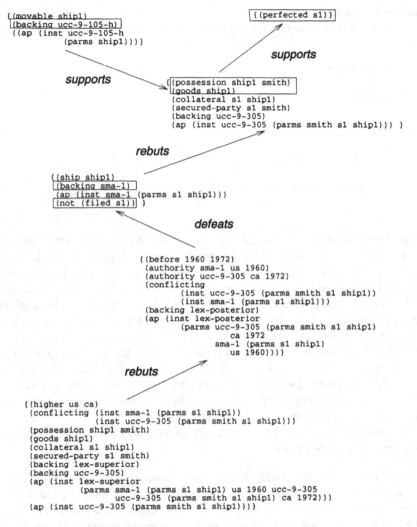

```
{(movable ship1)                              {(perfected s1)}
 (backing ucc-9-105-h)
  ((ap (inst ucc-9-105-h
              (parms ship1))))}
                                                        supports

            supports        {(possession ship1 smith)
                             (goods ship1)
                             (collateral s1 ship1)
                             (secured-party s1 smith)
                             (backing ucc-9-305)
                             (ap (inst ucc-9-305 (parms smith s1 ship1))) }

                rebuts

{(ship ship1)
 (backing sma-1)
  (ap (inst sma-1 (parms s1 ship1)))
 (not (filed s1))} }

                    defeats

            {(before 1960 1972)
             (authority sma-1 us 1960)
             (authority ucc-9-305 ca 1972)
             (conflicting
                    (inst ucc-9-305 (parms smith s1 ship1))
                    (inst sma-1 (parms s1 ship1)))
             (backing lex-posterior)
             (ap (inst lex-posterior
                    (parms ucc-9-305 (parms smith s1 ship1)
                             ca 1972
                             sma-1 (parms s1 ship1)
                             us 1960))))}

                rebuts

{(higher us ca)
 (conflicting (inst sma-1 (parms s1 ship1))
              (inst ucc-9-305 (parms smith s1 ship1)))
 (possession ship1 smith)
 (goods ship1)
 (collateral s1 ship1)
 (secured-party s1 smith)
 (backing lex-superior)
 (backing ucc-9-305)
 (ap (inst lex-superior
            (parms sma-1 (parms s1 ship1) us 1960 ucc-9-305
                   ucc-9-305 (parms smith s1 ship1) ca 1972)))
 (ap (inst ucc-9-305 (parms smith s1 ship1))))}
```

Figure 5.3. The issues regarding (`perfected s1`)

in the graph will be the root node, for the formula itself.) Notice that these and/or graphs are orthogonal to the dialectical graph of arguments concerning a formula. Each formula in the dialectical graph has its own and/or graph. A *leaf* of such an and/or graph is a node which has no successors in the graph. The leaves of an argument are the union of the leaves of the and/or graphs for each formula in the argument.

Definition 24 (Leaves of an Argument)

Let $\{p_1, ..., p_n\}$ be an argument. The leaves : $2^L \to 2^L$ of an argument are defined recursively as follows:

$$\text{leaves}(\{p_1, ..., p_n\}) = \bigcup_1^n l(p_i),$$

where the auxiliary function l is defined as follows.
If supports$(p) = \varnothing$ then $l(p) = \{p\}$. Otherwise let

$$\{S_1, ..., S_n\} = \text{supports}(p)$$

in

$$l(\{S_1, ..., S_n\}) = \bigcup_1^n \text{leaves}(S_i).$$

The active issues of a *layer* of a dialectical graph of arguments are the claims of the union of the leaves of all arguments of that layer. The active issues of the *trial proceedings* are the active issues of the first layer with active issues of the complete dialectical graph for the main claim.

Definition 25 (Active Issues)

Let first : $(2^A \to A) \times [2^A] \to A$ be a function which iterates over the 2^A sequence looking for the first set of arguments for which the $2^A \to A$ function maps to a non-empty argument. If one is found, then first returns this argument, otherwise the empty argument is returned. Let active : $2^A \to 2^L$ be the following function. If L is a layer $\{A_1, ..., A_n\}$ of a dialectical graph of arguments, then active(L) is the set of *issues* in

$$\bigcup_1^n \text{leaves}(A_i).$$

Now, let ϕ be the main claim of the trial proceedings, $S = \text{supports}(\phi)$, and

$$[L_1, ..., L_n] = \text{append}(S, \text{successors}(S)).$$

The *active issues* of the proceedings are

$$\text{first}(\text{active}, [L_1, ..., L_n]).$$

To return to our example, Figure 5.4 shows the and/or graph for the arguments of the first layer of the dialectical graph for the main claim (perfected s1), which was shown above in Figure 5.7. The issues of this and/or graph, which happens to be a tree, are highlighted. (All of the other formulas have been conceded or are applicability assumptions.) As the graph does contain issues, they are the only issues which are active at the beginning of trial, and must be decided first.

One of these issues is a legal question, (backing ucc-9-105-h), and the other is a question of fact, (possession ship1 smith). In this model, issues of fact and law are distinguished syntactically. The only legal issues are backing claims. The question of possession could have involved legal issues, but the parties didn't make arguments raising such issues, so it remains a question of fact in this case. The Trial Game does not impose an order on legal and factual issues. In a more elaborate model, presumably factual issues should be tried first, perhaps by a jury, to avoid deciding legal questions unnecessarily. In our example, if the trier of fact decides that the plaintiff does not have possession of the ship, then all other issues become moot and the plaintiff looses.

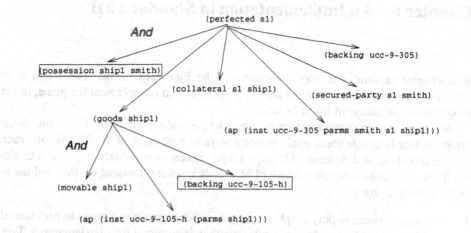

Figure 5.4. Active Issues at the Beginning of the Trial Game

Chapter 6   An Implementation in Standard ML

This chapter explains one way to implement the Pleadings Game. The intent is to provide just enough detail to allow any AI programmer to reimplement the game, in the programming language of his or her choice.

My own implementation was programmed in Standard ML [50; 87], a functional programming language comparable in many ways to languages of the Lisp family, such as Common Lisp and Scheme. Although Lisp is much more widely used for artificial intelligence programming than Standard ML (SML), several features of SML led me to prefer it for this project:

1. It has an expressive polymorphic type system which permits a much larger class of typing errors to be caught at compile time than is common for Lisp languages. Type declarations are optional; they are inferred by the compiler. Although the type system is somewhat more restrictive than Lisp's, this has not been a problem in practice. SML's type system is a good compromise between expressiveness and safety.

2. It has an advanced module system, which allows programs to be designed and organized in a way which very closely resembles algebraic specifications. The module system also supports type-safe, separate compilation and information hiding.

3. There are several good compilers available, including an excellent, free and portable compiler, Standard ML of New Jersey.[1]

The rest of this chapter is organized as follows. The next section provides a very brief overview of SML's module system. This is followed by an overview of the modules and their relationships in my implementation of the Pleadings Game. Finally, there are sections describing each of the main modules of the system in somewhat more detail.

6.1   Standard ML's Module System

As SML is not very well known, I will assume as little knowledge about the language as possible. It will be assumed, however, that the reader is familiar with functional

---

[1]This compiler is available for most Unix workstations and Macintosh computers via Internet FTP, from `research.att.com`, in the `dist/ml` directory.

170

programming in general. For more information about SML, Paulson's *ML for the Working Programmer* [87] is a good programming manual and introduction to the language.

SML's module system is likely to be the most unfamiliar part of the language. There are three language constructs at the module level:

Structures.

A structure is a collection of values, types and exceptions. A structure may also include substructures. That is, structures may be organized in a hierarchy. A *value* may be any object-level data, including functions, which are "first-class" objects. Exceptions, types, and the module-level constructs explained here, such as structures, are not values.

Signatures.

A signature is a *description* of structures. Unlike the interfaces of some module systems, a signature need not be associated with a single structure. Rather, any number of structures may *match* or *satisfy* a signature. Conversely, a structure may satisfy more than one signature. This is not unlike the relationship between formulas and models in logic.

Functors.

A functor is a mapping from structures to structures. They may be viewed as functions at the module level.

To help make these ideas clearer, here is a standard example, for the queue abstract data type. Here is one possible signature for queues:

```
signature QUEUE =
  sig
    structure E : ELEMENT

    type queue

    exception EmptyQueue

    val empty_queue : queue
    val enqueue : queue -> E.element -> queue

    val empty : queue -> bool

    val dequeue : queue -> (E.element * queue)
    val front : queue -> E.element
  end;
```

Structures which match the QUEUE signature have a substructure E, for the type of elements of the queue, an exception, EmptyQueue, a constructur function,

empty_queue, and four other operations on queues. enqueue adds a element to a
queue, empty tests whether a queue has elements, dequeue returns a pair of the front
of the queue and the rest of the queue, and front returns the front element without
removing it. The EmptyQueue exception is raised by dequeue and front if the queue
is empty.

The signature specifies the syntax of a module. In a formal language for algebraic
specifications, there would also be the possibility of formally specifying the semantics
of modules for this signature. In SML, the semantics is given by a natural language
description, as I have done here for the QUEUE signature, perhaps augumented by a clear
reference implementation in SML.

Here is a simple structure which implements queues of integers using lists. (A list
of integers in SML is represented as [1,3,4].) It is not necessary for our purposes to
understand this code in detail. However, it may be interesting to notice that functions can
be defined in SML using pattern matching over data structures.

```
structure Queue1  =
struct

    structure E =
        struct
            type element = int
        end

    type queue =  E.element list

    exception EmptyQueue

    val empty_queue = []

    fun empty [] = true
      | empty _ = false

    fun enqueue [] x = [x]
      | enqueue q  x = q@[x]

    fun dequeue [] = raise EmptyQueue
      | dequeue (hd::tl) = (hd,tl)

    fun front [] = raise EmptyQueue
      | front (hd::tl) = hd

end;
```

An SML compiler can check that `Queue1` indeed matches the `QUEUE` signature. As mentioned previously, it will also match other signatures, such as the *empty signature*, `sig end`, or any portion of the `QUEUE` signature, such as

```
sig
    type queue
    val empty : queue -> bool
end
```

The `Queue1` structure is restricted to queues of integers. To avoid having to reimplement queues for other types of elements, an SML functor may be used to abstract the element type from the implementation. For example:

```
functor ListQueue(E : ELEMENT) =
struct
    structure E = E
    type queue = E.element list
    exception EmptyQueue
    val empty_queue = []
    ...
end;
```

The `ListQueue` functor can be used to generate `QUEUE` structures for any kind of element. For example, to create a structure for queues of strings, one could type:

```
structure StringQueue =
    ListQueue (struct
                  type element = string
               end);
```

This description of SML's module system should be sufficient for our purposes here. Other features of SML will be explained only as necessary to clarify some aspect of the implementation of the Pleadings Game.

6.2 Modules Overview

Six functors are of primary interest to us here:

Cil.
This is a theorem prover for McCarty's Clausal Intuitionistic Logic [80; 81].

Rules.

This module implements my language for defeasible rules with explicit exceptions, and is responsible for mapping these rules into default theories for conditional entailment.

Mrms.

This is my *Minimal Reason Maintenance System*. It caches theorems and computes the minimal, supporting arguments for a formula, as defined by my tractable theory of abduction.

Record.

This module implements the representation of the record, which is the "game board" of the Pleadings Game, including the statements of the parties and the background. It also includes various functions for querying the state of the record after each move.

Ce.

This is a theorem prover for Geffner and Pearl's defeasible logic of *conditional entailment*. In the Pleadings Game, this module is also responsible for testing whether proposed arguments are rebuttals or defeating counterarguments.

Clerk.

This module is reponsible for mediating the Pleadings Game. It controls access to the record and checks whether the preconditions of a move are satisfied before permitting the record to be modified according to the effects of the move.

To construct an executable program for the Pleadings Game, these functors are applied as shown in Figure 6.1. In terms of its functionality, a functor may be viewed as a source code generator, such as the Unix parser generator utility, yacc. (However, source code is *not* actually generated here.) Viewed this way, the process of applying functors to create an executable program is comparable to generating, compiling and linking modules using more conventional languages.

In this figure, the boxes represent functors and the circles represent structures. The figure gives only a rough overview of the relationships between the main functors and structures of the Pleadings Game. Not everything available in a structure may be required by the functor using it. For example, the Ce functor requires only a small portion of the facilities made available by the Rd structure, representing the record. Just what each of these functors requires and produces will be explained in more detail below.

The figure is drawn so that the top-level modules are at the top. The C structure is the main structure of the Pleadings Game. It contains the *read-eval-print* loop for playing the game. (A graphical user interface would be quite useful, but has not been implemented.)

Although it would be possible to describe these modules in either a top-down or bottom-up fashion, I have chosen the latter alternative. It has the advantage that each feature will be explained before it is used.

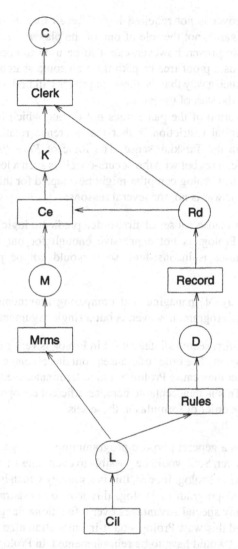

Figure 6.1. Main Functors and Structures

6.3   Cil — A Theorem Prover for Clausal Intuitionistic Logic

Recall that to assert a supporting argument A for a claim $p;$, the proponent has the burden of proving $A \cup \Theta \models p$, where Θ is the current context of conceded formulas. Also, when asserting a counterargument D of an argument A, the propopent has the burden of proving $D \cup A \cup \Theta \models$ false.

As it is the proponent who has the burden of proof, and not the mediator, strictly speaking a theorem prover is not required here. (Recall that the model plays the role of the mediator of the game, not the role of one of the players.) A *proof checker* would be sufficient. A theorem prover, however, can also be used to check proofs. Instead of representing the proof as a proof tree or path through some search space, the argument itself is represented in such a way that the theorem prover will find a proof within resource bounds agreed upon at the start of the game.

The formal specification of the game does not dictate which logic to use for these purposes. The only formal restriction is that the inference relation of the logic be a *consequence relation* in the Tarskian sense. The logic of *Pure Prolog*, that is, Prolog without its imperative features but with the occurs-check, is such a logic. So it would make sense to ask whether a fast Prolog compiler might be adapted for this purpose.

Unfortunately, the answer is no, for several reasons:

1. The definite Horn clause subset of first-order predicate logic, which is the subset realized in Pure Prolog, is not expressive enough for our purposes. No set of definite Horn clauses is inconsistent, so it would not be possible to represent counterarguments.

2. We need some way of managing and comparing arguments, which are *sets* of formulas. A Prolog program, however, is but a single argument in this sense.

3. The simple, depth-first search strategy used in Prolog is very sensitive to the order of clauses in the program. The order of clauses contains crucial control information. A poorly chosen order may cause Prolog to fail to terminate, even when trying to prove trivial theorems. This is unacceptable here, as efficient set operations on arguments do not preserve the order of formulas in these sets.

Prolog, of course, is a general purpose programming language and not just, or even primarily, a theorem prover. So it would be possible to overcome all of these limitations by writing a theorem prover *in* Prolog. Indeed, this is a strategy which is often recommended. For those who prefer to program in Prolog, this may be an attractive alternative, but Prolog does not offer any special advantages over a functional language such as Lisp or Standard ML when used this way. Prolog's built-in unification algorithm, search strategy and database features all would have to be reimplemented, in Prolog, to write the kind of theorem prover required for the Pleadings Game.

Having decided to implement a more powerful theorem prover in Standard ML, it still remained to choose an appropriate logic. I chose Thorne McCarty's Clausal Intuitionistic Logic (CIL), because it is a conservative extension to Pure Prolog with the additional expressiveness required for the Pleadings Game. In particular, CIL supports a monotonic form of negation, as required for counterarguments. The theorems of the logic are a subset of the classical theorems, so a theorem prover for CIL may be viewed, like Pure Prolog, as an incomplete prover for classical logic. Its incompleteness is not, however, ad hoc, but well-defined by McCarty's intuitionistic semantics [80].

Here is a Standard ML signature for that part of the CIL prover of interest to us here.

The components of this signature will be explained in detail below.

```
signature CIL =
sig
    type term

    val bottom : term      (* "false" in surface syntax *)
    val constant : symbol -> term
    val number : int -> term
    val term : { args  : term list ref,
                 arity : int ref,
                 symr  : symbol ref } -> term

    type wff

    val atom : term -> wff
    val all : symbol list * wff -> wff
    val implication : term * wff list -> wff

    type formula

    structure F : sig
                    type element
                    val bottom : element
                    val eq : element -> element -> bool
                    val less : element -> element -> bool
                  end

    sharing type formula = F.element

    val intern : wff -> formula
    val extern : formula -> wff
    val eqFormula : formula -> formula -> bool

    structure C : SET
    sharing type formula = C.E.element

    type context
    sharing type context = C.set

    val initialDepth : int ref
    val depthLimit : int ref
    val step : int ref
```

```
      exception Fail
      val entails : context -> formula -> bool
end
```

The language of CIL is also a subset of first-order logic. The constructor functions for the `term` and `wff` types, above, define its abstract syntax. Essentially, CIL extends Pure Prolog with *embedded implications* and *universal quantification* in the bodies of clauses. The heads of clauses, and of embedded implications, are restricted to atomic formulas, as before. (`not p`) is just syntactic sugar for (`if p false`), using my concrete syntax.[2]

Contexts are sets of formulas, managed by the C substructure.

For reasons discussed below, a formula is not represented as a `wff`, but as an index into a table of formulas. The `intern` and `extern` functions are used to convert between `wff` and `formula` values.

The F substructure and the *sharing constraint* are used to state that the `formula` type is partially ordered with a bottom element. This information will be used, below, to create a reason maintenance structure for caching CIL proofs.

For our purposes, the most important function of the CIL signature is `entails`, which searches for a proof of a formula from a set of formulas, using the *iterative deepening* strategy. The `entails` function raises the `Fail` exception if it fails to find a proof within the depth limit. Iterative deepening is a strategy which combines the space efficiency of depth-first search with the completeness of breadth-first search. Search proceeds depth-first until the `initialDepth` limit is reached. If a proof has not yet been found, the search begins again, with a deeper limit, using the `step` to increment the limit. This process repeats until either a proof is found or the `depthLimit` is reached. The disadvantage of this strategy is of course that the upper part of the space is searched again on each iteration.

The `Cil` functor implements a structure providing the facilities of the CIL signature. The theorem prover structure used in the Pleadings Game, named L, is generated as follows:

```
structure L = Cil (struct
                     val maxterms = 20000
                     val maxvars  = 100000
                   end)
```

The `maxterms` and `maxvars` values here specify the maximum number of copy terms and logical variables to be allocated to the prover. These upper limits are only necessary because fixed size arrays were used to implement the variable binding array and

---

[2]Some of the modules described in this chapter include parsers and printers for reading and writing some readable concrete syntax like this. As parsing is conventional technology, these utilities will not be discussed further, and have been omitted from the signatures shown.

heap of copy terms.

As in Prolog, the Cil implementation uses backward chaining from the goal to be proved. Experience has shown, however, that this is not a very effective strategy for Clausal Intuitionistic Logic, in general. In retrospect, it is easy to see why. Suppose one of the formulas is (if (if p q) r) and the goal to prove is r. There are two ways to prove the embedded implication (if p q). First, p is added to the context and one tries to prove either q or false. That is, if the attempt to prove q in this extended context fails, the system will try to find a proof for false.

At first glance, this may not seem to present a problem, as false is an atomic formula, just like any other. However, this does turn out to be a practical problem, for two reasons:

1. As the heads of clauses must be atomic formulas, formulas such as

   (all (x) (if (instrument x) (not (goods x))))

   must be represented as

   (all (x) (if (and (instrument x) (goods x)) false))

   This means that there will usually be many more formulas for false than for other predicates.

2. Recall that negated subgoals, such as (not p), are just syntatic sugar for (if p false). Thus, there will also usually be many more attempts to prove false than any other formula.

In search terms, the branching factor of a goal directed search for a proof of false is very high. An interesting project might be to design a prover for CIL which uses backwards chaining to prove all goals except false, as usual, but foward chaining to prove contradictions.

There are a couple of other implementation hints worth mentioning. The implementation of the Cil functor is based on the data structures and algorithms described in the book by Maier and Warren [72], for efficiently implementing Prolog interpreters. In my experience, the performance of this implementation is considerably better than that obtained using the methods typically explained in Lisp and Scheme books for implementing Prolog, at the cost of some additional complexity. These other methods are suitable only for didactic purposes. One of the suggestions adopted from Maier and Warren's book is to manage the storage of terms and variable bindings explicitly, instead of relying on SML's automatic storage management (i.e., garbage collection.) This is why the fields of compound terms are represented as mutable data structures, using SML references.

I promised to explain above why formulas are not represented by the wff data type, but instead by an index into a table of wffs. The set operations on arguments would be intolerably expensive if formulas were represented using the wff data type directly. The usual set operations, such as testing membership in a set or forming the union of two sets, require testing elements for equality. If equality of formulas is defined as structural equality, this test would require, in the worst case, a recursive walk over the entire abstract syntax tree of both wffs. Using a table, the equality test involves a simple comparison of two integers.

In Prolog implementations, it is usual to index formulas by the predicate of the head of the formula, and perhaps by some of its arguments as well. This avoids attempting to unify some goal with the head of every formula in the context. Only those formulas with the same predicate need be considered. In CIL, one needs to consider not only a single database of formulas, but a dynamically changing database, as formulas are asserted hypothetically to prove embedded implications. The C structure, which manages sets of formulas, is implemented so that all set operations preserve this efficient indexing.

6.4 Rules — A Rule Language Translator

Recall that rules in my language are mapped into the background context of a conditional entailment default theory. For example, the rule

```
(rule s9-105 (x)
       if (movable x)
       then (goods x)
       unless (or (money x) (instrument x)))
```

would be mapped into the set of formulas

```
(all (x)
     (if (and (movable x)
              (backing s9-105))
         (antecedent (inst s9-105 (parms x)))))

(all (x)
     (if (and (movable x)
              (backing s9-105)
              (ap (inst s9-105 (parms x))))
         (applies (inst s9-105 (parms x)))))

(all (x)
     (if (applies (inst s9-105 (parms x)))
         (goods x)))

(all (x)
     (if (and (or (money x) (instrument x))
              (ap (inst s9-105 (parms x))))
         false))
```

and a default

```
(antecedent (ap (inst s9-105 (parms x)))) =>
(ap (inst s9-105 (parms x)))
```

The `Rules` functor maps a `CIL` structure into a `RULES` structure. That is, given a theorem prover for CIL, it creates a structure for managing defeasible rules. Here is the signature:

```
signature RULES =
sig
    structure L  : CIL
    structure R  : SET          (* Rules *)
    structure D  : SET          (* Defaults *)

    type default
    sharing type D.element = default

    type rule
    sharing type R.element = rule

    type formula
    sharing type formula = L.formula

    val rule : symbol
             * symbol list
             * L.wff list
             * L.term
             * L.wff list -> rule

    val name       : rule -> symbol
    val parameters : rule -> symbol list
    val antecedent : rule -> L.wff list
    val consequent : rule -> L.term
    val unless     : rule -> L.wff list

    val eq : rule -> rule -> bool

    type backcontext

    val backcontext : L.C.set * D.set -> backcontext
    val strict      : backcontext -> L.C.set
    val defaults    : backcontext -> D.set
```

```
val meaning   : rule -> backcontext
val combine   : R.set -> backcontext

val instance : symbol * (L.term list) -> L.term
val assumption : formula -> bool

exception Precondition
val precondition : backcontext -> formula ->
                   formula list
```
end

First, there are three substructures, for the CIL prover and for sets of rules and defaults, L, R, and D, respectively.

Next, there is a constructor function for rules, `rule`, and several accessor functions for the components of rules, `name`, `parameters`, `antecedent`, `consequent`, and `unless`. There is also an equality predicate, `eq`. Two rules are equal if they have the same name. This avoids a structural comparison of rules.

Background contexts are also provided here. As for rules, there is a constructor function, `backcontext`, and some selector functions, `strict` and `defaults`, which access the nondefeasible formulas and defaults of the background context, respectively.

The `meaning` function translates a rule into a background context. `combine` does the same for a set of rules.

Finally, there are a few utilities: for constructing terms naming rule instances, `instance`; testing whether a formula is an applicability assumption, `assumption`; and for retrieving the precondition of a default instance from a background context, `precondition`.

The RULES structure for the Pleadings Game is generated as follows, using the L prover for CIL.

```
structure D = Rules (L)
```

The implementation of the `Rules` functor is quite straightforward. The bulk of the work went into implementing the parser for the surface syntax of rules, which need not interest us here. The only detail worth mentioning is that the R structure for managing sets of rules is implemented using balanced trees. (See [111]).

6.5 Mrms — A Minimal Reason Maintenance System

The Mrms functor implements what I call a *Minimal Reason Maintenance System*. It provides a number of critical services in the Pleadings Game, including caching inferences made by the Cil theorem prover and computing minimal supporting arguments and minimal inconsistent arguments. These minimal arguments are required for computing the dialectical graph of arguments for some claim, and in the computation of the *and/or* argument graphs. In turn, these graphs are used to compute issues and active issues. The known consequence relation is also implemented using the MRMS.

The structure generated by Mrms satisfies this signature:

```
signature MRMS =
    sig
            structure D : DATUM
            structure E : SET
            structure S : STREAM

            type datum
            type environment

            sharing type datum = D.element = E.E.element
                and type environment = E.set

            val env : datum list -> environment
            val justify : environment -> datum -> unit

            val reset : unit -> unit

            val derivable : environment -> datum -> bool
            val inconsistent : environment -> bool
            val nogoods : unit -> environment S.stream
            val supports : datum -> environment S.stream
    end
```

For those familiar with de Kleer's Assumption-Based Truth Maintenance System (ATMS) [27], it may be clear that the terminology used in this signature has been borrowed from the ATMS. In fact, an ATMS could be implemented so as to satisfy this signature. The *semantics* of the MRMS, however, differs considerably from that of the ATMS. A detailed comparison of the ATMS and MRMS would be inappropriate here, as our goal is to explain how to implement the Pleadings Game. For this purpose, a brief description of the MRMS semantics of this signature should suffice. A very brief comparison with the ATMS is at the end of this section.

The D substructure defines the type of data managed by the reason maintenance system. In the Pleadings Game, this data will be CIL formulas, but the MRMS is designed to be independent of the particular type of data managed. All that is required is that equality be defined and that there be a distinguished element, bottom:

```
signature DATUM =
sig
    type element
```

```
    val bottom : element
    val eq : element -> element -> bool
end
```

In the MRMS signature, the datum type is a synonym for D.element.

In the Pleadings Game, the bottom element is L.bottom, the term of CIL denoting inconsistency. (Again, in the surface syntax for formulas L.bottom is denoted by false.)

The E substructure manages sets of data. The environment type is just a synonym for E.set. There is a constructor function for environments, env, which maps a list of data to an environment. Duplicates in the list are ignored.

Dependencies between data are stored in the MRMS by asserting so-called "justifications", using the justify function. In the Pleadings Game application, justications are used to cache CIL proofs. For example, a proof of L.entails A f can be cached by executing justify A f.

Each justification changes the internal state of the MRMS. Notice that the MRMS *structure* implements a single reason maintenance object. There is no reason maintenance data type as such. The reset function reinitializes this internal state, essentially by erasing all justifications.

There are four types of queries. The derivable function checks whether a datum depends on some environment. In our application, if derivable A f is true, then so is L.entails A f. Again, the MRMS is used to cache CIL proofs. But it is not simply a cache, as it performs some simple inferences on its own. Precisely, given the set of justifications in the MRMS, derivable A f if and only if:

1. f ∈ A, or

2. The MRMS contains a justification, justify D f, such that derivable A p for each proposition p in D.

    Similarly, inconsistent A if and only if:

1. bottom ∈ A, or

2. The MRMS contains a justification, justify D bottom, such that derivable A p for each proposition p in D.

Justifications can be viewed as propositional Horn clauses. From this perspective, a formula f is propositionally entailed by the union of a set of formulas A and the propositions encoded by the justifications in the MRMS, if and only if:

1. derivable A f, or

2. inconsistent A.

Unlike CIL, propositional Horn clause derivability is decidable, and efficiently so [29]. This explains why it can make sense to consult the MRMS before trying to find a proof using CIL.

There are only two more functions to explain, nogoods and supports. The nogoods function returns a stream of the minimal, inconsistent environments. (A stream is a sequence whose elements are computed as needed.) Precisely, an environment A is in nogoods () if and only if:

1. inconsistent A, and

2. There does not exist a justification justify D bottom in the MRMS such that D ⊂ A.

The supports function is similar. An environment A is in supports f if and only if:

1. derivable A f;

2. It is not the case that inconsistent A; and

3. There is not a justification justify D f in the MRMS such that D ⊂ A.

Very briefly, the MRMS differs from de Kleer's ATMS as follows. In an ATMS, there are three, disjunct kinds of data: *presumptions, assumptions* and the rest. A presumption p is implicitly justified by an empty environment, as if one had asserted justify [] p. The derivability and consistency tests of the ATMS are complete only for sets of assumptions. For example, derivable A f may be false even though justify D f has been asserted, for some D which is a subset of A, if D contains data which have not been declared to be assumptions. On the other hand, the nogoods and supports computed by the ATMS are constrained to consist entirely of assumptions. It has been shown by Selman and Levesque that the problem of computing even a single nogood or supporting environment from a set of the assumptions is intractable [112]. The ATMS computes *all* of the nogoods and supports for *all* of the conclusions of the justifications which have been asserted, each time a justification is asserted. Thus, the ATMS tries to solve many intractable problems each time a justification is asserted.

The MRMS, on the other hand, solves much simpler problems, as the nogoods and supports are not constrained to be subsets of some set of assumptions. All of the MRMS operations are both theoretically and practically efficient. This is not to claim that the MRMS is superior to the ATMS for all applications. According to Selman and Levesque, in applications where supports and nogoods consisting only of assumptions are required, the ATMS may perform as well as possible. Fortunately, an ATMS is not required for the Pleadings Game.

Let us now turn our attention to the Mrms implementation. It maps a structure matching the following signature into an MRMS.

```
sig
    structure D :
        sig
            type element
            val bottom : element
            val eq : element -> element -> bool
            val less : element -> element -> relation
        end
    and Env : SET
    sharing type D.element = Env.E.element
end
```

The D substructure is just a DATUM structure in which the elements are partially ordered by the less relation. The Env substructure manages environments.

One of the strengths of Standard ML is that a module like the Mrms can be implemented as generically as desired. The Mrms implementation does not depend on the type of the data or the method used for managing environments. In the Pleadings Game, the MRMS for clausal intuitionistic logic is generated with a single line of code, as follows:

```
structure M = Mrms (structure D = L.F and Env = L.C)
```

Here, the data managed are CIL formulas and environments are sets of formulas. In particular, notice that the data are not restricted to ground, atomic formulas.

6.6 Record — The Pleadings Game Playing Board

The "playing board" of the Pleadings Game is called the *record*. The Record functor maps a RULES structure into a structure for managing the state of the record and responding to various queries about this state. The implementation itself is straightforward. This section just describes the RECORD signature it satisfies.

First of all, some of the structures and types imported from the RULES structure are renamed to make them easier to use here.

```
structure D : RULES
structure L : CIL
structure R : SET
structure C : SET

sharing L = D.L
    and R = D.R
    and C = D.L.C

type formula
sharing type formula = L.formula
```

```
type argument
sharing type argument = C.set
```

Here, D is a new name for the imported RULES structure. L is just an abbreviation for D.L; i.e., it is another name for the CIL theorem prover. R and C manage sets of rules and formulas, respectively. The type declarations just make it unnecessary to use the qualified names within the RECORD structure. For example, one can just type formula instead of L.formula.

Recall that there are four kinds of statements, which can be inductively defined in Standard ML as follows:

```
datatype statement =
    Claim of formula
          | Argument of argument * formula
          | Rebuttal of argument * formula * argument
          | Denial of statement
```

An SML datatype declaration like this exhaustively defines the constructor functions for the type. Accessor functions need not be defined, as pattern matching can be used in SML to select the parts of a datatype value. Conventionally, the names of the constructor functions for a datatype begin with an uppercase letter.

The *statements* of a party is a triple for his open, conceded and denied statements:

```
structure StSet : SET
sharing type statement = StSet.E.element

datatype statements =
    Statements of StSet.set * StSet.set * StSet.set
```

The *background* consists of the formula which is the *main claim* of the game, a set of nondefeasible formulas and a set of defeasible rules.

```
datatype background = Background of formula * C.set * R.set
```

Now, the *record* itself is a tuple consisting of a background, the statements of the plaintiff and the statements of the defendant.

```
datatype record =
    Record of background * statements * statements
```

Finally, there are several functions for querying the record:

```
val K : record -> D.backcontext
val L : record -> C.set
```

```
val facts : record -> C.set
val Theta : record -> C.set
val rules : record -> R.set
val uissue : record -> formula
```

Here, K is the background context of the record, L is the set of nondefeasible formulas, the facts are the conceded formulas of both parties, Theta is the current *context*, i.e., the union of the facts and L, the rules function retrieves the current set of defeasible rules, and finally uissue is the main claim of the record.

In the definition of the rules of the game, it will be convenient to be able to refer to the statements of the proponent and opponent of the move. The following functions provide this service.

```
datatype party = Plaintiff | Defendant
val opponent : record -> party -> statements
val proponent : record -> party -> statements
```

The complete RECORD signature has now been explained. Recall that D is a RULES structure. The RECORD structure used in my implementation of the Pleadings Game is generated using D as follows.

```
structure Rd : sig
                  include RECORD
                      val r : record ref
                      val p : party ref
                  end =
struct
    structure R = Record (D)
    open R

    val p = ref Plaintiff

    val initStatements =
        Statements(StSet.empty_set,
                   StSet.empty_set,
                   StSet.empty_set)

    val r = ref (Record (Background (bottom,
                                     C.empty_set,
                                     R.empty_set),
                         initStatements,
                         initStatements))
end
```

The structure generated by `Record` is completely applicative; it has no internal state. The `Rd` structure here extends this structure with two references, `r` and `p`. `r` represents *the* record of the Pleadings Game. This reference is changed by the moves made during the game. `p` points to the player whose turn it is to move.

6.7   `Ce` — A Theorem Prover for Conditional Entailment

Geffner and Pearl's nonmonotonic logic, called conditional entailment, is used extensively in the rules of the Pleadings Game. Whether or not an argument is permitted depends on whether or not it is a *supporting* argument, *rebuttal*, or *defeating counterargument*. Moreover, whether a party is entitled to a summary judgment at the end of pleading depends in part on whether or not the main claim is conditionally entailed by formulas conceded by both parties.

My implementation of a theorem prover for conditional entailment is based on Geffner and Pearl's description [41, pp. 230-231]. However, in their implementation, arguments are restricted to sets of applicability assumptions and an ATMS is used to manage dependencies between these arguments. In the Pleadings Game, arguments may consist of arbitrary formulas, not just applicability assumptions. Moreover, as discussed above, the computational complexity of the abduction problem solved by an ATMS is unacceptably high, and unnecessary for our purposes. Fortunately it is possible to implement a theorem prover for conditional entailment which is not subject to these limitations. As this implementation is novel and required for the Pleadings Game, it will be described in some detail later in this section. First, here is an overview of the signature for conditional entailment to be implemented:

```
signature CE =
sig

        structure S : STREAM

        type argument
        type formula


        val supports  : formula  -> argument S.stream
        val defeaters : argument -> argument S.stream
        val rebuttals : argument -> argument S.stream
        val entailed  : formula  -> bool


        val preferred : formula  -> argument -> bool
        val counters  : argument -> argument -> bool
```

```
      val dominates : argument -> argument -> bool
      val protected : argument -> argument -> bool
      val defeats    : argument -> argument -> bool
      val rebuts     : argument -> argument -> bool
  end
```

Recall that conditional entailment is defined relative to a consequence relation and a default theory. In CE structures, the underlying consequence relation and default theory are implicit. There is one default theory per CE structure, but implemenations may differ about how this theory is represented. As usual, the signature here specifies only the necessary parts of a prover for conditional entailment. Structures matching this signature may offer additional facilities for constructing or manipulating the default theory.

The rest of the functions in this signature should be self-explanatory to those familiar with the proof theory of conditional entailment. The main function is entailed, which tests whether a formula is conditionally entailed by the default theory.

Before explaining in detail how the Ce functor for this signature is implemented, let me show how it is applied in the Pleadings Game.

```
structure K : CE =
    Ce (struct
            structure Rms : MRMS = M
            open Rd

            fun evidence () = Rd.facts (!r)

            val assumption = D.assumption

            exception Precondition

            fun precondition f =
                (D.precondition (K (!r))) f)
                handle D.Precondition =>
                    raise Precondition
        end)
```

The default theory is represented by the MRMS and the evidence function. The nondefeasible formulas of the background context of the default theory are represented by asserting justifications into the MRMS. The underlying consequence relation is also represented by the MRMS derivable and inconsistent functions. A function for testing whether a formula is an applicability assumption, assumption is also required, as is a function for computing the precondition of the default instance named by an applicability assumption, precondition. The Precondition exception should be raised if the formula is not an applicability assumption.

Notice that the evidence may not be encoded in the MRMS. This would make it impossible to distinguish between the evidence and the formulas of the background context. When computing dominance relations between assumptions, only the information in the background context may be considered, according to the semantics of conditional entailment.

In my application the reason maintenance system used is the M structure mentioned earlier in this chapter. The background context is computed from the r record in the Rd structure. The assumption and precondition functions are defined using the functions of the same name from the RULES structure D.

For those interested only in how conditional entailment is used in the Pleadings Game, the information above should be sufficient. For those interested in implementation details, the rest of this section explains one way to implement the Ce functor.

First, here are some convenient synonyms for the structures we will be using.

```
structure S = Rms.S
structure C = R.C
type argument = Rms.environment
type formula = Rms.datum
open Rms
```

S is a structure for streams of formulas and C manages sets of formulas. The Rms has been opened so its components can be accessed without qualifying their names.

The next two functions are local utilities. They just select the assumptions and claims of an argument, respectively. Recall that all non-assumptions are claims.

```
fun assumptions (arg : argument) : argument =
    C.filter R.assumption  arg

fun claims (arg : argument) : argument =
    C.filter (fn w => (not (R.assumption w))) arg
```

The preferred function tests whether a formula is preferred to any formula in a set of formulas, in *every* admissible priority ordering on defaults. This is a direct implementation of Geffner and Pearl's syntactic test of preference. Thus, unlike in Geffner and Pearl's own implementation [41, p. 230], it is not required here that we "further commit ourselves to a single minimal admissible priority ordering."

```
fun preferred (wff1 : formula) (arg : argument) : bool =
let val pre = (precondition wff1)
                handle Precondition => []
in
    inconsistent (C.union (C.set (wff1::pre)) arg)
end
```

Notice again that the evidence is not included in this inconsistency test, as the admissible priority orderings on defaults depend only on the background context.

One argument *dominates* another if and only if every assumption of the first argument is preferred to some assumption of the second argument. The empty argument dominates every argument.

```
fun dominates (arg1 : argument) (arg2 : argument) : bool =
let val A1 = assumptions arg1
    val A2 = assumptions arg2
in
    C.empty (C.filter (fn w => not (preferred w A2))
                       A1)
end
```

Unlike in Geffner and Pearl's implementation, arguments here may contain claims as well as assumptions. These claims are added hypothetically to the evidence of the default theory. Intuitively, when trying to show (rebuts arg1 arg2), one accepts the claims of arg2 for the sake of argument, and says, even if these claims are accepted, the argument would be rebutted by arg1 assuming its claims are also accepted. For this purpose, some of the operations below are defined relative to the current value of a variable, E, which will contain the union of these hypotheses and the evidence.

```
val E = ref (evidence ())
```

Two arguments are counterarguments if and only if they are together inconsistent with the union of L and the evidence, E. Unlike when checking preference, the claims of the arguments and evidence are considered here. In this code, L is implicit; it is encoded in the justifications of the MRMS.

```
fun counters arg1 arg2 : bool =
    inconsistent (C.union arg1 (C.union arg2 (!E)))
```

To compute rebuttals and defeating counterarguments, we will be using two implementation-level concepts: *minimal conflict sets* and *basic defeat pairs*. A minimal conflict set is a minimal set of *assumptions* which is inconsisent with $L \cup E$. The nogoods of the MRMS are minimal sets of inconsistent formulas, but these sets may include claims, i.e., formulas which are not applicability assumptions. However, the nogoods can be used to compute the minimal conflict sets as follows. First, recall that formulas in the evidence, E, are assumed to be true. If a nogood D contains formulas in E then $D \cap E$ must be inconsistent. If $D \cap E$ contains only assumptions, then it is a minimal conflict set. If, on the other hand, it contains claims, it is not a minimal conflict set; consistency can be restored by deciding that any one of these claims is false, rather than choosing between the applicability assumptions.

```
fun noContestedClaims arg =
    C.empty (C.difference (claims arg) (!E))
```

```
fun conflictSets () =
    S.map (fn arg => C.difference arg (!E))
        (S.filter noContestedClaims
            (nogoods ()))
```

The conflict sets computed by conflictSets are minimal.

A minimal conflict set c can be partitioned into a pair of sets, (c0,c1) such that c1 is the largest subset of c which dominates c0. If c1 is not empty, then (c0,c1) is a *basic defeat pair*. All minimal rebutters and defeaters of an argument can be computed from the set of basic defeat pairs.

Next, the basicDefeatPairs function is defined. Breadth-first search is used to partition the minimal conflict sets. The code for performing this search is conventional and so has been omitted.

```
fun basicDefeatPairs () : (argument * argument) S.stream =
let fun partition (nogood : argument) :
        argument * argument = ...
in
    S.filter (fn (_,s1) => not (C.empty s1))
            (S.map partition (conflictSets ()))
end
```

There are two versions of most of rest of the functions to be described, one that assumes the hypotheses have been added to the evidence, foo, and one that is responsible for adding the hypotheses to the evidence, foo'. The functions which add hypotheses are all local, hidden in the implementation of the Ce functor.

The extend1 and extend2 functionals just makes it easy to define the version of the functions which first adds the hypotheses to the evidence.

```
fun extend1 f arg1 =
    (E := C.union (claims arg1) (evidence ());
     let val result = f (assumptions arg1)
     in
         E := evidence ();
         result
     end handle x => (E := evidence (); raise x))

fun extend2 f arg1 arg2 =
    (E := C.union (claims arg1)
                    (C.union (claims arg2) (evidence ())));
     let val result = f (assumptions arg1)
                        (assumptions arg2)
     in
         E := evidence ();
         result
```

```
      end handle x => (E := evidence (); raise x))
```

Given the basic defeat pairs, it is now easy to compute the minimal defeating
counterarguments of an argument.

```
fun defeaters' (arg : argument) : argument S.stream =
    S.map (fn (_,c1) => C.difference c1 arg)
         (S.filter (fn (c0,_) => C.subset c0 arg)
                  (basicDefeatPairs ()))

val defeaters = extend1 defeaters'
```

An argument, arg1, is protected from another, arg2 if and only if arg1 contains a
subset which defeats arg2.

```
fun protected' arg1 arg2 : bool =
    exists (fn arg3 => C.subset arg3 arg1)
          (defeaters' arg2)

val protected = extend2 protected'
```

Computing rebuttals can be more difficult, as two passes over the minimal conflicts sets
is made in the worst case: once to find a counterargument and then again to check that the
counterargument is not (known to be) protected.

```
fun rebuttals' arg =
let fun f (nogood, str) =
    if not (C.empty (C.intersection
                          nogood arg)) then
        let val r = C.difference nogood arg
        in
            if not (protected' arg r) then
                S.stream (r, str)
            else
                str
        end
    else
        str
in
    S.accumulate f (S.empty_stream ())
                  (conflictSets ())
end

val rebuttals = extend1 rebuttals'
```

An argument is `stable` if there is a defeating counterargument for every rebuttal.

```
fun stable' (arg : argument) : bool =
    forall (fn r =>
                exists (fn d => stable' (C.union arg d))
                    (defeaters' r))
        (rebuttals' arg)

val stable = extend1 stable'
```

The minimal supporting arguments of a formula, for the purposes of computing conditional entailment, are the applicability assumptions of the MRMS supporting arguments which do not contain contested claims and which are not (known to be) inconsistent with the evidence. A formula in the evidence is supported by the empty argument.

```
fun supports (wff1 : formula) : argument S.stream =
    if C.member wff1 (!E) then
        S.singleton C.empty_set
    else
        (S.filter (fn arg =>
                    not (inconsistent
                        (C.union arg (!E))))
            (S.map assumptions
                (S.filter noContestedClaims
                    (Rms.supports wff1))))
```

It might be thought that MRMS supporting arguments which are found here to be inconsistent with the evidence could be deleted from the MRMS. However, it must be remembered that the MRMS encodes the nondefeasible formulas L of the background context of the default theory. Although A may not be satisfiable given the evidence, deleting this argument from the reason maintenance system would in effect change L, which may cause the computation of the dominance relation between defaults to be incorrect.

A formula is conditionally entailed if it is supported by a stable argument.

```
fun entailed (wff1 : formula) : bool =
    exists stable (supports wff1)
```

This implementation of conditional entailment should be correct and complete. Correctness follows from Geffner and Pearl's lemma 5.6 [41, p. 227], which states that a proposition is conditionally entailed if it is supported by a stable argument. The test is not complete when the underlying logic supports disjunctive arguments. However, I conjecture it is complete here, because the MRMS does not support disjunctive justifications. As discussed above, the justifications of the MRMS are isomorphic to definite, propositional Horn clauses.

The `supports`, `rebuttals` and `defeaters` functions, above, are used to generate the dialectical graph of arguments. However, when checking the preconditions of moves in the Pleadings Game, there will be occassion to just check whether a given argument defeats or rebuts another. The `defeats` and `rebuts` functions perform this service.

```
fun defeats' A1 A2 =
    (counters A1 A2) andalso
    (dominates A1 A2)

fun rebuts' A1 A2 =
    (counters A1 A2) andalso
    (not (protected A2 A1))

val defeats = extend2 defeats'
val rebuts  = extend2 rebuts'
```

We are finished with the implementation of the Ce functor. This implemenation is somewhat more complex than Geffner and Pearl's, as we have been careful to keep the evidence separate from the formulas of the background context, and have allowed arguments to contain arbitrary formulas, rather than just applicability assumptions. Certain possibilities to improve performance have been omitted here, to avoid still more complexity. For example, computing the basic defeat pairs can be expensive. In the implementation shown here, they are computed once to generate the rebuttals of an argument and again to generate the defeating counterarguments. In the Pleadings Game, the set of permitted moves depends on the current set of issues. Computing the issues requires a traversal of the dialectical graph for the main claim and thus, in this implementation, redundant computation of the basic defeat pairs, once for each level of the graph. It would be nice to be able to cache these basic defeat pairs, so as to avoid this redundacy. But as these pairs depend on the default theory, including whatever formulas are hypothetically added to the evidence, one must be careful that these cached pairs are properly updated when the default theory changes. Alternatively, the CE signature and this implementation could be extended with a function for computing the issues for some claim. The implementation here could eliminate the redundant computation of the defeat pairs. This alternative has the conceptual disadvantage that issues have nothing to do with conditional entailment per se, but rather with just one of its applications.

6.8   Clerk — The Pleadings Game Mediator

The `Clerk` functor is the final module of the Pleadings Game to be described. Its main responsibility is mediating the moves of the Pleading Game to make sure that the rules of the game are not violated. The functor maps a structure matching this signature

```
sig
      structure Rd : RECORD
          and K  : CE
      sharing type Rd.argument = K.argument
          and type Rd.formula = K.formula
end
```

into a structure matching the following:

```
signature CLERK =
sig
      structure Rd  : RECORD
      structure Str : STREAM

      open Rd Str

      datatype assertion =
          Declare of D.rule
        | Concede of statement
        | Deny of statement
        | Defend of statement * argument

      val known : C.set -> formula -> bool
      val entails : C.set -> formula -> bool

      val successors : argument stream ->
                          argument stream stream
      val issues : unit -> C.set
      val issue : formula -> bool
      val relevant : statement -> bool

      val summaryJudgment :  unit -> party option

      exception Objection
      val move : party -> assertion -> unit
end
```

The clerk for my implementation of the Pleadings Game was generated by this code:

```
structure C = Clerk (structure Rd = Rd and K = K)
```

The Clerk also provides a simple user-interface for playing the game, just a command language and a read-eval-print loop, but this need not be of further interest to us here.

In the CLERK signature, above, the Rd structure is the same RECORD structure as the imported structure. The Str structure provides sequences whose elements are generated only as needed. Both of these are opened so that their identifiers can be used without qualifiers. For example, we can write simply statement instead of Rd.statement and stream instead of Str.stream. The C and D structures are from the RECORD; they are for sets of formulas and rules, respectively.

The assertion datatype is just a Standard ML transliteration of the formal definition of assertions in the Pleadings Game.

The known function implements a decidable subset of the underlying logic chosen for the game, which in my implementation is Clausal Intuitionistic Logic. It is simply implemented using the reason maintenance system, M, as follows:

```
fun known (Gamma : C.set) (phis : L.formula) : bool =
let val context = C.union (Theta (!r)) Gamma
in
    (M.derivable context phis) orelse
    (M.inconsistent context)
end
```

Recall that the r reference points to the current record of the game.

The entails function is a "wrapper" for the entailment function of the Clausal Intuitionistic Logic (CIL) theorem prover, L. It is responsible for caching proofs found by L in M. (In the code below, be careful not to confuse the *value* L with the *structure* L. The naming environments for values and structures is disjunct in Standard ML. The L structure is the CIL prover; the L value is the RECORD function which computes the nondefeasible formulas of the background context of the record.)

```
fun entails (A : C.set) (f : L.formula) : bool =
    if L.entails A f then
        (M.justify (C.difference A (L (!r))) f;
         true)
    else
        false
```

Notice that the proof is strengthened before it is cached, by removing formulas from the argument A that are in also in L of the background.

The successors function generates layers of a dialectical graph of arguments. It differs from the specification of the previous chapter only in returning a stream of a stream of arguments, instead of a sequence of a *set* of arguments. Conceptually, the arguments of a layer are not ordered. However, in practice it can be more efficient to generate only one argument of a layer at a time. This is achieved using streams.

The issues function computes the issues relative to the main claim of the record, uissue (!r). Its implementation is a straightforward encoding of the definition of issues in the previous chapter. The issue function just checks whether a formula is a member of the issues.

A statement is relevant if it concerns an issue. The implementation is trivial, but is a nice example of defining functions using pattern matching over inductively defined data types in SML:

```
fun relevant (Claim c) : bool = issue c
  | relevant (Argument (_,c)) = issue c
  | relevant (Rebuttal (_,c,_)) = issue c
  | relevant (Denial s) = relevant s
```

The summaryJudgment function just checks whether one of the parties is entitled to a summary judgment. An option is an SML idiom for constructing any value or, optionally, nothing:

```
datatype 'a option = NONE | SOME of 'a
```

If the plaintiff, e.g., is entitled to summary judgment, then summaryJudgment () returns SOME Plaintiff.

The most interesting function of this module is move, which checks that the precondition of the applicable rule of the Pleadings Game is satisfied, before executing the move and modifying the state of the record. The move function is defined by cases over the inductively defined assertion datatype. There is one case for each rule of the game. Pattern matching is used to select the applicable rule. If the precondition of the applicable rule is not satisfied, the Objection exception is raised. As the implementation of the preconditions and effects of these rules is also straightforward, only an outline of the implementation has been included below. The code for rule 1 of the game, which regulates when claims may be conceded, is shown in full. The others are similarly implemented. Notice that Rules 9 and 10 of the game, regarding the assertion of defeating counterarguments, are coalesced into one case here, as the empty set cannot be recognized by pattern matching.

```
exception Objection

fun move (p : party)
         (Concede (cl as (Claim c))) : unit =
    let val os = opponent (!r) p
        val ps = proponent (!r) p
    in
        if (StSet.member cl (openStatements os))
            andalso
            (not (known (C.add c (claims ps)) bottom))
        then
            (update p
                    (proponent (!r) p)
                    (Statements
```

```
                        (StSet.remove cl
                                (openStatements os),
                        StSet.add cl (conceded os),
                        denied os)))
        else
                raise Objection
    end

| move p (Concede (s as (Argument _))) = ...
| move p (Concede (s as (Rebuttal _ ))) =  ...
| move p (Deny (cl as (Claim c))) = ...
| move p (Deny (s as (Denial _))) = ...
| move _ (Declare r) = ...
| move p (Defend (s as (Denial (Claim c)), A)) = ...
| move p (Defend (s as (Argument (A, c)), D)) = ...
| move p (Defend (s as (Rebuttal (A, c, R)), D)) = ...
| move _ _ = raise Objection
```

This completes the overview of my implementation of the Pleadings Game in Standard ML. Many details have been omitted from this description, about such things as parsing and the command interpreter, but nonetheless it is should now be sufficiently clear how to reimplement the system.

Chapter 7 Conclusion

The Pleadings Game is a theoretical model of Alexy's discourse theory of legal argumentation. The norms of civil pleading are modeled by the preconditions and effects of rules for making certain kinds of claims and arguments during pleading. Legal arguments are not found or constructed by the model. It is not a model of the legal reasoning behavior of lawyers.[1] Analytical, empirical and normative claims have been made for the Pleadings Game model. Keeping its purpose and object in mind, let us now try to evaluate to what extent these claims are supported by the game.

Analytical Claims.

The analytical claims are the least problematical. The Pleadings Game is an existence proof that judicial discretion *can* be limited by the issues and arguments of the record constructed during pleading, that conflicting arguments can be resolved by ordering them according to such principles as specificity, authority and time, and that the concept of an issue can be used to focus pleading. It is hard to imagine that anyone might have trouble accepting these as *possibilities*.

---

[1]Some might question whether the Pleadings Game should be considered an artificial intelligence model, since it does not model intelligent behavior. But "AI" is another open-textured term which should not be limited to its literal meaning. AI can be understood to be the study of computer models of cognitive processes, including communication. From this perspective, computational dialectics is a subfield of AI, focusing on normative models of communication. (See also [49].)

Empirical Claims.

Cautiously, I have only claimed that *some* legislation is in fact structured as defeasible rules with exceptions. Article Nine is clearly an example of this. In retrospect, it should have perhaps been apparent that it has this structure without the assistance of a formal model like the Pleadings Game. However, traditional legal logicians have argued so insistently for such a long time against any form of logic other than monotonic, first-order classical logic, that legislation structured like Article Nine appeared malformed. Indeed, authors like Rödig have argued, in effect, that the exceptions are not *really* there, that the surface organization of the legislation is just an awkward, if not inept, representation of a set of exceptionless rules for a monotonic logic. The Pleadings Game lends further support to the view that this traditional surface structure reflects the deep analytical structure of the rules with which one directly reasons and argues.

Not only are the rules of Article Nine defeasible, they are also "higher-order": Some statutes refer not only to objects in the domain of secured transactions, such as goods, but also to other legal rules and principles. The Pleadings Game shows one way to represent this structure, by reifying rules.

Normative Claims.

My three normative claims are the strongest, and presumably the most controversial. The first of these is that a deductive argument alone is neither a necessary nor sufficient justification for a legal decision. The judge should take the issues raised and arguments made by the parties during pleading into account. Although Alexy too is an adherent of this traditional theory of justification, the Pleadings Game shows how his theory of argumentation can support a more adequate conception of justification.

Next, I have argued again here that legislation should be formulated using defeasible rules, due to the normative and conflict resolution purposes of the law. The Pleading Game lends further support to this argument by showing how legal reasoning can proceed rationally when legislation is structured this way, without first "axiomatizing" the law as a theory in a monotonic logic.

Finally, the claim that judicial discretion should be limited by fair procedural rules, rather than by Hart's distinction between clear and hard cases, is supported more by the moral and ethical arguments justifying the rules of the Pleadings Game than by the model itself. As usual, the importance of the model is that it animates the theory. Perhaps the model will encourage some of those in AI and Law interested in clarifying the limits of judicial discretion to look beyond relational models of legal reasoning and alternative conceptions of clearness towards better procedural models of justice.

In stating and defending these claims, I have tried to avoid placing undo emphasis on the technical details of the Pleadings Game model. Keeping in mind that all models are abstractions, it should be no surprise that certain important features of legal argumentation are only inadequately accounted for in the model, if at all. To the AI and Law community, the most obvious limitation is the failure to account for arguing with cases, in addition to statutes. Although Ashley's model of case-based argumentation is an empirical model of how lawyers construct arguments using cases, I suspect it contains important insights which may be useful in a unified, normative model for arguing with statutes *and* cases. HYPO's *3-Ply Arguments* have an analytical structure similar to supporting arguments, rebuttals and defeating counterarguments. Just as statutes have been represent by rules mapped into default theories for conditional entailment, perhaps an encoding for cases with their dimensions can be found which permits a similar mapping into default theories. We have seen that Geffner and Pearl's syntactic test for the priority relation on defaults can be used to model any explicit partial order on defaults, not just the intended specificity relation. Can a representation of cases as default theories be found which properly orders examples and counterexamples using this syntactic test?

Another limitation of the model is that it does not explicitly account for the use of ideals (i.e., topoi), metaphors and purpose in legal argumentation. This is related to the previous limitation concerning case-based reasoning. It may be possible to subsume all of these problems under a general theory of backing. Perhaps an ideal such as liberty can be used in way similar to a statute, case or principle to back a legal rule. The problem of ranking conflicting rules would be reduced to the problem of ranking these various kinds of backing. These kinds of arguments are possible in Pleadings Game as it is, but I suspect there should be special discourse norms for each kind of backing.

In retrospect, the choice of conditional entailment as the underlying logic for the Pleadings Game is not without its problems. The most serious is that it give undue prefence to specificity over all other criteria for resolving conflicts between rules. In the law, most people agree that a more specific law from a lower authority does not override the more general law from a higher authority. For example, a specific state law would not override the federal constitution. Another problem with conditional entailment is its enormous complexity. The basic ideas of the Pleadings Game are not difficult, but they are obscured by the complexity of conditional entailment. Nonetheless, I am still aware of no alternative which does not suffer from problems at least as severe as these.

Finally, the Pleadings Game is only another step along the path toward a full account of the limits of judicial discretion. As its name suggests, it is first of all a model of pleading, where the judge is not yet a party to the proceeding. Although, as I hope to have demonstrated, pleading does restrict discretion, it is not the only constraint. A fuller treatment of discretion may involve investigating the discourse norms regulating such activities as trial and the writing of the decision.

Up until now in this conclusion, we have been discussing the contributions of the Pleadings Game model to legal philosophy. Although this dissertation is primarily an application of artificial intelligence to a legal problem, there have also been several contributions to the field of artificial intelligence:

1. To my knowledge, the Pleadings Game is the first formal model of dialogical argumentation in which 1) the concepts of issue and relevance are used to focus discourse; 2) a tractable inference relation is used to commit players to some of the consequences of their claims; 3) the goal of argumentation is to identify issues, rather than decide the main claim[2]; and 4) conflicts between arguments may be resolved by arguing about the validity and priority of defeasible rules, at any "level".

2. The rule language of the Pleadings Game supports a natural representation of defeasible rules with explicit exceptions. Principles for ordering rules can easily be expressed within the language.

3. The game is also a contribution to the field of nonmonotonic logic. The legal examples demonstrate well that specificity is only one among many principles for ordering conflicting rules. These principles are shown to be domain dependent, calling into question efforts within the nonmonotonic logic community to find and formalize a univeral priority principle within a logic. Instead, in the Pleadings Game a way of encoding many kinds of priority relationships within domain theories is developed. Finally, the model shows how to avoid the problem of the undecidability or intractability of expressive logics, by dividing the burden of proof among those whose interests are affected by the decision.

4. Similarly, the game suggests what may be a practical solution to the knowledge acquisition problem in some applications: distributing the burdens and rights of representation among the various classes of users of the system.

5. A new theory of abduction was developed and shown to subsume a number of existing abduction systems, such as Poole's Theorist system. The problem of computing the minimal, supporting arguments for a formula is shown to be an abduction problem in this theory. This abduction problem is interesting because it is tractable without being trivial.

6. The tractable theory of abduction led to a new, efficient system for reason maintenance, the Minimal Reason Maintenance System (MRMS). It is a new, efficient tool for caching inferences and computing the abductive supports of formulas, given a set of arguments. Depending on the needs of the application, the MRMS may be an attractive alternative to an ATMS.

7. Finally, the implementation of the model features new theorem provers for clausal intuitionistic logic and conditional entailment.

Although the purpose of the Pleadings Game is theoretical, there may be practical ramifications. The game demonstrates that a machine can monitor a discussion, helping

---

[2]Anne Gardner's model also spotted issues, but not in a dialogical context.

to ensure that some discourse norms are respected. A *mediation system* of this kind may be more practical and appropriate in domains where users have conflicting interests and opinions. Such a system should also be somewhat easier to implement, as responsibility for encoding knowledge is distributed among the users, rather than borne solely by the system developers. When interests conflict, such a system could also be less controversial, as the rights to access and modify the knowledge base are granted to the users affected by the decisions of the system. In legal applications, mediation systems are not "computer judges", but more limited *computer clerks*. The judge in this model remains a person.

There are plentiful opportunities for future work in the area of discourse models of legal reasoning. An AI system which plays the Pleadings Game, or supports a person playing the game by helping to find arguments and select moves, would be an interesting challenge. Some possible extensions have already been mentioned, such as trying to find a unifying normative account of arguing with statutes and cases. Then there are other kinds of legal language games to attend to, such as discovery, trial, appeal and arbitration. Arbitration would be an especially interesting challenge, as its goal is compromise and consensus, rather than a complete win for one party at the expense of the other. Perhaps a formal discourse game can be designed which does justice to the famed triad of thesis, antithesis and synthesis.

Appendix A   The Article Nine World

Just as Winograd's SHRDLU system conversed in the famous *blocks world*, variants of which have continued to be of great service in AI planning research [130], the examples used in this book are based, not on the real Article Nine, with all its complexity, but on a "micro-world" version of it. Let's call it the "Article Nine World", or simply "A9W". Our goal is a simplified version of Article Nine which, although certainly inadequate for solving real secured transactions problems, retains the features required to demonstrate my model of legal argumentation.[1] What are those features? My aim is to understand how legal arguments should be constructed and challenged from a set of conflicting statutes. However, it is not enough that the statutes in micro-world version conflict. They should conflict in the same variety of ways identified in Chapter 2. Thus, explicit and implicit exceptions, blanket exceptions, scoping provisions, conflicts between levels of authority and so on, will all be retained in A9W.

A9W is more incomplete than incorrect. For solving priority problems, it should be adequate, at least as a first approximation, unless the type of collateral is one of the types I've ignored, such as fixtures and farm products. Also, nothing is included about remedies on default, or even what constitutes default, or about the requirements of a security agreement, the financing statement, or filing.

A9W, like the real Article Nine, will be expressed here in natural language. However, alongside the natural language version of many of these statutes, a formal representation will also be given, using the rule language presented in Chapter 5. *The formalization is not A9W, per se, but a representation of A9W.* Its purpose is to demonstrate the expressiveness of the representation language, provide more examples of its use, and to support my claim that programs in this language can retain the structure of the original statutes. It would be antithetical for me to claim these formal versions of the natural language statutes are adequate for all purposes. The natural language versions in this micro-world play the role of an authoritative primary source of law; the formal restatements are one kind of nonauthoritative secondary source. When constructing arguments, a lawyer should not restrict his arguments to these prefabricated restatements, but should instead be ready to construct alternative representations through a process of creative interpretation of the law, which takes into account, among other things, the unique circumstances of his client's case.

First some conventions. To assist in comparing the original UCC sections with those of A9W, the UCC's numbering scheme will be used, even though this will seem somewhat

---

[1]Those of you familiar with SHRDLU will recognize, however, that A9W is considerably more complex and realistic than the blocks world.

odd, as some numbers (or letters) may be skipped in A9W. Also, to avoid confusion, references to A9W sections in others chapters of this book will always be preceded by "A9W", such as "A9W § 9-201". There will be rules in A9W which are not from Article Nine of the UCC, but from other UCC articles, or other legal sources. The original source will be made apparent. My comments about the model, which are not part of the "authoritative" text of A9W, are in italics. At the end of this chapter there is a dictionary of predicate and function symbols used in the formal restatements.

A.1 A9W Article 1; General Provisions

A.1.1 § 1-103. Supplementary General Principles of Law Applicable

Unless displaced by the particular provisions of the Act, the principles of law and equity, including estoppel, fraud, misrepresentation, duress, coercion and mistake shall supplement its provisions.

A.1.2 A9W § 1-201. General Definitions

Subject to additional definitions contained in the subsequent Articles of this Act which are applicable to specific Articles, and unless the context otherwise requires, in this Act:

(3) "Agreement" means the bargain of the parties in fact as found in their language or by implication from other circumstances.

(37) "Security Interest" means an interest in personal property which secures payment or performance of an obligation.

A.1.3 A9W § 1-105. Territorial Application of the Act; Parties' Power to Choose Applicable Law

(1) Except as provided hereafter in this section, when a transaction bears a reasonable relation to this state and another state the parties may agree that the law of either this state or the other state shall govern their rights and duties.

(2) When § 9-103 specifies the applicable law, it governs.

A.2 A9W Article 2; Sales

A.2.1   A9W § 2-505. Seller's Shipment Under Reservation

(1) Where the seller has identified goods to the contract before shipment:

(a) his procurement of a negotiable bill of lading to his own order reserves in him a security interest in the goods.

A.3   A9W Article 9; Secured Transactions

A.3.1   A9W § 9-102. Policy and Subject Matter of Article

(1) Except as provided in Section 9-104 on excluded transactions, this Article applies

(a) to any transaction which is intended to create a security interest in personal property, and

(b) to any sale of chattel paper.

A.3.2   A9W § 9-103. Perfection of Security Interests in Multiple State Transactions.

(1) Instruments and ordinary goods.

(b) Except as otherwise provided in this subsection, perfection is governed by the law of the jurisdiction where the collateral is when the last event occurs on which is based the assertion that the security interest is perfected.

(c) If the parties to a transaction creating a purchase money security interest in goods in one jurisdiction understand at the time that the interest attaches that the goods will be kept in another jurisdiction, the law of the other jurisdiction governs perfection.

§ 9-103 is an interesting example of a rule which orders other rules, where this ordering rule itself is defeasible.

A.3.3   A9W § 9-104. Transactions Excluded From Article

This Article does not apply

(h) to a right represented by a judgment

(j) to the creation or transfer of an interest in real estate.

A.3.4   A9W § 9-105. Definitions

(1) In this Article unless the context otherwise requires:

(b) "Chattel paper" means a writing which evidences both a monetary obligation and a security interest in specific goods.

```
(rule s9-105-b (p)
        if (exists (r1 r2 e1)
                (and (writing p)
                        (evidence p r1)
                        (right-to-payment r1)
                        (evidence p r2)
                        (holds (security-interest r2) e1)))
        then (chattel-paper p))
```

(c) "Collateral" means the property subject to a security interest.

(d) "Debtor" means the person who owes payment or other performance of the obligation secured.

(h) "Goods" includes all things which are movable at the time the security interest attaches but does not include money or instruments.

```
(rule s9-105-h (s c)
        if (exists (a)
                (and (collateral s c)
                        (attachment s a)
                        (holds (movable c) a)))
        the (goods s c)
        unless (or (money c) (instrument c)))
```

(i) "Instrument" means a writing which evidences a right to the payment of money and is not itself a security agreement.

```
(rule s9-105-i (p)
        if (exists (r)
                (and (writing p)
                        (evidence p r)
                        (right-to-payment r)
                        (not (security-agreement p))))
        then (instrument p))
```

(l) "Security agreement" means an agreement which creates a security interest.

```
(rule s9-105-1 (a)
        if (exist (i)
                (and (agreement a)
                        (initiates a (security-interest i))))
        then (security-agreement a))
```

(m) "Secured Party" means a lender, seller or other person in whose favor there is a security interest.

A.3.5   A9W § 9-107. Definitions: "Purchase Money Security Interest"

A security interest is a "purchase money security interest" to the extent that it is retained by the seller of the collateral to secure its price.

```
(rule s9-107 (si sp c d s)
        if (exists (sp d s)
                  (and (secured-party si sp)
                       (debtor si d)
                       (collateral si c)
                       (seller s sp)
                       (buyer s d)
                       (goods s c)))
        then (pmsi si c))
```

A.3.6   A9W § 9-109. Classification of Goods;

Goods are
  (1) "consumer goods" if they are used primarily for personal purposes;

```
(rule s9-109-1 (s c)
        if (exists (p)
                  (and (goods s c)
                       (debtor s p)
                       (uses p c)))
        then (consumer-goods s c))
```

  (4) "inventory" if they held by a person who holds them for sale;

```
(rule s9-109-4 (s c)
        if (exists (p)
                  (and (collateral s c)
                       (debtor s d)
                       (sells d c)))
        then (inventory s c))
```

A.3.7 A9W § 9-113. Security Interest Arising Under Article on Sales

A security interest arising solely under the Article on Sales (Article 2) is subject to the provisions of this Article except that so long as the debtor does not have possession of the goods

(a) no security agreement is necessary to make the security interest enforceable; and

(b) no filing is required to perfect the security interest.

A.3.8 A9W § 9-201. General Validity of Security Agreement

Except as otherwise provided by this Act a security agreement is effective according to its terms between the parties, against purchasers of the collateral and against creditors.

A.3.9 A9W § 9-203. Attachment and Enforceability of Security Interest

(1) Subject to the provisions of Section 9-113, a security interest is not enforceable against the debtor or third parties and does not attach unless

(a) the collateral is in the possession of the secured party or the debtor has signed a security agreement which contains a description of the collateral;

(b) value has been given; and

(c) the debtor has rights in the collateral.

(2) A security interest attaches as soon as all of the events specified in subsection (1) have taken place unless explicit agreement postpones the time of attaching.

A.3.10 A9W § 9-301. Persons Who Take Priority Over Unperfected Security Interests; Right of "Lien Creditor"

(1) Except as otherwise provided in subsection (2), an unperfected security interest is subordinate to the rights of

(a) persons entitled to priority under Section 9-312;

(b) a person who becomes a lien creditor before the security interest is perfected.

(c) in the case of goods, instruments or chattel papers, a buyer not in the ordinary course of business, to the extent that he gives value and receives delivery of the collateral without knowledge of the security interest and before it is perfected.

(2) If the secured party files with respect to a purchase money security interest within ten days after the buyer receives possession of the collateral, he takes priority over the rights of a lien creditor which arise between the time the security interest attaches and the time of filing.

A.3.11 A9W § 9-302. When Filing is Required to Perfect Security Interest

(1) A financing statement must be filed to perfect all security interests except the following:

(a) a security interest in collateral in possession of the secured party under Section 9-305;

(d) a purchase money security interest in consumer goods; but filing is required for a motor vehicle.

```
(rule s9-302 (s c)
        if (exists (f t)
                (and (holds (perfection-steps s c) t)
                     (collateral s c)
                     (not (and (filing s f)
                               (collateral f c)))))
        then false
        unless (or (applies (inst s9-305 (parms s c)))
                   (applies (inst s9-302d (parms s c)))))

(rule s9-302d (s c)
        if (pmsi s c)
        then (applies (inst s9-302d (parms s c)))
        unless (motor-vehicle c))
```

Notice that the conclusion of rule s9-302d is just it applies. This avoids introducing a predicate which does not appear in A9W.

A.3.12   A9W § 9-303. When Security Interest is Perfected.

(1) A security interest is perfected when it has attached and when all of the applicable steps required for perfection have been taken.

```
(rule s9-303 (s c e)
        if (exists (a p)
                (and (attachment s a)
                     (collateral a c)
                     (holds (perfection-steps s c) p)
                     (later p a e)))
        then (holds (perfected s c) e))
```

A.3.13   A9W § 9-304. Perfection of Security Interest in Instruments.

(1) A security interest in money or instruments can be perfected only by the secured party's taking possession, except as provided in subsection (4).

```
(rule s9-304 (s c e)
      if (exists (p)
            (and (holds (perfection-steps s c) e)
                 (collateral s c)
                 (money-or-instrument c)
                 (secured-party s p)
                 (not (holds (possesses p c) e))))
      then false
      unless (applies (inst s9-304-4 (parms s c e)))))
```

(4) A security interest in instruments is perfected without filing or the taking of possession for a period of 21 days from the time it attaches.

```
(rule s9-304-4a (s c a)
      if (and (collateral s c)
              (instrument c)
              (attachment s a)
              (collateral a c))
      then (initiates a (perfection-steps s c)))
```

```
(rule s9-304-4b (s c t2)
      if (exists (t1 a d e)
            (and (collateral s c)
                 (instrument c)
                 (attachment s a)
                 (collateral a c)
                 (time a t1)
                 (days 21 d)
                 (add t1 d t2)
                 (date t2 e)))
      then (terminates e (perfection-steps s c)))
```

A.3.14   A9W § 9-305. When Possession by Secured Party Perfects Security Interest Without Filing.

A security interest in goods, instruments, money, or chattel paper may be perfected by the secured party's taking possession of the collateral.

```
(rule s9-305 (s c e p)
      if (exists (p)
            (and (collateral s c)
                 (or (goods s c)
                     (instrument c)
```

```
                        (money c)
                        (chattel-paper c))
                  (secured-party s p)
                  (transfer e)
                  (object e c)
                  (recipient e p)))
         then (initiates e (perfection-steps s c)))
```

A.3.15 A9W § 9-306. "Proceeds"; Secured Party's Rights on Disposition of the Collateral

(1) "Proceeds" includes whatever is received upon the sale of collateral or proceeds.

```
(rule s9-306-1 (s p)
         if (exists (c d t)
                  (and (collateral s c)
                       (debtor s d)
                       (seller t d)
                       (goods t c)
                       (consideration s p)))
         then (proceeds s p))
```

That the sale of proceeds is also proceeds is implicitly represented by the code of s9-306-1 and s9-306-2b, below. According to my interpretation, proceeds are collateral, whose subsequent sale is proceeds using the above rule.

(2) A security interest continues in the collateral notwithstanding sale, and also continues in any proceeds.

```
(rule s9-306-2a ()
         if (exists (t c s)
                  (and (goods t c)
                       (collateral s c)
                       (terminates t (security-interest s))))
         then false)

(rule s9-306-2b (s c)
         if (proceeds s c)
         then (collateral s c))
```

(3) The security interest in proceeds is perfected if the interest in the original collateral was perfected, but it ceases to be a perfected security interest and becomes an unperfected security interest ten days after receipt of the proceeds by the debtor unless

(a) a filed financing statement covers the original collateral and the proceeds are collateral in which a security interest may be perfected by filing; or

(c) the security interest in proceeds is perfected within the ten day period.

```
(rule s9-306-3-1 (s p si e c)
       if   (and (goods s c)
                 (consideration s p)
                 (collateral si c)
                 (collateral si p)
                 (holds (perfected si c) e))
       then (holds (perfected si p) e)
       unless (exists (t2)
                 (applies (inst s9-306-3-2
                              (parms t2 si c p)))))

(rule s9-306-3-2 (s t2 si c p)
       if (exists (t1 d e)
              (and (date t1 e)
                   (time s e)
                   (days 10 d)
                   (add t1 d t2)))
       then (terminates e (perfected si p))
       unless (or (exists (f)
                        (and (filing si f)
                             (collateral f c)
                             (perfectable-by-filing si p)))
                  (exists (e)
                        (and (initiates e (perfected si p))
                             (before e t2))))))
```

A.3.16 A9W § 9-307. Protection of Buyers of Goods

(1) A buyer in the ordinary course of business takes free of a security interest created by the seller even though the security interest is perfected and even though the buyer knows of its existence.

(2) In the case of consumer goods, a buyer takes free of a security interest even though perfected if he buys without knowledge of the interest unless prior to the purchase the secured party has filed a financing statement covering such goods.

A.3.17 A9W § 9-308. Purchase of Chattel Paper and Instruments

A purchaser of chattel paper or an instrument who gives new value and takes possession of it in the ordinary course of business has priority over a security interest in the chattel paper or instrument

(b) which is claimed merely as proceeds of inventory subject to a security interest, even though he knows that the specific paper or instrument is subject to the security interest.

A.3.18   A9W § 9-312. Priorities Among Conflicting Security Interests in the Same Collateral

(4) A purchase money security interest in collateral other than inventory has priority over a conflicting security interest in the same collateral if the purchase money security interest is perfected at the time the debtor receives possession of the collateral or within ten days thereafter.

```
(rule s9-312-4 (s1 s2 c)
       if (exists (e1 e2 e3 d tr t1 t2 t3)
              (and (pmsi s1)
                    (collateral s1 c)
                    (not (inventory s1 c))
                    (collateral s2 c)
                    (different s1 s2)
                    (holds (perfected s1 c) e1)
                    (debtor s1 d)
                    (recipient tr d)
                    (object tr c)
                    (time e1 t1)
                    (date t2 e2)
                    (time tr e2)
                    (days 10 d)
                    (add t2 d t3)
                    (date t3 e3)
                    (before t1 e3)))
       then (priority s1 s2 c))
```

(5) In all cases not governed by other rules in this section, priority between conflicting security interests in the same collateral shall be determined according to the following rules:

(a) Conflicting security interests rank according to priority in time of filing or perfection, whichever is earlier.

```
(rule 9-312-5a-1 (s1 s2 c)
       if (exists (e1)
              (and (file-or-perfect s1 e1 c)
                    (not (exists (e2)
                          (file-or-perfect s2 e2 c)))))
```

```
            then (priority s1 s2 c))

(rule 9-312-5a-2 (s1 s2 c)
        if (exists (e1 e2)
                   (and (file-or-perfect s1 e1 c)
                        (file-or-perfect s2 e2 c)
                        (before e1 e2)))
           then (priority s1 s2 c))

(rule 9-312-5a-3 (s e c)
        if (exists (p f)
                   (and (holds (perfected s c) p)
                        (filing s f)
                        (collateral f c)
                        (earlier p f e)))
           then (file-or-perfect s e c))

(rule 9-312-5a-4 (s e c)
        if (and (filing s e)
                (collateral e c)))
           then (file-or-perfect s e c))

(rule 9-312-5a-5 (s e c)
        if (holds (perfected s c) e)
           then (file-or-perfected s e c))
```

The three rules for `file-or-perfect` are a good example of the use of specificity to order rules. If the security interest is both filed and perfected, and one of these events occurs before the other, than the 9-312-5a-3 has priority, as it is the most specific. If the interest was perfected by filing, then the two events are equivalent: both 9-312-5a-4 and 9-312-5a-5 are applicable, with the same result, so it is unimportant which rule is applied. Finally, if the interest has been perfected without filing, then only 9-312-5a-5 will be applicable.

(b) So long as conflicting security interests are unperfected, the first to attach has priority.

```
(rule s9-312-5b-1 (s1 s2 c)
        if (exists (a1 a2)
                   (and (attachment s1 a1)
                        (collateral a1 c)
                        (attachment s2 a2)
                        (collateral a2 c)
                        (before a1 a2)))
           then (priority s1 s2 c))
```

```
(rule s9-312-5b-2 (s1 s2 c)
      if (exists (a)
                (and (attachment s1 a)
                     (collateral s1 c)))
      then (priority s1 s2 c))
```

One need not show that the security interest is not perfected to use the above two rules. However, as all perfected security interest are attached, the priority rules for perfected security interests take precedence, because of specificity. Specificity is also used to order these two rules. The later , s9-312-5b-2, only applies if only one of the two interests is attached.

A.4   Legal Principles

Here are some generally accepted principles for ordering conflicting rules.

A.4.1   Lex Superior Derogat Inferior

Laws which are backed by a higher authority take precedence over conflicting laws backed by a lower authority. Federal law, for example, takes precedence over conflicting state law, and the decisions of appellate courts take precedence over conflicting decisions of lower courts.

```
(rule lex-superior (r1 p1 r2 p2)
      if (exists (a1 d1 a2 d2)
                (and (conflicting (inst r1 p1)
                                            (inst r2 p2))
                     (authority r1 a1 d1)
                     (authority r2 a2 d2)
                     (higher a1 a2)))
      then (preferred (inst r1 p1) (inst r2 p2)))
```

A.4.2   Lex Posterior Derogat Priori

Later rules have priority over conflicting earlier rules.

```
(rule lex-posterior (r1 p1 r2 p2)
      if (exists (a1 a2 d1 d2)
                (and (conflicting (inst r1 p1)
                                            (inst r2 p2))
                     (authority r1 a1 d1)
```

```
                        (authority r2 a2 d2)
                        (before d2 d1)))
       then (preferred (inst r1 p1) (inst r2 p2)))
```

A.4.3 Priority Between Lex Superior and Lex Posterior

In the case of conflict, an earlier rule supported by a higher authority has priority over a later rule supported by a lower authority.

```
(rule superior-over-posterior (p1 p2)
       if (conflicting (inst lex-superior p1)
                       (inst lex-posterior p2))
       then (preferred (inst lex-superior p1)
                       (inst lex-posterior p2)))
```

A.5   Common Sense Knowledge

These rules do not exhaust common sense, of course, but they are useful for the examples in this book.

The earlier of two events is the one which occurs before the other. Similarly, the later of two events is the one which occurs after the other.

```
(rule earlier-1 (e1 e2)
       if (before e1 e2)
       then (earlier e1 e2 e1))

(rule earlier-2 (e1 e2)
       if (before e2 e1)
       then (earlier e1 e2 e2))

(rule later-1 (e1 e2)
       if (before e2 e1)
       then (later e1 e2 e1))

(rule later-2 (e1 e2)
       if (before e1 e2)
       then (later e1 e2 e2))
```

Transferring an object from one person to another causes the recipient to obtain possession of the object. The person transferring the object no longer has possession after the transfer.

```
(rule begin-possession (p o e)
        if (and (transfer e)
                (recipient e p)
                (object e o))
        then (initiates e (possesses p o)))

(rule end-possession (p o e)
        if (and (transfer e)
                (agent e p)
                (object e o))
        then (terminates e (possesses p o)))
```

A time-dependent proposition holds at some particular time if a previous event successfully initiated the proposition, unless another event successfully terminated the proposition, after the initiating event, and before the time in question. (These rules are based on Shanahan's version of the Kowalski and Sergot's event calculus [61] [114; 85].)

```
(rule holds (e p t)
        if (and (happens e)
                (initiates e p)
                (succeeds e)
                (before e t))
        then (holds p t)
        unless (clipped e p t))

(rule clipped (t1 p t2)
        if (exists (e)
                (and (happens E)
                     (terminates E P)
                     (succeeds E)
                     (before T1 E)
                     (before E T2)))
        then (clipped t1 p t2))
```

The priority relation on security interests is not symmetric: If a security interest x has priority over another security interest y, then y does not have priority over x.

```
(rule priority-not-symmetric (s1 s2 c)
        if (and (priority s1 s2 c)
                (priority s2 s1 c))
        then false)
```

A.6   Dictionary of Predicate Symbols

The predicate symbols used in the formalization of the rules of A9W above are listed here alphabetically. The arity and type of each predicate will be indicated by a form such as

```
(agent <event> <person>).
```

In this example, the predicate `agent` is a binary relation between events and persons. The type declarations, such `<event>`, are an informal indication of the expected types of terms. The rule language, which is untyped, does not enforce these declarations.

```
(add <number> <number> <number>)
```
   `(add x y z)` means $x + y = z$. Notice that `add` is a predicate, not a function.

```
(agent <event> <person>)
```
   `(agent e1 p1)` means the agent of event e1 is person p1. The agent is the (legal) person who performs the event.

```
(agreement <object>)
```
   `(agreement o1)` means o1 is an agreement.

```
(ap <rule-instance>)
```
   `(ap r1)` is an applicability assumption. These are the propositions which are maximized by conditional entailment.

```
(applies <rule-instance>)
```
   `(applies r1)` means that the rule instance r1 applies. See also `ap`.

```
(attachment <security-interest> <event>)
```
   `(attachment s1 e1)` means the security interest s1 became attached at the time of event e1.

```
(before <event> <event>)
```
   `(before e1 e2)` means that e1 occurs before e2.

```
(buyer <sale> <person>)
```
   `(buyer s1 p1)` means p1 is the buyer at the selling event s1.

```
(chattel-paper <object>)
```
   `(chattel-paper o1)` means o1 is chattel paper.

```
(collateral <event> <property>)
```
   `(collateral e1 p1)` means the collateral of the event e1 is the property p1. The event may be one creating a security interest, such as a security agreement, or may be the attachment of such an interest, or the filing of a financing statement covering p1.

```
(consideration <sale> <object>)
```
(consideration s1 o1) means that o1 is the property received, or to be received, by the seller from the buyer in the sale s1.

```
(consumer-goods <security-interest> <property>)
```
(consumer-goods s1 p1) means that the collateral p1 of the security interest s1 is consumer goods.

```
(date <number> <event>)
```
(date n1 e1) means the n1 units of canonical time, from the beginning of measured time, is the event e1.

```
(days <number> <number>)
```
(days n1 n2) means n1 days are n2 canonical time units.

```
(debtor <security-interest> <person>)
```
(debtor s1 p1) means that p1 is the debtor of the security interest s1.

```
(different <object> <object>)
```
(different o1 o2) means that o1 and o2 do not denote the same object.

```
(earlier <event> <event> <event>)
```
(earlier e1 e2 e3) means that e3 is the earlier of e1 or e2. If e1 occurs at the same time as e2, then (earlier e1 e2 e1), for example, is false.

```
(evidence <object> <object>)
```
(evidence o1 o2) means that the existence of o1 is evidence for the existence of o2.[2]

```
(file-or-perfect <security-interest> <event>)
```
(file-or-perfect s1 e1) means e1 is the event of filing or perfecting the security interest s1, whichever occurred earlier.

```
(filing <security-interest> <event>)
```
(filing s1 e1) means that e1 is the event of filing a financing statement for the security interest s1.

```
(goods <event> <object>)
```
(goods e1 o1) means that o1 is the goods of the event e1. For example, if e1 is a sale, o1 is the goods sold at the sale. If e1 is a security-interest then o1 is the goods secured by the interest.

---

[2]This is admittedly an ad hoc approach to evidence. The model theoretic semantics of propositions of this kind is unclear. In any model of (evidence o1 o2), there are objects denoted by o1 and o2, by definition.

(happens <event>)
   (happens e1) means that the event e1 occurs.

(holds <fluent> <event>)
   Time-dependent atomic propositions are called "fluents". They are modeled as terms in the event calculus. (holds f1 e1) means that f1 is true just before the event e1. Events are instantaneous; it may that f1 is no longer true immediately after e1.

(initiates <event> <fluent>)
   (initiates e1 f1) means the f1 is true just after the event e1. That is, f1 is a postcondition of e1.

(instrument <object>)
   (instrument o1) means o1 is an instrument, which in the context of Article Nine is a written document evidencing a right to payment of money.

(inventory <security-interest> <property>)
   (inventory s1 p1) means that p1, the collateral of the security interest s1, is inventory.

(later <event> <event> <event>)
   (later e1 e2 e3) means that e3 is the later of e1 and e2. If e1 and e2 occur at the same time, then (later e1 e2 e1) and (later e1 e2 e2) are both false.

(money <object>)
   (money o1) means o1 is money.

(motor-vehicle <object>)
   (motor-vehicle o1) means o1 is a motor vehicle, such a car or truck.

(holds (movable <object>) <event>)
   movable is a fluent predicate. (holds (movable o1) e1) means o1 is a movable object at the time of event e1.

(object <transfer> <object>)
   (object t1 o1) means the o1 is the object transfered by the event t1.

(holds (perfection-steps <security-interest> <object>) <event>)
   perfection-steps is a fluent. (holds (perfections-steps s1 c1) e1) means the steps necessary to perfect the security interest s1 in the collateral c1 have been taken by the time of event e1.

(perfectable-by-filing <security-interest> <object>)
   (perfectable-by-filing s1 o1) means that the security interest s1 in the collateral o1 may be perfected by filing a financing statement.

`(holds (perfected <security-interest> <object>) <event>)`
    perfected is a fluent. `(holds (perfected s1 o1) e1)` means the security
    interest s1 in the collateral o1 is perfected at the time of event e1.

`(pmsi <security-interest>)`
    `(pmsi s1)` means s1 is a purchase money security interest.

`(holds (possesses <person> <object>) <event>)`
    possesses is a fluent. `(holds (possesses p1 o1) e1)` means person
    p1 has possession of o1 at the time of event e1.

`(priority <security-interest> <security-interest> <object>)`
    `(priority s1 s2 c1)` means the security interest s1 has priority over the
    security interest s2 in the collateral c1.

`(recipient <event> <person>)`
    `(recipient e1 p1)` means the person p1 received the object transferred by
    event e1.

`(right-to-payment <object>)`
    `(right-to-payment o1)` means o1 is a right to payment.

`(sale <event>)`
    `(sale e1)` means e1 is a selling event. See also buyer, seller, goods and
    consideration.

`(same <object> <object>)`
    `(same o1 o2)` is true if o1 and o2 denote the same object. The unique names
    assumption does not hold.

`(secured-party <security-interest> <person>)`
    `(secured-party s1 p1)` means that p1 is the person whose interest is secured
    by s1.

`(security-agreement <object>)`
    `(security-agreement o1)` means o1 is a security agreement. See also
    debtor, secured-party and collateral.

`(holds (security-interest s1) e1)`
    security-interest is a fluent. `(holds (security-interest s1)
    e1)` means s1 is a security interest at the time of event e1.

`(sells <person> <object>)`
    `(sells p1 o1)` means that p1 sells objects of the type of o1. For example,
    `(sells Joe car1)` means Joe sells cars. (It also means he sells vehicles and
    every other supertype of cars.)

`(succeeds <event>)`
>   `(succeeds e1)` means the event e1 was successful.

`(terminates <event> <fluent>)`
>   `(terminates e1 f1)` means that the fluent f1 is no longer true just after e1 occurs.

`(time <event> <time>)`
>   `(time e1 t1)` means the event e1 occured at time t1. A time is also a kind of event.

`(transfer <event>)`
>   `(transfer e1)` means e1 is an event in which some object was transferred from one person to another. See also `recipient`.

`(uses <person> <object>)`
>   `(uses p1 o1)` means the person p1 uses the object o1 primarily for personal purposes, rather than, for example, in a business.

`(writing <object>)`
>   `(writing o1)` means that o1 is a written document, such as a check or written agreement.

Appendix B   Glossary of Legal Terms

action
> *n* A suit brought in a court.

affirmative defense
> *n* In pleading, matter constituting a defense; new matter which, assuming the complaint to be true, constitutes a defense to it.

allegation
> *n* The assertion, claim, declaration, or statement of a party to an action, made in a pleading, setting out what he expects to prove.

borrower
> *n* He to whom a thing or money is lent at his request.

civil law
> *n* Laws concerned with civil or private rights and remedies, as contrasted with criminal laws.

civil procedure
> *n* Body of law concerned with methods, procedures and practices in civil litigation.

claim
> *n* A demand for something due or believed to be due. An assertion open to challenge.

collateral
> *n* Property which is pledged as security for the satisfaction of a debt.

commercial law
> *n* The law applicable to the rights and relations of persons engaged in commerce or trade.

common law
> *n* The body of law developed in England primarily from judicial decisions based on custom and precedent, unwritten in statute or code, and constituting the basis of the English legal system and of the system in all of the U.S. except Louisiana.

complaint
> *n* A formal allegation against a party.

constituent facts

    n The elements of a crime, tort or other type of action. Those matters which must be proved to sustain a cause of action because they consitute the action or crime.

counterclaim

    n A claim presented by a defendant in opposition to or deduction from the claim of the plaintiff.

damages

    n Compensation in money imposed by law for loss or injury.

defendant

    n The person against whom relief or recovery is sought in a action or suit.

defense

    n A defendant's denial, answer or plea. An argument in support or justification.

fact

    n A thing done; an action performed or an incident transpiring; an event or circumstance; an actual occurrence; an actual happening in time space or an event mental or physical.

file

    vb To deposit in the custody or among the records of a court.

financing statement

    n A written statement used as a public record of a security interest.

goods

    n All things movable at the time the security interest attaches except money or instruments.

instruments

    n A written document which evidences a right to payment of money and is not itself a security agreement or lease.

issue

    n A single, certain, and material point, deduced by the allegations and pleadings of the parties, which is affirmed on one side and denied on the other. A fact put in controversy by the pleadings; such may either be issues of law or fact.

lender

    n He from whom a thing or money is borrowed.

mortgage

    n An interest in land created by a document providing security for the performance of a duty or the payment of a debt.

perfection
> *n* The perfection of a security interest deals with those steps legally required to give a secured party an interest in the subject property against the debtor's other creditors.

plaintiff
> *n* One who commences a personal action or lawsuit to obtain a remedy for an injury to his rights. The complaining party in a litigation.

pleading
> *n* One of the formal and usually written allegations and counter allegations made alternately by the parties in a legal action or proceeding.

proceeds
> *n* Money or some other thing of value obtained by the sale of property.

reply
> *n* The plaintiff's answer to the defendant's counterclaim.

security interest
> *n* A form of interest in property which provides that the property may be sold on default in order to satisfy the obligation for which the security interest is given.

secured transaction
> *n* A transaction which is founded on a security agreement. Such an agreement creates or provides for a security interest.

suit
> *n* An action or process in a court.

summary judgment
> *n* Judgment for a party without trial, when there is no genuine issue of material fact and the party is entitled to judgment as a matter of law.

trial
> *n* A judicial examination and determination of issues between parties to an action.

ultimate issue
> *n* An issue which is sufficient and final for the disposition of the entire case.

References

1. E. Adams. *The Logic of Conditionals*. Reiter, Dordrecht, 1975.

2. Carlos E. Alchourrón and Eugenio Bulygin. Limits of Logic and Legal Reasoning. In Antonio A. Martino, *Expert Systems in Law*, pages 9–27. North-Holland, Amsterdam, 1992.

3. Robert Alexy. *Theorie der juristischen Argumentation*. Suhrkamp Verlag, Frankfurt am Main, 1978.

4. Robert Alexy. *A Theory of Legal Argumentation*. Clarendon Press, Oxford, 1989.

5. Layman E. Allen. Symbolic Logic: A Razor-Edged Tool for Drafting and Interpreting Legal Documents. *The Yale Law Journal* **66** (1957).

6. Layman E. Allen. Deontic Logic. *Modern Uses of Logic in Law* **13** (1960).

7. Layman E. Allen. *Wff 'n Proof: The Game of Modern Logic*. Autotelic Instructional Materials Publishers, New Haven, 1966.

8. Layman E. Allen. The Plain Language Game: Legal Writing Made Clear by Structuring it Well. In *Proceedings of the International Workshop on Formal Methods in Law*. German National Research Center for Computer Science (GMD), Sankt Augustin, 1982.

9. Layman E. Allen and Charles S. Saxon. More IA Needed in AI: Interpretation Assistance for Coping with the Problem of Multiple Structural Interpretations.. In *Proceedings of the Third International Conference on Artificial Intelligence and Law*, pages 53–61. ACM, 1991.

10. Ross Anderson and Nuel D. Belnap Jr.. *Entailment: The Logic of Relevance and Necessity*. Princeton University Press, 1974.

11. Kevin D. Ashley. Toward a Computational Theory of Arguing with Precedents: Accomodating Multiple Interpretations of Cases. In *The Second International Conference on Artificial Intelligence and Law*, pages 93–102. ACM, June 1989.

12. Kevin D. Ashley. *Modeling Legal Argument: Reasoning with Cases and Hypotheticals*. MIT Press, 1990.

13. Michael D. Bayles. *Procedural Justice; Allocating to Individuals*. Kluwer Academic Publishers, 1990.

14. Trevor Bench-Capon and Marek Sergot. Toward a Rule-Based Representation of Open Texture in Law. In Charles Walther, *Computer Power and Legal Language*, pages 39–60. Quorum Books, 1988.

15. Trevor Bench-Capon. Deep Models, Normative Reasoning and Legal Expert Systems. In *Proceedings of the Second International Conference on Artificial Intelligence and Law*. ACM Press, Vancouver, 1989.

16. Trevor Bench-Capon and Frans Coenen. Expoiting Isomorphism: Development of a KBS to Support British Coal Insurance Claims. In *Proceedings of the Third International Conference on Artificial Intelligence and Law*, pages 62–68. ACM Press, Oxford, 1991.

17. T.J.M. Bench-Capon, P.E.S. Dunne and P.H. Leng. Interacting with Knowledge Systems Through Dialogue Games. In *Proceedings of the 11th Annual Conference on Expert Systems and their Applications (vol. 1)*, pages 123–130, Avignon, 1991.

18. T.J.M. Bench-Capon, P.E.S. Dunne and P.H. Leng. A Dialogue Game for Dialectical Interaction with Expert Systems. In J.C. Rault, *Proceedings of AVIGNON-92 (vol. 1)*, Nanterre, 1992.

19. Donald H. Berman and Carole D. Hafner. Indeterminacy: A Challenge to Logic-based Models of Legal Reasoning. *Yearbook of Law, Computers and Technology* 3, 1–35 (1987).

20. Henry Campbell Black. *Black's Law Dictionary*. West Publishing Company, 1979.

21. Ronald J. Brachman and James G. Schmolze. An Overview of the KL-ONE Knowledge Representation System. *Cognitive Science* 9, 171–216 (1985).

22. L. Karl Branting. Representing and Reusing Explanations and Legal Precedents. In *Proceedings of the Second International Conference on Artificial Intelligence and Law*, pages 103-110. ACM, 1989.

23. Gerhard Brewka and Karl-Heinz Wittur. Nichtmonotone Logiken — Eine Untersuchung der Formalisierungen nichtmonotoner Schlußweisen und die Implementation eines nichtmonotonen Reasoning-Systems. Master's thesis (1984), Universität Bonn.

24. Gerhard Brewka. Tweety – Still Flying: Some Remarks on Abnormal Birds, Applicable Rules and a Default Prover. In *Proceedings of the National Conference on Artificial Intelligence*, pages 8–12. AAAI, Philadelphia, 1986.

25. Gerhard Brewka. Cumulative Default Logic: In Defense of Nonmonotonic Inference Rules. *Artificial Intelligence* 50 (2), 183–205 (1991).

26. Eugene Charniak and Drew McDermott. *Introduction to Artificial Intelligence*. World Student Series. Addison-Wesley, Reading, Massachusetts, 1985.

27. Johan de Kleer. An Assumption-Based TMS. *Artificial Intelligence* **28** (1986).

28. J. Delgrande. An Approach to Default Reasoning Based on a First-Order Conditional Logic. In *Proceedings of the National Conference on Artificial Intelligence*, pages 340–345. AAAI, Seattle, 1987.

29. W. F. Dowling and J. H. Gallier. Linear-Time Algorithms for Testing the Satisfiability of Propositional Horn Formulae. *Journal of Logic Programming* **3**, 267–284 (1984).

30. R. M. Dworkin. Is Law a System of Rules?. In R. M. Dworkin, *The Philosophy of Law*, pages 38–65. Oxford Unviersity Press, 1977.

31. Paul Edwards. *The Encyclopedia of Philosophy*. Macmillan Pub. Co, Inc. & The Free Press, 1972.

32. K. Eshghi and R. A. Kowalski. Abduction as Deduction. Technical Report (1988), Dept. of Computing, Imperial College of Science and Technology, London.

33. Walter Felscher. Dialogues as a Foundation for Intuitionistic Logic. In D. Gabby and F. Günthner, *Handbook of Philosophical Logic; Vol. III: Alternatives in Classical Logic*, pages 341–372. D. Reidel, 1986.

34. Herbert Fiedler. Juristische Logik in mathematischer Sicht. *ARSP* **52** (1966).

35. Herbert Fiedler. Zur logischen Konzeption der Rechtsfindung aus dem Gesetz und ihrem historichen Bedingungen. In U. Klug, Th. Ramm, F. Rittner and B. Schmiedel, *Gesetzgebungstheorie, Juristische Logik, Zivil- und Proceßrecht*, pages 129–139. Springer-Verlag, 1978.

36. Herbert Fiedler. Die Rechtsfindung aus dem Gesetz im Lichte der neueren Logik und Methodenlehre. In G. Kohlmann, *Festschrift für Ulrich Klug zum 70. Geburtstag*, pages 55–67. Deubner Verlag, Cologne, 1983.

37. Herbert Fiedler. Expert Systems as a Tool for Drafting Legal Decisions. In Antonio A. Martino and Fiorenza Socci Natali, *Logica, Informatica, Diritto*, pages 265–274. Consiglio Nazionale delle Richere, Florence, 1985.

38. Richard E. Fikes and Nils J. Nilsson. STRIPS: A New Approach to the Application of Theorem Proving to Problem Solving. *Artificial Intelligence* **2**, 189–208 (1971).

39. D.M. Gabbay and U. Reyle. N-PROLOG: An extension of PROLOG with Hypothetical Implications. *Journal of Logic Programming* **1**, 319–355 (1984).

232

40. Anne von der Lieth Gardner. *An Artificial Intelligence Approach to Legal Reasoning*. Artificial Intelligence and Legal Reasoning. MIT Press, 1987.

41. Hector Geffner and Judea Pearl. Conditional Entailment: Bridging Two Approaches to Default Reasoning. *Artificial Intelligence* **53** (2–3), 209–244 (1992).

42. Thomas F. Gordon. Object-Oriented Predicate Logic and its Role in Representing Legal Knowledge. In Charles Walter, *Computing Power and Legal Reasoning*, pages 163–203. West Publishing Company, 1985.

43. Thomas F. Gordon. Oblog-2, A Hybrid Knowledge Representation System for Defeasible Reasoning. In *The First International Conference on Artificial Intelligence and Law, Proceedings*, pages 231–239. ACM Press. ACM, May 1987.

44. Thomas F. Gordon. Some Problems with Prolog as a Knowledge Representation Language for Legal Expert Systems. In C. Arnold, *Yearbook of Law, Computers & Technology*, pages 52–67. Butterworths, London, 1987.

45. Thomas F. Gordon. The Importance of Nonmonotonicity for Legal Reasoning. In H. Fiedler, F. Haft and R. Traunmüller, *Expert Systems in Law; Impacts on Legal Theory and Computer Law*, pages 111–126. Attempto Verlag, Tübingen, 1988.

46. Thomas F. Gordon. Issue Spotting in a System for Searching Interpretation Spaces. In *Proceedings of the Second International Conference on Artificial Intelligence and Law*, pages 157–164. ACM, June 1989.

47. Thomas F. Gordon. An Abductive Theory of Legal Issues. *International Journal of Man-Machine Studies* **35**, 95–118 (July 1991).

48. Thomas F. Gordon. A Theory Construction Approach to Legal Document Assembly. In Antonio A. Martino, *Expert Systems in Law*, pages 211–225. North-Holland, Amsterdam, 1992.

49. Thomas F. Gordon. Artificial Intelligence: A Hermeneutic Defense. In Christiane Floyd, Heinz Züllighoven, Reinhard Budde and Reinhard Keil-Slawik, *Software Development and Reality Construction*, pages 280–290. Springer-Verlag, 1992.

50. Robert Harper, Robin Milner and Mads Tofte. The Definition of Standard ML, Version 2. Tech. Rep. (1988), Laboratory for Foundations of Computer Science, Department of Computer Science, University of Edinburgh.

51. H. L. A. Hart. The Ascription of Responsibility and Rights. In Antony Flew, *Logic and Language: First and Second Series*, pages 151–174. Anchor Books, Garden City, 1965.

52. H. L. A. Hart. *The Concept of Law*. Oxford University Press, 1961.

53. H. L. A. Hart. *Essays in Jurisprudence and Philosophy*. Oxford University Press, 1983.

54. Thomas Hobbes. *Leviathan*, 1651.

55. Oliver Wendel Holmes. *The Common Law*. Little, Brown, Boston, 1881.

56. Ulrich Junker. *Relationship Between Assumptions*. Ph.D. thesis, Kaiserslautern, 1992.

57. Immanuel Kant. *Critique of Pure Reason*. MacMillan, London, 1929. tr. Norman K. Smith.

58. Arthur Kaufmann and Winfried Hassemar. *Einführung in Rechtsphilosophie und Rechtstheorie der Gegenwart*. C. F. Müller, Heidelberg, 1981.

59. Ulrich Klug. *Juristische Logik*. Springer, 1982.

60. Kurt Konolige. A General Theory of Abduction. In *Working Notes of the AAAI Spring Symposium on Automated Abduction*, pages 62–66. American Association for Artificial Intelligence, 1990.

61. Robert Kowalski and Marek Sergot. A Logic-Based Calculus of Events. *New Generation Computing* **4**, 67–95 (1986).

62. S. Kraus, D. Lehmann and M. Magidor. Nonmonotonic Reasoning, Preferential Models and Cumulative Logics. *Artificial Intelligence* **44**, 167–207 (1990).

63. D. Lehmann and M. Magidor. Rational Logics and their Models: a Study in Cumulative Logic. Technical Report (1988), Department of Computer Science, Hebrew University, Jerusalem, Israel.

64. Hector J. Levesque. A Knowledge-Level Account of Abduction. In *IJCAI-89*, pages 1061-1067, Detroit, 1989.

65. Vladimir Lifschitz. On the Semantics of STRIPS. In M. Georgeff and A. Lansky, *Reasoning about Actions and Plans*. Morgan Kaufmann, Los Altos, California, 1987.

66. K. N. Llewellyn. *The Bramble Bush: On Our Law and Its Study*. Oceana Publications, Dobbs Ferry, New York, 1930. 1960 edition.

67. K. N. Llewellyn. *Jurisprudence: Realism in Theory and Practice*. The University of Chicago Press, London, 1962.

68. Kuno Lorenz. *Arithmetik und Logik als Spiele*. Ph.D. thesis, Kiel, 1961.

69. Ronald Loui and William Chen. An Argument Game. Technical Report WUCS-92-47 (1992), Department of Computer Science, Washington University.

70. R. Loui, J. Norman, K. Stiefvater, A. Merrill, A. Costello and J. Olson. Computing Specificity. Technical Report CS-TR93-03 (1993), Department of Computer Science, Washington University.

71. J. D. Mackenzie. Question-Begging in Non-Cumulative Systems. *Journal of Philosophical Logic* **8**, 159–177 (1979).

72. David Maier and David S. Warren. *Computing with Logic*. Benjamin/Cummings, 1988.

73. Catherine C. Marshall. Representing the Structure of a Legal Argument. In *The Second International Conference on Artificial Intelligence and Law*, pages 121–127. ACM, June 1989.

74. P. Martin-Löf. Constructive Mathematics and Computer Programming. In C.A.R. Hoare and J.C. Shepardson, *Mathematical Logic and Programming Languages*. Prentice-Hall, 1985.

75. John McCarthy. Circumscription – A Form of Nonmonotonic Reasoning. *Artificial Intelligence* **13**, 27–39 (1980).

76. John McCarthy. Applications of Circumscription to Formalizing Common-Sense Knowledge. *Artificial Intelligence* **28**, 89–116 (1986).

77. L. Thorne McCarty. Reflections on TAXMAN: An Experiment in Artificial Intelligence and Legal Reasoning. *Harvard Law Review* **90** (5) (1977).

78. L. Thorne McCarty and N. S. Sridharan. A Computational Theory of Legal Argument. Technical Report LRP-TR-13 (1982), Laboratory for Computer Science Research, Rutgers University.

79. L. Thorne McCarty. Intelligent Legal Information Systems: Problems and Prospects. *Rutgers Computer & Technnology Journal* **9**, 265–294 (1983).

80. L. Thorne McCarty. Clausal Intutionistic Logic, I. Fixed-Point Semantics. *The Journal of Logic Programming* **5**, 1–31 (1988).

81. L. Thorne McCarty. Clausal Intutitionistic Logic, II. Tableau Proof Procedures. *The Journal of Logic Programming* **5**, 93–132 (1988).

82. L. Thorne McCarty. A Language for Legal Discourse, I. Basic Features. In *The Second International Conference on Artificial Intelligence and Law*, pages 180–189. ACM, June 1989.

83. L. Thorne McCarty. AI and Law: How to Get There from Here. *Ratio Juris* **3** (2), 189–200 (July 1990).

84. L. Thorne McCarty and William W. Cohen. The Case for Explicit Exceptions, 1992.

85. Lode Missiaen and Maurice Bruynooghe. Localized Abductive Planning. In *Proceedings of the European Workshop on Planning (EWSP)*. GMD, Sankt Augustin, March 1991.

86. Robert C. Moore. Semantical Considerations on Nonmonotonic Logic. *Artificial Intelligence* **25**, 75–94 (1985).

87. Lawrence C. Paulson. *ML for the Working Programmer*. Cambridge University Press, 1991.

88. Judea Pearl. Probabilistic Semantics for Nonmonotonic Reasoning: A Survey. In R. Cummins and J. Pollock, *Philosophical AI: Computational Approaches to Reasoning*, pages 157–187. MIT Press, 1991.

89. Chaim Perelman. *Juristische Logik als Argumentationslehre*. Karl Alber Verlag, Freiburg/München, 1979.

90. Lothar Philipps. Rechtliche Regelung und formale Logik. *ARSP* **50** (1964).

91. John Pollock. Defeasible Reasoning. *Cognitive Science* **11**, 481-518 (1988).

92. David Poole. On the Comparison of Theories: Preferring the Most Specific Explanation. In *Proceedings of the International Joint Conference on Articial Intelligence*, pages 144–147, Los Angeles, 1985.

93. David Poole. A Logical Framework for Default Reasoning. *Artificial Intelligence* **36** (1) (1988).

94. David Poole. Hypo-deductive Reasoning for Abduction, Default Reasoning and Design. In *Working Notes of the AAAI Spring Symposium on Automated Abduction*, pages 106–110. American Association for Artificial Intelligence, 1990.

95. Richard A. Posner. *Economic Analysis of Law*. Little, Brown and Company, Boston. Second edition, 1977.

96. Henry Prakken. A Tool In Modelling Disagreement in Law: Preferring the Most Specific Argument. In *Proceedings of the Third International Conference on Artificial Intelligence and Law*, pages 165–174, Oxford, 1991.

97. Henry Prakken. *Logical Tools for Modelling Legal Argument*. Ph.D. thesis, Free University of Amsterdam, 1993.

98. Thomas M. Quinn. *Uniform Commercial Code Commentary and Law Digest*. Warren, Gorham & Lamont, Boston, 1978.

99. John Rawls. *A Theory of Justice*. Harvard University Press, 1971.

100. Raymond Reiter. A Logic for Default Reasoning. *Artificial Intelligence* **13**, 81–132 (1980).

101. Raymond Reiter and Johnan de Kleer. Foundations of Assumption-Based Truth Maintenance Systems, Preliminary Report. In *Sixth National Conference on Artificial Intelligence*, pages 183–188. AAAI, 1987.

102. Nicholas Rescher. *Dialectics*. State University of New York, Albany, 1977.

103. Edwina L. Rissland. Dimension-Based Analysis of Hypotheticals from Supreme Court Oral Argument. In *The Second International Conference on Artificial Intelligence and Law*, pages 111–120. ACM, June 1989.

104. Jürgen Rödig. *Die Denkform der Alternative in der Jurisprudenz*. Springer-Verlag, 1969.

105. Jürgen Rödig. *Schriften zur juristischen Logik*. Springer Verlag, Berlin, 1980.

106. Tom Routen and Trevor Bench-Capon. Hierarchical Formalizations. *International Journal of Man-Machine Studies* **35**, 69–93 (1991).

107. Giovanni Sartor. The Structure of Norm Conditions and Nonmonotonic Reasoning in Law. In *Proceedings of the Third International Conference on Artificial Intelligence and Law*, pages 155–164. ACM Press, Oxford, 1991.

108. R. Schreiber. *Logik des Rechts*. Springer-Verlag, Berlin, 1962.

109. Wolfgang Schuler and John B. Smith. Author's Argumentation Assistant (AAA): A Hypertext-Based Authoring Tool for Argumentative Texts. In A. Rizk, N. Streitz and J. Andre, *Hypertext: Concepts, Systems and Applications*. Cambridge University Press, 1990.

110. Karsten Schweichhart. Das Argument Construction Set. Arbeitspapier 348 (November 1988), GMD.

111. Robert Sedgewick. *Algorithms*. Series in Computer Science. Addison-Wesley, 1983.

112. Bart Selman and Hector J. Levesque. Abductive and Default Reasoning: A Computational Core. In *Proceedings of the Eight National Conference on Artificial Intelligence*, pages 343–348. AAAI Press, 1990.

113. Bart Selman. Computing Explanations. In *Working Notes of the AAAI Spring Symposium on Automated Abduction*, pages 82–84. AAAI, 1990.

114. Murray P. Shanahan. Prediction is deduction but explanation is abduction. In *Proceedings of the International Joint Conference on Artificial Intelligence*, 1989.

115. Yoav Shoham. A Semantical Approach to Nonmonotonic Logics. In Matthew L. Ginsberg, *Readings in Nonmonotonic Reasoning*, pages 227–250. Morgan Kaufmann, 1987.

116. Guillermo R. Simari and Ronald P. Loui. A Mathematical Treatment of Defeasible Reasoning and its Implementation. *Artificial Intelligence* **53** (2–3), 125–157 (1992).

117. David B. Skalak and Edwina L. Rissland. Arguments and Cases: An Inevitable Intertwining. *Aritificial Intelligence and Law* **1** (1), 3–45 (1992).

118. Richard E. Speidel, Robert S. Summers and James J. White. *Teaching Materials on Commercial and Consumer Law*. American Casebook Series. West Publishing Company, 1981.

119. Richard E. Susskind. *Expert Systems in Law*. Oxford, 1987.

120. Ilmar Tammelo. *Outlines of Modern Legal Logic*. Steiner, Wiesbaden, 1969.

121. Ilmar Tammelo. Rechtslogik. In A. Kaufmann and W. Hassemer, *Einführung in Rechtsphilosophie und Rechtstheorie der Gegenwart*, 8, pages 120–131. C. F. Müller, Heidelberg, 1981.

122. Stephen E. Toulmin. *The Place of Reason in Ethics*. Cambridge University Press, 1950.

123. Stephen E. Toulmin. *The Uses of Argument*. Cambridge University Press, 1958.

124. Dirk van Dalen. Intuitionistic Logic. In D. Gabbay and F. Günthner, *Handbook of Philosophical Logic; Vol. III: Alternatives in Classical Logic*, pages 225–339. D. Reidel, 1986.

125. George H. von Wright. Deontic Logic. *Mind* **60** (1) (1963).

126. Heinz Wagner. *Die moderne Logik in der Jurisprudenz*. Gehlen, Bad Homburg, 1970.

127. Ota Weinberger. *Rechtslogik. Versuch einer Anwendung moderner Logik auf das juristische Denken*. Springer-Verlag, 1970.

128. Ota Weinberger. *Rechtslogik*. Duncker & Humblot, Berlin. second edition, 1989.

129. James J. White and Robert S. Summers. *Handbook of the Law Under the Uniform Commercial Code*. American Casebook Series. West, 1980.

238

130. Terry Winograd. A Procedural Model of Language Understanding. In R. C. Schank and K. M. Colby, *Computer Models of Thought and Language*. Freeman, San Francisco, 1973.

131. Ludwig Wittgenstein. *Philosophical Investigations*. Macmillan, New York. Third edition, 1958.

Index

A9W, 206
Ashley, Kevin, 2
abduction, 159
  use in elliptical arguments, 51
  intractability of, 105
  use in issue spotting, 108
  propositional Horn clause, 157
  signature, 160
  use in explanation, 89
abnormality
  minimization of, 97
abstraction
  use in managing complexity, 39
absurdity, 81
acceptance
  of claims, 69
admissibility
  of priority order on assumptions, 100
  of preferential model structures, 98
adoption rules, 86
agreement
  in Habermas' theory of truth, 64
Alchourron, Carlos E., 8
Alexy, Robert, 1
  evaluation of his theory, 71
  theory of legal argumentation, 53
Allen, Layman E., 32
  contrapositive inference, 100
  logic games, 107
amicus curiae briefs, 67
analytical jurisprudence, 22
Anderson, Ross, 100
answer
  in Dialogue Logic, 77
  form of pleading, 111
antecedent
  of a default, 117
  of rules, 117
appeal, 109

arbitration, 205
Argument Construction Set, 108
arguments
  substantial vs. analytic, 61
Aristotle, 32
Article Nine World, 206
Artificial Intelligence, 76
  contributions to, 203
  open texture of term, 201
assertion
  in Dialogue Logic, 77
  in pleading, 111
  in the Pleadings Game, 127
Assumption Based Truth Maintenance, 104
  compared with the MRMS, 185
  signature, 183
assumptions
  in the ATMS, 185
  in Conditional Entailment, 97
  encoding in the Pleadings Game, 121
Austin, John L., 57
authority, 8
  in criticism of Habermas, 67
  in Hart's positivism, 22
  in isomorphic modeling, 12
  of judges to make law, 47
  representation of, 122
  priority of, 19
  in Susskind's theory, 38
Autoepistemic Logic, 96
automated theorem proving, 45
axiomatization, 34
  of the law, 35

background
  in Conditional Entailment, 98
  in the Pleadings Game, 126
backing
  use of reification to model, 122

239

244